70 0637647

D1639564

TRADE UNION
AND
SOCIAL HISTORY

Trade Union
and
Social History

A. E. Musson

Professor of Economic History
University of Manchester

FRANK CASS : LONDON

First published 1974 in Great Britain by
FRANK CASS AND COMPANY LIMITED
67 Great Russell Street, London WC1B 3BT, England

and in United States of America by
FRANK CASS AND COMPANY LIMITED
c/o International Scholarly Book Services, Inc.
P.O. Box 4347, Portland, Oregon 97208

Copyright © 1974 A. E. Musson

ISBN 0 7146 3031 4

Library of Congress Catalog Card No. 73-82609

Printed in Great Britain by
Northumberland Press Limited,
Gateshead

Contents

Preface

ALL the studies in this collection relate to working-class movements, mainly in the nineteenth century. They are mostly products of my interest in trade-union history, but include also contributions on the struggle for a free press, the early co-operative movement, and factory reform. They originally appeared in a wide variety of publications, some not very generally accessible, and it has therefore seemed worthwhile to bring them together, with revisions and interconnections where necessary. Chapter 1 is very largely new, but arises from an article on 'Writing Trade-Union History' in the *Amateur Historian*, January 1954, which, in a greatly revised and extended form, now serves as an introduction to this volume. Chapter 2 is based on a paper given at a conference of the Labour History Society on 'The Webbs as Trade-Union Historians', a synopsis of which was published in the Society's *Bulletin*, No. 4, Spring 1962; this was notable for its revision of the Webbs' views on Owenism and the trade-union movement and also on so-called 'New Model' unionism. Chapter 3 is a slightly amended version of my booklet on *The Congress of 1868: The Origins and Establishment of the Trades Union Congress*, produced by the T.U.C. in 1955; this was based on entirely new evidence, showing precisely how the T.U.C. came to be established, but it has never been commercially published and so opportunity is now taken of giving it wider circulation. Chapter 4 is based on a previously unpublished paper, originally read to the Manchester branch of the Fabian Society in 1953, on trends in trade-union development since the late nineteenth century. These first four chapters together provide a general review of trade-union history from the Industrial Revolution to modern times.

They are followed by three chapters on industrial relations in the printing and typefounding trades, and on the struggle for a free press. Chapter 5 is extracted from the early part of my book on *The Typographical Association* (1954), the printing industry providing probably the best opportunity for an account of early craft unionism. Chapter 6, by contrast, originally an article in *The Library* (Bibliographical Society, June 1955), produces even rarer evidence on the existence of an early *employers'* association, that of the London master letter-founders, or typefounders, including relations with their workmen's trade society; it needs emphasising that combinations and restrictive practices are not confined to labour. Chapter 7 is based on three articles in *Parliamentary Affairs* (Hansard Society), Vol. IX (1956), Nos. 2, 3, and 4, on 'Parliament and the Press', tracing the growth of press freedom from the sixteenth century to modern times, and also on an article in the *Manchester Guardian,* 28 June 1955, on 'Freeing the Press: the First Provincial Dailies', celebrating the repeal of the newspaper stamp tax and the first appearance of the *Guardian* as a daily; the growth of the radical and trade-union movements was closely connected with the struggle for a free press in the early nineteenth century.

The final chapters are on two other important elements in the working-class movement of that period, namely the early co-operative and factory reform movements. Chapter 8 is a reprint of an article which originally appeared in the Lancashire and Cheshire Antiquarian Society's *Transactions,* Vol. LXVIII (1958), dealing with the ideology of early co-operation in that area, emphasising the importance and analysing the main characteristics of the pre-Rochdale movement in the North-West, which had hitherto been very largely neglected. Chapter 9 is a revised version of my article on 'Robert Blincoe and the Early Factory System', in the *Derbyshire Miscellany,* February 1958: the circumstances surrounding Blincoe's career and the publication of his famous *Memoir* were here revealed for the first time, showing incidentally the links between the factory reform movement and such leading radicals and trade unionists as Richard Carlile and John Doherty.

These publications, based on research into original records, have provided new insights and interpretations in several areas of working-class history. They are all related to a central theme—the working-class struggle to defend their standard of life, to obtain improvements in working conditions, and to secure freedom of association and free expression of opinion on political and social affairs. The basic attitude is summed up in a trade-union motto fairly common in the first half of the nineteenth century, 'United to Protect, but not Combined to Injure', which illustrates the mainly defensive outlook of working-class organisations in that period. Trade unionists and others were struggling to protect their traditional standards of living and working, in a time of revolutionary industrial and social change, when old crafts were declining under the competition of new machinery, while unemployment and poverty were widespread, and workers' associations were liable to legal prosecution. Yet they were almost entirely non-revolutionary, striving to achieve their aims by peaceful, constitutional means, by patient negotiation and agitation, without violently attacking other classes; violence did, of course, occur sporadically, against non-unionists as well as employers, but was generally condemned by trade unions.

Gradually, as trade unions and other labour organisations grew in strength, they were able to achieve considerable improvements in wages and hours of work, to better factory conditions, to bring pressure for other social and political reforms, and eventually, by creating first the Trades Union Congress and then the Labour Party, to help bring about the great socio-political changes of the present century. But throughout they have continued to maintain a non-revolutionary, reformist attitude, and trade unions especially still retain many of their traditional characteristics and defensive policies; though today there might be some doubt, especially in widely disruptive strikes, as to whether they are 'not Combined to Injure', the great majority of trade unions today still see themselves as essentially protective of their members' employment and living standards, condemn violence, and express regard for the public interest. Nevertheless, despite the growth of the Welfare State and rising living standards, this country is faced today with strikes, and threats of strikes, on a greater scale than ever in the nineteenth century. These studies will, it is hoped, throw some light on the historical background to such modern problems.

Chapter 1

WRITING TRADE-UNION HISTORY*

THE pioneering scholarly work of the Webbs[1] has stood almost unchallenged until recent years, describing and analysing the development of trade unionism from the Industrial Revolution to the twentieth century. G. D. H. Cole was, for a long time, the only historian to make any really significant reassessment.[2] During the past two decades, however, Labour history generally has attracted increasing attention and the range and depth of trade-union studies have been considerably extended.[3] The modern tendency is to view the growth of trade unions as part of general social history, part of the wider class struggle between capital and labour, linked with the socio-political movements of Radicalism, Chartism, Co-operation, Socialism, and the modern Labour Party, originating from the same socio-economic causes, swayed by the same ideological influences.[4] At the same time, the level of expertise in economic and sociological analysis of such related problems as class structure, real wages and the standard of living has risen markedly. The result has been a considerable increase in the scope and sophistication of trade-union history.

This tendency was already visible twenty years ago, when it was emphasised that 'no [trade-union] history can be written *in vacuo*. A trade-union historian must have a good general knowledge of the changing economic, legal, and political environment in which trade unions have developed. The trade cycle will be found to have had a particularly dominant influence.'[5] Since then the present writer has increased this emphasis on cyclical factors, because trade-union records demonstrate that the pattern of boom and slump was of greater significance than the more usually emphasised ideological fluctuations. Hobsbawm has also

---

* This is virtually a new chapter, though it draws to some extent on an article published in the *Amateur Historian*, Jan. 1954. It aims to provide some insight into the problems of research and writing on trade-union history, indicating what are regarded as the major themes. It also serves as an introduction to the following chapters.

laid stress upon the trade cycle,[6] though some of his observations as to its operation are open to criticism: it is very doubtful, for example, that in the first half of the nineteenth century 'slump explosions' in trade-unionism were the rule. Throughout the nineteenth century, before as well as after 1850, it was more usual, especially in the stronger craft trades, for increases in trade-union strength and activity to coincide with trade revival and boom, though weaker depressed trades might become more desperate in slumps.

Whatever difference of opinion may exist on timing and effects, however, there can be no doubt of the powerful influence of general economic forces upon trade-union development. Nowadays, therefore, one would need to recommend, even to an amateur historian, something beyond Clapham's *Economic History of Modern Britain* for general economic background. Cyclical studies such as those of Rostow and Matthews would be illuminating; Habakkuk's economic-technological comparison of Britain and America would draw attention to forces of supply and demand in the labour market and the influences of technological change; even studies of overseas trade, such as those of Imlah, are relevant to understanding the influence of export fluctuations on employment and the effects of changing terms of trade upon living standards; while investigations into the growth and distribution of national wealth and income, into population growth and distribution (geographical and occupational), and into changes in employment, retail prices, etc., are obviously significant.

Against this general economic and social background, as the author's researches into printing trade unionism demonstrated,[7] 'the historian of a trade union must have a thorough knowledge of the industrial development of the particular trade concerned, since this will have had directly important effects upon working conditions and upon the policy and growth of the union'.[8] He must acquire close familiarity with the changing business structure, technology and working practices of the industry, because these are of basic importance not only to employment and wages but also to labour relations, trade customs, and the whole environment in which any union operates. It is necessary to know how wages are paid, whether on time or piece rates, how rates vary according to different kinds of work—often in a highly complicated way on different machines, or materials, or jobs of varying difficulty—how the quantity and quality of work may be checked, what kinds of bonus systems are operated, how hours and overtime are regulated, and many other trade practices often peculiar to a particular industry. Contemporary technical accounts are usually available for most industries, together with general encyclopaedias or 'dictionaries of arts and sciences', while many local guides and histories also provide industrial descriptions; more general information is available in numerous parliamentary papers on trade and industry, factory and mines inspectors' reports, censuses of population and industry, and other official papers such as those of the Board of Trade and Ministry of Labour.

It is necessary, moreover, to delve beneath accounts and statistics of industries, especially in the nineteenth century, when wide variations were to be found in the industrial structures and customs of different areas. These variations have been stressed particularly by historians of coal-miners' unions, notably J. E. Williams,[9] on account of diverse geographical, geological, land-tenurial and economic factors which have brought about differences in business organisation, mining operations, and working conditions in different coalfields, and caused the characteristic strength of miners' district unions. But similar variations are to be found in other industries: there have always been marked differences between London and the provinces in the printing trade for example; London dockers' working conditions and unions differ from those in Liverpool; agricultural labourers in different parts of the country have always worked under different conditions of climate, soil, land tenure, etc.; nineteenth-century engineering workers in London did different kinds of work, and had different trade practices, from those in Lancashire.

The same is true if one is comparing trade unionism in different areas rather than in different industries; in fact, with growing localisation of industries the two kinds of differences tended to merge. Thus the trade unionism of London, with its multiplicity of skilled handicrafts and small workshops, contrasted strongly with that of Lancashire, where the workers were increasingly concentrated in factories, tending machines; workers in the small metal trades of the Birmingham area likewise experienced different conditions, productive of different union organisation and attitudes, from those of the engineering and shipbuilding workers of Clydeside. These local variations have been reflected, therefore, in recent histories of trades councils, as well as in studies of the differing responses of trade societies in different parts of the country to general movements such as Owenism and Chartism, as demonstrated by Asa Briggs and others.

For much the same reason, it is difficult to generalise about the experiences of trade unions under the law. This, however, has never been sufficiently emphasised, mainly because most histories of trade-union law have tended to be written from a legal point of view, depicting general statutory or common law changes, but inadequately investigating how variously the law was applied, or not applied, in different industries and areas. Dr. Dorothy George's pioneering work in this field[10] has never been adequately followed up, and trade-union historians are still apt to make subjective, prejudiced generalisations, backed by little historical investigation. In regard to the Combination Laws, for example, E. P. Thompson admits that 'no count has been made of the number of cases brought under them', but nevertheless he reaffirms the view—exploded by Dr. George—that the Combination Laws 'were often employed' and that trade societies were constantly repressed.[11]

Thus although several studies have been made of the legal aspects of trade unionism since R. V. Hedges and A. Winterbottom produced theirs in 1930,[12] there is still need for more painstaking research into the innumerable legal cases of the eighteenth and nineteenth centuries. One suspects that such research might reveal considerable variations in the application of the law between different industries, areas, and periods, reflecting the differences and changes in the underlying industrial structure and economic conditions.

Here again, then, in the legal as well as in the industrial sphere, one is impressed by the variety of trade-union experiences. This is equally so if one examines their varied roles in general socio-political movements, in which trade-union historians have frequently presented a false picture of trade-union solidarity. A notable example is provided by E. P. Thompson in his book on 'the making of the English working class'. The extent to which emotional and ideological influences can sway historical judgement is well illustrated by the contrast between his sound historical evidence on the wide differences between different sections of the working *classes*—especially between skilled artisans organised in trade societies and others—and his insistence, nevertheless, on the existence of a united, self-conscious, working *class* by as early as 1832. Other left-wing historians, such as Hobsbawm and Harrison, by contrast, whilst emphasising the solidarity shown in such movements as Owenism and Chartism, and slurring over the deep-rooted sectionalism of trade societies, recognised by Thompson, emphasise the gulf between the skilled, so-called 'New Model' unions and the depressed sections of the working class after mid-century.[13] There is, in fact, plentiful evidence to show that neither Owenism nor Chartism came anywhere near to being united, class-conscious workers' movements; certainly the extent of support which they gained from trade unions has often been greatly exaggerated. In fact, as Pelling has concluded, it is 'a mistake . . . to speak of a homogeneous "working class" in Britain at any time before the later nineteenth century'.[14] Indeed, it does not exist even today, with the continuance of wide differences in wages and outlook, strong sectionalism of trade unions, complexities of status and class structure, and the existence of a Conservative Government helped into office by working-class votes.

For all the talk of 'brotherhood', in fact, the most striking feature of trade-union history has always been its profound sectionalism. A trade union is, by its very nature, a union of workers in a particular trade, concerned with maintaining or advancing their own material interests. Throughout the nineteenth century, schemes of general trades' union or federation broke on this rock, and even when trade unions did collaborate, as in the Trades Union Congress or in the Labour Party, they maintained—and still retain—their basic sectional interests, their insistence on autonomy in trade affairs, especially in wages-bargaining, and are prepared to strike, even under a Labour Government and in nationalised industries, to secure as large a slice of the national cake for themselves as they can.

It is not, therefore, in general histories of trade-unionism or of working-class movements that the basic characteristics of trade unionism are to be found, but in the histories of individual unions. Owenism, Chartism, and modern Socialism undoubtedly have a wide and idealistic appeal, and trade unions have, to varying degrees, been captivated by it in the past and present, but these movements have really transcended trade unionism, and, indeed, have often clashed with it. Mass movements and revolutionary slogans have an excitement which generally attracts students of working-class history, especially young ones these days, but most trade-union activity has always been concerned with more limited mundane affairs relating to wages, hours, and working conditions, with patient organising and negotiations, and—before the Welfare State—with careful administration of friendly benefits. It is at bench and forge, in workshop and factory, in branch, district, and national office, that one must seek trade unionism.

Unfortunately, this kind of trade–union history can hardly be written for the early years, in the eighteenth and early nineteenth centuries, from which trade-union records (minute-books, reports, etc.) have rarely survived, and then only in a scrappy, incomplete form. Recourse must therefore be had to other evidence, necessarily second-hand. Many valuable documents for this period —contemporary pamphlets, parliamentary petitions, etc., copies of trade-union rules, and even some correspondence—are to be found in the British Museum (among the Place papers, for example), in the Goldsmiths' Library (London University), and in various public libraries. There is also much valuable material in the Public Record Office (especially among Home Office papers) and in the evidence before Parliamentary Committees and Royal Commissions on trade unionism, such as those of 1824, 1838, and 1867. The *Report on Trade Societies and Strikes*, published by the Social Science Association in 1860, is also very valuable. An enormous amount of evidence can also be gleaned from local newspapers and periodicals, most notably from the *Beehive* in the 1860s and 70s.

From the mid-century onwards, however, as national unions came to be more numerously and strongly established, records of the trade-unions themselves become more abundant and the main sources for their history over the past hundred years are to be found at union headquarters—in the volumes of Executive Council minutes, monthly periodicals, yearly or half-yearly reports, delegate meeting reports, reports of conferences with employers and with other unions, rule-books, wage-scales, branch circulars and 'memorials', collections of statistics and miscellaneous papers, together with a growing volume of correspondence, which have accumulated in the filing cabinets and cellars of national trade unions. These records become enormous in modern times: in the Typographical Association, for example, 'the Executive Council Minutes for 1853–65 were contained in one small book, but a large 500 page volume was needed for six months minutes by the end of the century'.[15]

At the same time, however, it is necessary to examine branch records in order to gain knowledge of local affairs. This is especially important in the nineteenth century, when unions were much less centralised, when branches and workshops played a more important role, and wages and working conditions varied more widely than in modern times. Indeed, records of this kind frequently date back to a period long before any national union came into being, to the early days when trade unionism was an affair of small independent, local societies in towns and districts. In the same way, these small societies frequently co-operated in local trades associations, mostly for mutual support in strikes, leading eventually to the formation of permanent trades councils, from the mid-century onwards, before a national trades council—the Trades Union Congress—was established in 1868.

As the T.U.C. developed, together with national unions in the later nineteenth century, it tended to become the national focus for trade-union interests in the political sphere, just as trades' councils developed locally into what the Webbs called 'the political organs of the Labour world'. Indeed, before the T.U.C. was established, the London Trades Council, controlled by the famous 'Junta', had begun to play such a role at the national centre, and its records, still surviving, mirror these widening trade-union interests. Later, of course, these interests came to be recorded in the T.U.C. archives, in the minutes of the Parliamentary Committee, annual Congress reports, etc., and thus a great quantity of records was eventually accumulated, raw material not only for the T.U.C.'s own history by B. C. Roberts, but a mine of information on general union affairs. Together with these, there are other collections of national importance transcending the affairs of individual unions, though again mainly concerned with political matters, such as the George Howell collection in the Bishopsgate Institute, London, and the John Burns collection, in the British Museum, as well as in Congress House.

The T.U.C., however, has never been able to exercise much control—save in a conciliatory role in major trade disputes—over the trade policies of individual unions, which to this day have jealously guarded their autonomy in matters relating to the wages and working conditions of their members. (Hence, of course, the present-day difficulty in getting a 'national incomes policy' negotiated through the T.U.C., the Confederation of British Industry, and any Government, Labour or Conservative.) On these 'trade' matters, therefore, the records of individual unions are all-important.

A plea may be put in here, however, for more attention to the records of employers' associations, where these are available. Nearly all trade-union histories are based on union evidence alone and are inevitably one-sided: they generally fail to take account of problems on the employers' side relating to trading difficulties, competition, costs, credit restrictions, labour discipline, and the objections to 'restrictive practices' (ca'canny', 'go-slow', and other output limitations) and 'closed shop' policies. Employers generally appear in trade-union histories as the enemy, as profiteering oppressors of the working class, and no account is taken of the role of entrepreneurs in providing capital, business enterprise, technological innovation, and organising skill, in bearing responsibility and taking risks: it is capitalist entrepreneurs who have been the dynamic driving force behind increasing industrial production, trade and wealth, resulting in rising living standards, whereas trade unions have almost always played a purely defensive, conservative role. That unions should have played such a role is understandable: faced by uncertainties of employment and fears of poverty, their essential purpose has been to safeguard their jobs, wages, and working conditions, and also to provide mutual help in times of distress. There is no doubt, moreover, that workers have suffered from profiteering exploitation and from grossly unequal distribution of national wealth and income. It is, however, a salutary exercise for a trade-union historian also to undertake a business history and to see things from 'the other side'. It is true that he will find there are many things to confirm his suspicions of employers: the records of firms and employers' associations undoubtedly display an emphasis on maximising profits and reducing labour costs, and they also reveal many 'restrictive practices' among employers themselves, limiting output, fixing markets, keeping up prices, etc.[16]—'free competition' is largely a figment of economic theory. But an awareness of the complexity of business problems, of which labour is only one, will emerge from such a study, while many examples of employers' concern for good labour relations and for the welfare of their employees will also be evident.

Our trade-union historian will thus be faced with a vast quantity of factual material, growing prodigiously in modern times. He is therefore confronted, like any other historian, with the problem of methodology: how to arrange the miscellaneous multitude of facts which he has collected into intelligible and interesting order and yet not present an over-rationalised and artifical picture of the past. Many trade-union histories, particularly older ones, are merely hotchpot collections of random snippets from voluminous records. This mode of writing is doubtless quick and easy, and only such popular presentations are likely to interest the average trade-union member; but they do not provide a thorough and penetrating analysis. This is impossible to achieve in a general chronological narrative. The complex mass of historical material has to be arranged under subject headings—growth and organisation; relations with employers; wages, hours, and working regulations; apprentices; friendly benefits; relations with other unions; political action, etc.—probably in several broad chronological divisions, so as to provide an intelligible and connected account of union policy in each of these fields. This mode of treatment, of course, has itself several drawbacks: it involves much more work for the historian, with problems of overlapping and cross references, while division into compartments is unreal historically and does not present the day-to-day problems of union affairs, as portrayed for example in Executive Council minute-books, with their plethora of miscellaneous matters from branches all over the country. But history is not mere chronicling: it must be analytical, it must seek to demonstrate the main continuous themes and their interconnections.

There is, in fact, a basic continuity in trade-union history, a gradual evolution, with few if any major breaks or watersheds. The early history, in the eighteenth and well into the nineteenth century, is concerned with small local societies, in some cases perhaps evolving from journeymen 'fraternities' and workshop organisations (like the printers' 'chapels') within the older craft gilds. These local societies were often linked together by 'tramp relief'—a form of unemployment relief which continued in many trades throughout the nineteenth and even into the twentieth century—and they also began to collaborate in trade affairs. But although loose national associations are to be discerned in some trades, such as weavers, hatters, woolcombers, shoemakers, etc., in the late eighteenth and early nineteenth centuries, truly national unions did not begin to emerge until around 1830, and many of these collapsed or became only shadowy remnants in subsequent trade depression, before reviving more strongly and continuously from the 1840s and 1850s onwards. This strong and successful revival, notably the creation of the Amalgamated Society of Engineers in 1851, led the Webbs to create the fiction of a 'New Model', but, in fact, as we shall see, there was little or nothing new in the organisation and policies of these unions.[17] They remained, as they always had been, exclusive craft organisations of skilled, relatively well-paid workers, with entry usually by apprenticeship, separated by demarcation lines from other trades and also closed against semi-skilled or unskilled workers from below. There are a few examples of sporadic unions among the latter, among dock-labourers, seamen, gas-stokers, agricultural labourers (such as the famous 'Tolpuddle martyrs'), and others, from the late eighteenth century onwards, but such workers remained mostly unorganised and efforts at unionism among them remained ephemeral until the later nineteenth century.

From a legal point of view also, trade unionism presents a pattern of gradual change. Too much importance has generally been attached to legal landmarks such as those of 1799–1800, 1825, and 1871–5. Repression of early trade societies, under the common law of conspiracy, the law of master and servant, and various parliamentary statutes, pre-dated the Combination Laws, and evidence of trade-union growth and activity, as well as examination of legal evidence, shows that the extent and severity of legal repression under this general legislation of 1799–1800 has often been, and often still is, exaggerated, despite Dr. Dorothy George's findings.[18] Similarly, and probably in consequence, the effects of the repeal of the Combination Laws have also been exaggerated. Unions had only very narrowly circumscribed legal status after 1825, and prosecutions at common law or under the law of master and servant were by no means unusual right down to the legislation of 1871–5.[19] Most unions, however, remained untroubled by the law, so that the Acts of the early 'seventies did not seriously alter the pattern of trade-union growth and policies. Many unions, indeed, never bothered about registering, or even deliberately refrained from doing so, under the 1871 Act. Nevertheless, the renewed legal threat posed by the Taff Vale Case of 1901 certainly caused a furore among trade unions, leading to the 1906 Trade Disputes Act, and to this day trade unions have remained apprehensive, distrustful, and doggedly opposed to any further threat of legislative control—hence the present fierce opposition to the Industrial Relations Act.

Gradual change is also apparent, and deep-rooted traditions have long continued, in the industrial sphere. Early trade societies were predominantly of handicraft workers in small workshops, because master-servant (or employer-employee) relationships, and confrontations between capital and labour, long preceded the Industrial Revolution. It is true that the 'factory system' did begin, from the late eighteenth century onwards, to have an important effect, massing large numbers of workers together and deepening the division between capital and labour, but knowledge of industrial history demonstrates that even after a century of 'industrial revolution', in 1850, factory workers were still a small minority of the total labour force, and the majority of trade societies were still composed of handicraftsmen. Certainly as mechanisation and factories continued to develop in the later nineteenth and twentieth centuries, the large battalions of factory workers and miners tended to predominate, but it is often forgotten how long many trades remained unmechanised, or only partially mechanised: the building trades, for example, clothing and boot-and-shoe trades, printing, dockwork, and many others. Moreover, it must be remembered that in the new factory industries, it was for long only among the skilled workers, the new *élite* of cotton spinners, engineers, etc., that trade unionism developed, with exclusive characteristics similar to those of the older skilled handicraft trades. Many of the latter, moreover, managed to survive the gradual transition from handicraft-workshop to mechanised-factory organisation, the printers being probably the most successful example, still preserving many of their older craft traditions. Others, of course, such as the handloom weavers' trade societies, were destroyed in the march of mechanisation, and the history of these depressed trades has tended to be neglected, until the recent researches of Bythell and Prothero,[20] because trade-union histories are almost all concerned with the development of successful, surviving modern unions; the casualities of industrialisation have largely been forgotten.

It was among these depressed trades that Owenism and Chartism secured most support in the 1830s and 1840s. Unable, because of unemployment and depressed wages, to maintain strong unions and trade policies, they turned desperately to Owenite-Socialist and Chartist ideas, hoping to ameliorate their conditions by social revolution or political democracy. The stronger societies, in both old and new trades, mostly held aloof from what they regarded as Utopian movements, preferring to rely on industrial bargaining for improvements in wages and hours, and on their friendly benefits for relief in unemployment, etc.

This type of Old Unionism grew from strength to strength in the third quarter of the nineteenth century, still predominantly concerned with sectional trade affairs. Except for their agitation on the Labour Laws, crowned with success in 1871–5, they continued to eschew political activity, which was mainly confined to the trades councils. It was not until the 1880s that a distinctively new trend in trade unionism developed. This new phase was not, like the so-called 'New Model', a figment of historical imagination, but was clearly evident to contemporary unionists themselves, as a clash developed between what they termed 'Old' and 'New' Unionism. Even so, one must beware of exaggerating this change, which did not occur so rapidly or completely as has often been suggested. 'New Unionism' is usually associated with the 1880s, but one of its most marked features, the organisation of semi-skilled and un-skilled workers, had been strongly foreshadowed in the late 'sixties and early 'seventies, with the formation of trade unions among railwaymen, dockers, agricultural labourers, etc., although collapse had followed in the subsequent trade depression. The new trends certainly became more strongly evident in the 'eighties, but a similar relapse occurred in the depression of the early and mid-'nineties. Nevertheless the new unions—the general and industrial unions of labourers, dockers, etc.—were now becoming an established feature, instead of collapsing completely as they had done in earlier depressions, and so the total membership and occupational coverage of trade unionism expanded very considerably.

But 'New Unionism' was by no means confined to new unions. Old-established craft unions also expanded their membership substantially and imbibed the new spirit, often assisting in the formation of new unions and also tending to join more readily in trades federations or amalgamations; a more democratic spirit was also evident in more numerous representative councils, delegate meetings, and ballot votes. Most noticeably of all, however, they were influenced by the new political spirit, by Socialism and the idea of 'independent Labour representation' on local councils and in Parliament. Trade-union periodicals, previously rather arid trade journals, were now enlivened with discussion of political and social questions, ranging from the Eight Hours Bill and workmen's compensation to unemployment, education, and housing. Trade societies began to establish labour representation funds and eventually they joined with the T.U.C. and Socialist organisations in founding the Labour Party.

This swing into politics was undoubtedly the most profound change in the whole history of British trade unionism. Nevertheless, it did not mean abandonment of traditional trade-union methods: the 'Old' unionists, who had argued against political involvement and in favour of reliance on collective trade bargaining for improvement of workers' living standards, may have been defeated, but much of the spirit of 'Old Unionism' still survived, and still does. Sectionalism still remained strong, despite the growth of 'industrial' and 'general' unionism,[21] and it soon became evident—and has remained evident, even under Labour Governments—that political action would not fulfil all their hopes. At first this was because of the weakness and futility of the infant Labour Party, but in modern times, when Labour has achieved political power, the trade unions have certainly not been prepared to abandon their trade autonomy and subsume their traditional sectional bargaining under Socialist planning.

The Labour Movement has continued, in the twentieth century, to have two distinct wings, and trade unions have certainly shown no signs of withering away with the growth of political democracy and a semi-Socialist society. Indeed, the growing strength of trade unions has in some ways posed a threat to the State, whether under Conservative or Labour governments. Threats of a General Strike have faded since the fiasco of 1926, but individual trade unions have not hesitated to use their industrial power against the general public in order to enforce their wages demands. Nationalisation has not proved the panacea it was once hoped, and miners and railwaymen have remained as sectionally aggressive as workers in private industries. The danger of crippling national strikes has increased in the present century, with the growing centralisation of union government and the development of national bargaining with employers' national organisations, in place of the workshop and branch bargaining of the nineteenth century.

On the other hand, however, national agreements and union diplomacy have greatly reduced the number of petty local stikes, while at national level unions have generally been prepared, in the event of negiotiating deadlock, to accept conciliation or arbitration machinery for settlement of disputes. Consequently, the number of 'days lost' through strikes in Britain compares favourably with those in most other countries. At the same time, however, the growing power of central union executives and officials has given rise to certain weaknesses—loss of contact with the rank-and-file and hence either apathy among the membership or local discontent, 'unofficial' action, and 'splinter' groups.[22]

To understand basic trade unionism, therefore, in the twentieth century as in the nineteenth, it is necessary to go to the 'grass roots'. In recent years their aggressive, materialist, sectional motives have been most apparent: these have certainly been strengthened, paradoxically, by the unprecedented rise in living standards since the Second World War. But trade unions remain staunchly defensive, despite the Welfare State, as demonstrated particularly by their increasing emphasis on job-security, with the associated fear of unemployment. This underlay much of nineteenth-century trade unionism: their efforts to reduce hours and overtime, their limitation of apprentices, their demarcations, exclusion of 'illegal' men, opposition to female labour, hostility towards mechanisation, regulation of machine-manning, restrictive 'go-slow' practices, and antipathy towards incentive schemes. The great slump of the inter-war years deepened these fears, and memories of the past have combined with renewed fears of technological change to cause modern trade unions to cling tenaciously to old attitudes and policies.

NOTES

1. S. and B. Webb, *The History of Trade Unionism* (rev. edn., 1920).
2. G. D. H. Cole, 'Some Notes on British Trade Unionism in the Third Quarter of the Ninteenth Century', *Int. Rev. for Soc. Hist.*, Vol. II (1937), reprinted in E. M. Carus-Wilson (ed.), *Essays in Economic History*, Vol. III (1962).
3. For recent general reviews, see E. J. Hobsbawm, 'Trade Union Historiography', Labour History Society *Bulletin*, No. 8, Spring 1964, and A. E. Musson, *British Trade Unions, 1800–1875* (Macmillan, Studies in Economic History, 1972).
4. The most outstanding recent example of this kind of history is E. P. Thompson, *The Making of the British Working Class* (rev. ed., 1968).
5. Musson, *Amateur Historian*, Jan. 1954.
6. E. J. Hobsbawm, *Labouring Men* (1964), Chap. 8.
7. A. E. Musson, *The Typographical Association: Origins and History up to 1949* (1954).
8. *Amateur Historian*, Jan. 1954.
9. J. E. Williams, 'Labour in the Coalfields: A Critical Bibliography', Labour History Society *Bulletin*, No. 4, Spring 1962.

10. M. D. George, 'The Combination Laws Reconsidered', *Economic History* (supplement to *Economic Journal*), No. 2, May 1927, and 'The Combination Laws', *Econ. Hist. Rev.*, Vol. VI (1936).
11. Thompson, *op. cit.*, Chap. 13, sec. iii.
12. R. V. Hedges and A. Winterbottom, *The Legal History of Trade Unionism* (1930); W. Milne-Bailey, *Trade Unions and the State* (1934); D. F. Macdonald, *The State and the Trade Unions* (1960); D. Simon, 'Master and Servant', in J. Saville (ed.), *Democracy and the Labour Movement* (1954).
13. See below, Chap. 2.
14. H. M. Pelling, *A History of British Trade Unionism* (1963), pp. 4–6.
15. Musson, *op. cit.*, p. 131.
16. See below, Chapter 6, for example.
17. See below, pp. 17–21.
18. See above, pp. 3–4.
19. See below, Chap. 3.
20. D. Bythell, *The Handloom Weavers* (1969); I. Prothero, 'Chartism in London', *Past and Present*, No. 44, Aug. 1969, and 'London Chartism and the Trades', *Econ. Hist. Rev.*, 2nd ser., Vol. XXIV, No. 2, May 1971.
21. See below. Chapter 4.
22. See below, pp. 75–6.

Chapter 2

TRENDS IN TRADE-UNION DEVELOPMENT, 1825–75*

THE Webbs interpreted trade-union history according to their Fabian Socialist views of social evolution. They highlighted those developments which demonstrated the evolution of Socialism among trade unions, while they dealt inadequately with the more purely trade-union aspects. There is plenty of evidence, however, that the latter constituted the most essential, solid, and continuous features of trade-union history in the nineteenth century, i.e. patient organisation of local societies and development of district and national unions, collective bargaining on wages, hours, apprentices, and working conditions, and arrangement of friendly benefits for unemployment, sickness, superannuation, and death. The practical effects of Owenite ideology, or later of classical economics, upon the actual organisation and policies of trade unions appear to have been superficial, and were exaggerated in importance by the Webbs.

The outburst of trade-union activity during the years 1829–34 was not a product of Owenite Socialist enthusiasm, but was a mainly endogenous movement. It was encouraged psychologically, if not legally, by the repeal of the Combination Laws. (The full effects of repeal were delayed by the economic crisis and serious depression of 1826 and the following years.) There had been, however, a similar outburst in 1818–19, even including an attempt at general trades' union. The practical aims were also unaltered: to deal with wages reductions, the breakdown of apprenticeship regulations and heavy unemployment. The cotton spinners, for example, in organising their Grand General Union in 1829—preceded by similar general movements in 1810 and 1825—were motivated by purely trade-union aims regarding wages, entry to the trade, and establishment of a strike fund. So, too, were the

* This chapter is based on a paper dealing with 'The Webbs and their phasing of trade-union development between the 1830s and the 1860s', a synopsis of which appeared in the *Bulletin of the Society for the Study of Labour History*, No. 4, Spring 1962. For a fuller discussion, see A. E. Musson, *British Trade Unions, 1800–1875* (1972).

letterpress printers in establishing their Northern Union in 1830; organisation of tramp relief for the unemployed was also a strong motive. The same is true of the miners, builders, potters, and other workers who began to organise wider district or national unions during these years.

Many trade societies, it is true, were influenced by Owenite ideas. A small minority of idealists wrote and spoke in favour of 'general union' and a Socialist millennium, but their propaganda had very little practical effect. It is clearly evident, in fact, from the literature of the early 'thirties that there were clashes between trade unionism and socialism (or co-operation) and that most trade societies were not prepared to subordinate their autonomy or their traditional policies to Owen's 'new view of society', though they might express sympathy with his aims. A few started small schemes of co-operative production, but mostly as a means of relieving unemployed or strike members rather than as serious attempts at altering the social system. The National Association for the Protection of Labour—an attempt at general union or trades' federation—grew out of the failure of the Lancashire cotton spinners' strike in 1829 and was primarily an attempt at organising a large strike fund. This above all is what attracted other trade societies into it—though it did provide wider social and political horizons—and it collapsed when piecemeal strikes broke out and failed. Most trade societies were primarily concerned with their sectional trade objectives. Doherty was unable to carry even the cotton spinners with him in his more radical schemes of political and social reform, while some societies, such as that of the Manchester letterpress printers, declined to have any connection with the Association.[1]

Owen's Grand National Consolidated Trades' Union was mainly a revival of Doherty's earlier organisation. The upsurge of trade unionism in 1833–4 must also be attributed to trade recovery. It should be emphasised, however, that the Grand National lasted for less than a year; that many of the skilled societies such as those of cotton spinners, engineers, and printers, held aloof; that, though some labourers were briefly organised, unionism spread only to a very limited extent beyond traditional craft boundaries; and that the Dorchester labourers, or 'Tolpuddle martyrs', were mainly concerned with trying to improve agricultural wages, not with revolutionising society. Careful research has demonstrated that the Webbs' guess of half-a-million members was ridiculously exaggerated: total paid-up membership was probably no more than about 16,000, consisting mostly of London tailors, shoe-makers, and silk-weavers, though a good many more were vaguely associated with the Union.[2] Owen himself was not really interested in trade unions, but only in using them as instruments for his own non-militant, co-operative-socialist schemes, and he quickly abandoned them when trade unionists themselves showed far more interest in strikes about wages and other trade matters. The whole Owenite episode, in fact, was grossly inflated by the Webbs.

This inflation, moreover, tended to warp their interpretation of subsequent trade-union development. There was not such a catastrophic collapse after 1834 as they tend to suggest. Most of the traditionally organised craft societies remained in existence, pursuing much the same policies as they had always done. It is, as the Webbs point out, extremely difficult to make a reliable estimate of total trade-union membership at this time; but their estimate of 100,000 in the late 1830s, contrasted with the inflated figure of half-a-million in the Grand National, certainly creates a very misleading impression. It is doubtful whether the hard core of continuously organised trade unionists was any less in the late 1830s than in the late 1820s, though it had certainly been higher in the upswing of 1833–4. There is plenty of evidence, *e.g.* that given in the report of the Select Committee on Combinations in 1838, and also in surviving though scrappy trade-union records and periodicals such as the *Northern Star*, to show that most trade societies survived after the collapse of the Grand National in 1834. They did, however, have to face very great difficulties between 1836 and 1843, in perhaps the most serious trade depression of the nineteenth century. Indeed the phasing of trade-union development, not only in this period but throughout the whole century coincided very closely with the trade cycle: in boom periods new unions were founded, while old ones were strengthened, membership grew, and advance movements began, while in depressions some societies collapsed, membership declined, and rearguard actions had to be fought against wage-cuts. This pattern of boom and slump is much more clearly evident than the ideological fluctuations propounded by the Webbs.

It was, in fact, reviving trade that brought about a strong recovery of trade unionism from 1843. This was noted by the Webbs, but given less importance than the development of so-called 'New Model' unionism from 1851, with the establishment of the Amalgamated Society of Engineers. The evidence indicates, in fact, that the real recovery began at the earlier date; although it was interrupted by another trade depression from 1846–7, this was less serious and hit the unions less hard than that in the late 'thirties and early 'forties. Moreover, there is very little, if any, justification for the term 'New Model', since the unions of the engineers, masons, carpenters, printers, etc., of the 'fifties and 'sixties preserved the main characteristics of earlier years. There was no radical change in organisation, not even in the engineers' society, which adopted the constitution of the 'Old Mechanics' or Journeymen Steam Engine and Machine Makers' Society;[3] since the late 'twenties (and earlier in some cases) local societies in many trades had been tending to federate or amalgamate into district and national unions, and central executives and permanent secretaries had begun to emerge. Restriction of membership to apprenticed craftsmen, payment of high subscriptions, and provision of friendly benefits were also long-established features. Nor was there any change in objectives: craft societies had always been primarily concerned with sectionalist trade policies regarding wages, hours, apprenticeship, and the 'closed shop'. Socialism and Chartism had never made much impression upon most of them, though some of the depressed trades, such as weavers and shoemakers, weakened by unemployment and reduced wages, had vainly sought salvation in political and social reform. Some of these weaker societies also participated in a renewed attempt at general union, the National Association of United Trades in 1845, but the larger, more powerful unions again held aloof and the scheme gradually fizzled out; Dr. Prothero's recent attempt to resurrect it, though interesting in drawing attention to the participation of many of these 'lower grades' in London,[4] cannot dispose of the fact that the Association failed to attract support from the trade-union movement as a whole.

To some extent there may appear to have been a narrowing of trade-union horizons. Owenite Socialism and Chartism, with their Utopian ideas of political and social revolution, faded into the past and trade unionists concentrated more intensively on down-to-earth, more realistic, practical objectives. The socio-political atmosphere certainly seemed less charged and exciting than in the earlier period, as reflected in trade-union and radical periodicals. This was probably because of the improvement in social conditions, the more buoyant economy of the third quarter of the century, the gradual rise in living standards, the effects of factory legislation and other social reforms: the worst of the Industrial Revolution was past, and the benefits of increasing national production and wealth were percolating down more widely in society. But even in the darker years of the preceding period, the great majority of trade societies had never abandoned their traditional means of defence in favour of political and social revolt, but had stuck tenaciously to their craft organisations and their efforts to maintain or improve wages and working conditions in their own particular trades. And this is what they continued to do. What happened in the 'fifties and 'sixties was not the creation of a 'New Model', but a strengthening of the old.

Hobsbawm and Harrison have recently endeavoured to maintain the myth created by the Webbs, adding the notion of dominance from mid-century by an exclusive and selfish 'labour aristocracy'.[5] But as the Webbs' own evidence demonstrated, and as other historians such as Thompson have strongly confirmed,[6] trade societies had always consisted of a 'labour aristocracy', divided by wide economic and social differentials from the mass of the 'labouring poor' beneath them, and they had always fought to maintain these differentials, by exclusive, sectionalist, trade policies, restricting entry to the trade by apprenticeship and admission fees, by demarcation lines and exclusion of 'illegal' men, trying to maintain craft status and wages, opposing the use of machinery, etc., and at the same time protecting their members against socio-economic disaster and parish relief by friendly benefits in unemployment, sickness, old age, and death. These well-tried methods they had always preferred to chimerical hopes of political and social revolution. So for the great majority of trade unionists there was no narrowing of horizons after mid-century, no abandonment or betrayal of noble ideals. They continued patiently, and successfully, in fact, to build on the well-established foundations of earlier trade unionism.

Nor did these unions, as the Webbs maintained, pursue more pacific policies than the earlier unions had done, abandoning an aggressive, even revolutionary, policy of strikes in favour of industrial pacifism. Collective bargaining with employers had long been developing as a means of settling disputes. Most unions had always endeavoured to avoid strikes, to arrange compromise agreements, trying to safeguard their meagre funds, to avoid loss of work, unemployment and perhaps even break-up of their union. Strikes had long been regarded as a necessary evil, a weapon only to be used in the last resort: 'United to Protect, but not Combined to Injure' had been the motto of the printers' Northern Union and this attitude was typical of the older craft societies. This had not, however, prevented the occurrence of numerous strikes, nor does their number appear to have diminished in the third quarter of the century. The engineers' strike of 1852 and the builders' of 1859 are only the two most outstanding examples: myriads of smaller disputes occurred, as shown in trade-union minute-books, reports and periodicals such as the *Beehive*.

This was so even in the so-called 'New Model' or amalgamated societies, on which the Webbs concentrated their attention. It is true that with the growing strength of trade unionism and the more favourable economic climate, employers were generally becoming readier to recognise and negotiate with trade unions, and that conciliation and arbitration were more strongly advocated from the 'fifties onwards, unions joining with employers to secure enabling legislation, but they certainly never abandoned the strike weapon. Increasingly centralised control did, however, exercise more restraint upon local militancy. Smaller societies in London and the provinces—neglected by the Webbs—still tended to be more actively aggressive. On the other hand, centralisation could also be associated with militancy, as in the case of Halliday's Amalgamated Association of Miners. Indeed, as G. D. H. Cole showed more than a quarter-century ago, militancy and strikes were still characteristic of many societies.[7]

Cole also pointed out that the Webbs were mistaken in depicting the typical or dominant trade society as the amalgamated type, like that created by the engineers and carpenters. In London there were still numerous small societies, and in the provinces many trades were still organised on a town or district basis, as were the miners and also the cotton operatives, among whom, as Turner has shown, 'the basic unit remained the autonomous local society'.[8] In fact, the typical trade society still remained fairly small, with only a few hundred members, while even the larger unions generally had only a few thousands. No doubt the amalgamated societies and the 'Junta' in the London Trades Council played a leading role in trade-union affairs, but the Webbs, influenced especially by Robert Applegarth of the Carpenters' Amalgamated Society, considerably exaggerated their role, deliberately minimising that of the smaller metropolitan societies, led by George Potter, and neglecting the provincial societies, from among whom, in fact, the Trades Union Congress eventually originated.[9]

Similarly, there is little truth in the Webbs' assertion that trade-union leaders in the third quarter of the nineteenth century were dominated by middle-class economic philosophy. Whatever lip-service they may have paid to it, when it suited their purposes, they did not, in fact, accept the wage-fund theory, or the immutability of the 'laws' of supply and demand, nor did they regard strikes as harmful and useless interferences with freedom of contract.[10] Trade unions, in fact, continued to pursue their traditional craft policies, endeavouring to peg up wages, to reduce hours of work, to limit overtime, to enforce apprenticeship restrictions, and to apply the 'closed shop' policy wherever they could, despite the tenets of economic theory, and they did not shrink from strikes to attain their ends.

To sum up, then, the Webbs' account of trade-union history in this period presents far too strong a contrast between what they regard as the generally militant trade unionism of the second quarter of the century, strongly influenced by Owenite Socialist ideas, and the pacific, narrow-minded 'New Model' unionism of the third quarter, curbed by orthodox economics. On the one hand, they grossly inflate the importance and even distort the character of 'revolutionary' Owenism, while, on the other hand, they greatly exaggerate the novelty and pacifism of the so-called 'New Model' unions. In actual fact, there was a strong thread of continuity, both in organisation and policy, through the whole period. Sectional craft societies, gradually extending and strengthening their traditional organisations, and concerned with bread-and-butter questions of wages and employment, formed the backbone of trade unionism all through these years.

In the later part of this period, however, the Webbs overlooked or underestimated the significance of certain more novel features. Already one can discern the emergence of a 'New Unionism' usually associated with the 1880s and 1890s. Among the cotton weavers for example, as Turner has shown, there was a strong development from mid-century onwards of a 'mass' unionism, of semi-skilled machine-minding workers, different from 'aristocratic' craft unionism,[11] and in the late 'sixties and early 'seventies there was a remarkable upsurge of trade unionism among other non-craft workers, including railwaymen, dockers, gas stokers, and building and agricultural labourers.[12] There was also a swing towards political action, in the Reform League, agitating for working-class parliamentary representation, and helping to achieve the 1867 Reform Act; in the Labour Representation League, founded in 1869; in the agitation over the Labour Laws; and in the Land and Labour League, with more extreme demands for land nationalisation and links with the First Socialist International.

The legislative achievements of 1867 and 1871–5, however, were followed by trade depression in the later 'seventies, which caused a recession in trade-union growth and activity. Trade unionism continued upon the old traditional lines, until the greater upheaval and expansion of 'New Unionism' and Socialism in the following decades.

NOTES

1. See below, p. 125.
2. W. H. Oliver, 'The Consolidated Trades' Union of 1934', *Econ. Hist. Rev.*, 2nd ser., Vol. XVII, no. 1, Aug. 1964.
3. J. B. Jefferys, *The Story of the Engineers, 1800–1945* (1946).

4. I. Prothero, 'London Chartism and the Trades', *Econ. Hist. Rev.*, 2nd ser., Vol. XXIV, No. 2, May 1971.
5. E. J. Hobsbawm, *Labouring Men* (1964), Chap. 15, and R. Harrison, *Before the Socialists: Studies in Labour and Politics. 1861–1881* (1965), Chap. 1.
6. Thompson, *op. cit.*, Chapter 8, on 'Artisans and Others'. V. L. Alien also agrees with the present writer that 'New Model Unionism ranks as a piece of historical fiction': 'A Methodological Criticism of the Webbs as Trade Union Historians', Labour History Society *Bulletin*, No. 4, Spring 1962.
7. See above, p. 13, n. 2.
8. H. A. Turner, *Trade Union Growth, Structure and Policy: A Comparative Study of the Cotton Unions* (1962), p. 109.
9. See below, Chapter 3.
10. This has been convincingly demonstrated by R. V. Clements, 'British Trade Unions and Popular Political Economy, 1850–1875', *Econ. Hist. Rev.*, 2nd ser., Vol. XIV (1961–2), pp. 93–104.
11. Turner, *op. cit.*, Chapters 3 and 4.
12. Pelling, *op. cit.*, pp. 72–7.

Chapter 3

THE ORIGINS AND ESTABLISHMENT OF THE TRADES UNION CONGRESS*

The founding of the Trades Union Congress is generally recognised as a landmark in the history of British trade unionism and of the whole Labour movement. Yet before this study was first published, in 1955, it had never been satisfactorily investigated and explained. George Howell wrote brief historical sketches in an article, 'Trades Union Congresses and Social Legislation', in the Contemporary Review, *September 1889, and in his* Labour Legislation, Labour Movements and Labour Leaders *(1905); he also appears to have been the author of a special article which appeared in the* Manchester Guardian *in September 1882, on the occasion of the second Congress to be held in Manchester, where it had first met fourteen years before.[1] The Webbs wrote a great deal about earlier attempts at general union, but their account of immediate T.U.C. origins was contained in a mere footnote to their trade-union history.[2] W. J. Davis, in his* History of the British Trades Union Congress *(1910) was extremely sketchy. Professor G. D. H. Cole wrote some notes on British trade unionism in that period,[3] which threw interesting light on T.U.C. origins, but his purpose was not to make a detailed study of that subject. No other writer had done much to illuminate it before this study appeared. Since then, Professor B. C. Roberts has written* The Trades Union Congress, 1868–1921 *(1958) which provides a scholarly history of the Congress over that whole period, but adds nothing of substance to the account of the T.U.C.'s establishment. As* The Congress of 1868 *remains authoritative, it is reprinted here with only minor modifications.*

1 FORERUNNERS OF THE T.U.C.

ORGANISED workers in different trades had frequently co-operated and met in conference before what is officially regarded as the first Trades Union Congress in 1868. Sidney and Beatrice

---

* A slightly revised version of *The Congress of 1868: The Origins and Establishment of the Trades Union Congress* (1955).

Webb and Professor Cole have provided accounts of the attempts at general trades' union or federation in the period up to 1834,[4] with the national trades' conferences organised by John Doherty and Robert Owen. One of these conferences, that in London in October 1833, was described as a 'Co-operative and Trades' Union Congress,'[5] the name deriving from the earlier 'congresses' of Owenite co-operative societies.[6]

These efforts collapsed in 1834 and trade unionism declined in the following years. Failure produced widespread disillusionment with general unionism, while many individual societies broke up and others only survived with difficulty in the trade depression of 1836–42. Owen continued to summon annual 'Socialist Congresses', and Chartist 'Conventions' were held in 1839 and 1842, but in these trade unions had little part. The famous trial of the Glasgow cotton spinners, followed by the appointment of a Parliamentary Committee of Inquiry into trade combinations in 1838, revived trade union solidarity, joint trades' defence committees being organised in several towns, led by London; but the fillip was only temporary.[7]

It was not until 1845 that another serious attempt at general trades' federation was made, with the establishment of the 'National Association of United Trades for the Protection of Labour'.[8] Again we find trade union delegates from all parts of the country attending national conferences or 'Labour Parliaments', but the Association proved a failure, most of the larger societies refusing to join. There was still strong opposition to 'general union' or trades' federation, the majority of unions preferring to concentrate on organising their own individual trades. The Association also suffered from renewed trade depression in 1846–7, sporadic strikes, and inter-union differences. It lingered on until the sixties, but was of little practical importance.[9] Nevertheless, it is an interesting fore-runner of the T.U.C., as 'a premature and imperfect Parliamentary Committee of the trade union world',[10] with its aim of federated trades' union action not merely for mutual support in strikes, but also for promoting 'all measures, political and social and educational, which are intended to improve the condition of the labouring classes'.

Sectionalism remained strong among trade unions in the 1850s, but mutual financial assistance was often given in strikes and there was another attempt at national trades' federation. In 1853–4, during the widespread strikes and lock-outs in Lancashire (the lock-out of the Preston cotton operatives, the Manchester dyers' strike, etc.) and elsewhere, Ernest Jones, the Chartist leader, tried to organise a national 'Mass Movement' and 'Labour Parliament' among trade unionists, in view of 'the futility of sectional struggles on the part of isolated bodies of working men, to maintain a just standard of wages and to achieve the emancipation of labour'.[11] A national conference was held in Manchester in March 1854, attended by trade union delegates from all over the country,[12] and efforts were made to raise a national subscription for the assistance of those on strike or locked out; meanwhile, in London, Manchester, Birmingham, and other cities there were local meetings of trades' delegates to rally support, and considerable sums were collected. The movement was short-lived, but the London Committee of Metropolitan Trades' Delegates pointed out 'that the time cannot be far distant when a more complete association of trades must exist than does at present and when the means of rendering support to others must be systematically and universally organised'.[13]

The builders' strike in London in 1859–60 over the nine-hour day again revived the feeling of solidarity between different trades, weekly meetings of metropolitan delegates being held and subscriptions received from all parts of the kingdom.[14] As a result the London Trades Council was established in 1860, a permanent association of metropolitan trade societies, for mutual aid in strikes and concerted action on matters of general concern such as labour legislation. Similar organisations were also established in other cities round about this time. Local meetings of trades' delegates had often been held since the early part of the century, but only in particular emergencies—during strikes, for example, or to agitate against threatened legislation—without having a continuous existence. Now permanent organisations were coming into being in London, Liverpool, Sheffield, Birmingham, Manchester, and other towns.[15] It was from these local trades councils that a national Trades Union Congress was to arise.

The London Trades Council soon came to be dominated by the general secretaries of several national amalgamated societies with their headquarters in the metropolis—William Allan of the Engineers, Robert Applegarth of the Carpenters and Joiners, Daniel Guile of the Ironfounders—together with some of the leading officials of London societies, such as George Odger of the Ladies Shoemakers and Edwin Coulson of the Bricklayers. This small group, nicknamed the 'Junta' by the Webbs, became 'an informal cabinet of the trade union world', assuming leadership of the whole movement, so that the minutes of the Council 'present a mirror of the trade union history of this period'.[16] The Council's power of granting 'credentials' to societies which appealed for aid in strikes or lock-outs, recommending them for financial aid to the metropolitan trades, gave them great influence over the conduct of disputes all over the country, especially as the powerful amalgamated societies provided most of the money. Their policy was a cautious one of conciliation and arbitration, with financial support only where negotiations proved futile—a policy which was dictated largely by their concern for safeguarding their funds, which were primarily for the provision of friendly benefits. But this cautious trade policy they combined with energetic agitation for political reforms. The duties of the London Trades Council were 'to watch over the general interests of labour, political and social, both in and out of Parliament', and 'to use their influence in supporting any measure likely to benefit trades' unions'.[17] Thus we find the Council campaigning in the early 'sixties for the franchise, for amendment of the Master and Servant Law, for Conciliation and Arbitration Acts, for new Mines Regulation Acts, and other labour legislation. Moreover, their political interests extended to foreign as well as domestic affairs, to the American Civil War, Italian liberation, and the Polish revolt of 1863, on all of which demonstrations were organised.[18] The chief reason for this changeover by British trade unionism from its former non-political attitude was 'its sense of the legal restraints under which it operated'[19]—the law regarding combinations and the master and servant law—and the desire for legislative enactments to improve the conditions of the workers. It was in united political action of this sort that the Trades Union Congress was to originate, for, as we shall see, the Congress was to be an embodiment of trade union solidarity in the political rather than the industrial sphere; its main purpose, that is, was originally to organise trade unions in political agitation for their own defence rather than for joint action in trade affairs.

The Junta's industrial and political activity brought them into touch with provincial leaders such as Alexander Macdonald of the Miners' National Union, Alexander Campbell of the Glasgow Trades Council, John Kane of the North of England Ironworkers, and William Dronfield of the Sheffield Association of Organised Trades. These men were generally in agreement with the Junta's policy, but gradually they began to seek a more nationally representative organisation for securing their aims, instead of the narrow control exercised by the Junta. Moreover, the smaller, locally organised, provincial societies were generally more militant than the large amalgamated unions with their headquarters in London, and did not always take kindly to the Junta's policy of industrial pacifism.

One of the first proposals, however, for united political action by the trade unions on a national scale came from the metropolitan building trades—which, as we have seen, were in the van of trade unionism in the early 'sixties—and was, it appears, a product of their struggle against their employers. In 1861 we find the Brick-layers' Society advocating the union of all trades in a Labour Parliament to 'legislate for labour' and to exercise influence 'upon all social and political questions affecting their common interests'.[20] Nothing concrete, however, came of this proposal. There was still strong opposition in many trades to such mixing of trade unionism with politics.

Nevertheless, the idea was gaining ground and not only in Lon-don. In November 1861 the Glasgow Trades Council issued an address to the trades of the United Kingdom urging united political action, with the ultimate object of gaining manhood suffrage and the more immediate aims of reforming the law regarding combina-tions and the law of master and servant, and securing the establish-ment of councils of conciliation and arbitration.[21] They suggested 'that all trades' councils, trade societies and suchlike associated bodies at once memorialise the Government' on the question of parliamentary reform, and that 'a monster national petition' should be 'put up for presentation to Parliament on the day of its opening'.

This proposal was rejected by the London Trades Council be-cause the metropolitan societies generally were not yet converted to the idea of trade union political action. But it was not long before the Junta brought about a change of policy and the minutes of the Council soon came to be filled with examples of activity on various political questions. Moreover, the Junta were largely responsible for the establishment in 1862 of the 'Manhood Suffrage and Vote by Ballot Association', which was designed to enlist the trades of the United Kingdom in an agitation for the franchise, and was the forerunner of the Reform League established in 1865.[22]

It was the Glasgow Trades Council, however, which initiated the first successful political action by the trades generally, when, in 1863–4, under the leadership of Campbell and Macdonald, they launched a campaign for reform of the Master and Servant Acts. They secured the support of trades councils in other towns and then, in May 1864, convened a conference of trade union representatives in London, in order 'to give a national character to the Move-ment'.[23] Owing partly to short notice, there were only about twenty representatives present, but they included such leading figures in the trade union movement as Applegarth, Odger, Coulson, Guile, Potter, Campbell, Macdonald, and Dronfield—delegates not only from the trades councils of London, Glasgow, Sheffield, Liverpool, and Nottingham, but also from unions of engineers, carpenters and joiners, bricklayers, stonemasons, miners, bookbinders, compositors, etc. They proceeded to organise a vigorous political campaign of deputations, lobbying, and petitions to M.P.s, as a result of which a Parliamentary Committee was appointed in 1865, on whose report an amending Act was eventually passed in 1867. This was a notable success for united trades' action and the policy of political agitation.

The 1864 Conference also passed a resolution, on the proposal of William Dronfield, of Sheffield, 'with a view of some combined action being taken' to secure the establishment of Courts of Conciliation and Arbitration. After the opinions of the trades had been obtained, they were to be forwarded to the London Trades Council, who were 'to deal with it by calling delegate meetings from all parts of the country, or taking such other steps as may be most desirable'.[24] The London Trades Council subsequently devoted a good deal of attention to this subject and organised political agitation upon it. Its report for 1864–5 stressed the value of united action among the trades, and the importance of the London Trades Council as 'a central and rallying point for all good projects effecting [sic] the cause of labour'. It pointed out 'the convenience of having a trades' council in London, ready to use the influence of the trades' societies upon the government at any time when the rights of labour may be assailed'. The Council 'should be the great centre for bringing together at proper times, and always when emergencies require them, representatives of the various societies, not only of London but of all parts of the United Kingdom'. The Council did not, however, consider it necessary to summon a national conference on the subject of Courts of Conciliation and Arbitration. An Act for the establishment of such courts was eventually passed in 1867, largely as a result of trade union agitation.

Meanwhile, however, the cautious trade policy and close control of the Junta were meeting with strong criticism in the metropolis. There the Junta's chief opponent and leader of the militant section was George Potter.[25] Born in 1832 at Kenilworth, the son of a carpenter, Potter, after serving an apprenticeship in his father's trade, had come to London in 1853 to find work. He soon became the secretary of the small Progressive Society of Carpenters and Joiners and from 1857 onwards was virtually leader of the London building trades.[26] He led the Conference of the United Building Trades during the great strike and lock-out over the nine-hour day in 1859 and, in January 1861, was the leading figure at the builders' conference in Derby which established the short-lived 'United Kingdom Association for Shortening the Hours of Labour in the Building Trades'. Potter's leadership, however, was challenged by Robert Applegarth, who established the Amalgamated Society of

Carpenters and Joiners in 1860. There soon developed a strong rivalry and personal dislike between the two. Potter was opposed to the cautious, bureaucratic, centralised control of Applegarth and the other officials of the large amalgamated societies, and to their pacific, friendly-society policy, preferring the personal contacts, direct action, and more aggressive methods of the older local societies. He was able to attract considerable support among the smaller London societies and in the provinces, where there was also opposition to the conservative policy and cliquish control of the Junta.

Potter was no mean opponent. Handsome of person, a fine speaker, and capable organiser, he was also an expert in the arts of agitation and keeping himself in the limelight. He had established the Trades Newspaper Company in 1861 to publish the *Beehive*, of which he was manager and real controller, and which became the official organ of the London Trades Council. The rivalry between Potter and the Junta, however, soon created a split in the Council. The Junta's dislike of him was due not merely to disagreement over trade union policy, but also to personal factors: Potter was a younger man than most of them and they disliked his self-advertisement, his control of the *Beehive*, his demagogic methods, his irresponsibility, and also, it appears, his drinking habits. They were altogether more serious, cautious, and conservative than the flamboyant Potter. The growing rivalry between them is writ large in the records of the Trades Council and in the *Beehive*. The Webbs adopted the Junta's opinion of Potter as an irresponsible agitator of no real importance,[27] but this view does not appear to be either just or correct. Potter had a considerable body of support both in London and the provinces, and was one of the leading figures in the events leading up to the establishment of the Trades Union Congress.[28]

The differences between Potter and the Junta became increasingly pronounced during the numerous strikes and lock-outs of the middle 'sixties, in which Potter was a strong advocate of an aggressive policy as opposed to the conciliatory methods of the Junta. Bitter feelings were aroused during the building trades' strike in the Midlands early in 1864, and in that of the North Staffordshire iron puddlers later in the same year. The latter dispute, in fact, brought about an open split.[29] The men, who were resisting a 10 per cent cut in wage rates, were encouraged by Potter, against the advice of the Ironfounders' executive and the London Trades Council, to reject the Earl of Lichfield's proposal that they should return to work pending arbitration. This, the London Trades Council considered, put them 'entirely in the wrong', as they thus threw away the only reasonable method of settling the dispute, and the Council, therefore, could hardly be expected to give them financial aid. Potter, on the other hand, gave them enthusiastic support and, on his own responsibility and without consulting the Council, of which he was a member, summoned 'irresponsible meetings' of trades' delegates in London to organise the raising of subscriptions. His actions aroused considerable indignation and he was strongly denounced at a special meeting of the Trades Council in March 1865.[30] Danter, president of the Amalgamated Society of Engineers, declared that Potter 'had become the aider and abettor of strikes. He thought of nothing else; he followed no other business; strikes were his bread and cheese; in short, he was a strike-jobber, and he made the *Beehive* newspaper his instrument for pushing his nose into every unfortunate dispute that sprung up.' Potter was accused of seeking personal power and prestige by dubious means, *e.g.*, by biased reports in the *Beehive* and by packing meetings. Similar strictures were included in the Council's annual report presented to the annual delegate meeting in August 1865, with the result that there was a great row and Potter was excluded from the Council. Moreover, an adjourned meeting later decided to withdraw support from the *Beehive*.[31]

The Junta's great dislike of the prominence which Potter was achieving is rather amusingly illustrated by another incident in 1864. When Mr. Gladstone introduced his Post Office Annuities Bill in February, Potter summoned a meeting of the London trades to oppose it as an insidious attempt to divert the savings of working men from their trade unions and benefit societies into an exchequer controlled by the governing classes. This opposition was condemned by Gladstone in the House of Commons on March 7, when he referred to Potter as 'the far-famed secretary of the trades' unions'.[32] The Junta were furious and sent a deputation to enlighten the Chancellor and to support the Bill.[33] Potter was strongly denounced for having 'arrogated to himself the title of secretary of the trades of England'.[34]

Potter declared at the annual delegate meeting of the London Trades Council in August 1865, that if the strictures upon him in the report were passed, the result might be 'the establishment of a counter-association'. In March 1866, therefore, he founded the London Working Men's Association, of which he was president and Robert Hartwell, the veteran Chartist, secretary. By this means and through the *Beehive* he sought to maintain his position in the working-class trade union and political movements, despite the opposition of the Junta.[35] He could still reckon on the support of the more militant trade societies both in London and in the provinces, and he continued to assist strikes by numerous reports in the *Beehive*, by summoning meetings of the London trades, and collecting subscriptions.

The middle 'sixties saw the outbreak of many such strikes and lock-outs, one of the greatest of which was that in the Sheffield file trade, beginning in February 1866, over a request by the grinders for a wage increase.[36] This lock-out was denounced by the Sheffield Association of Organised Trades, at a meeting on March 8, as 'an evident attempt to break up trade associations in Sheffield', and they appealed 'for the assistance of not only the united trades of this town, but of every trades union in the Kingdom, in order to prevent such associations from becoming destroyed by the lock-out system'. Their appeal was favourably received by the London Trades Council, which gave the necessary 'credentials' and urged the metropolitan societies to render all possible support.[37] Potter meanwhile was writing stirring appeals in the *Beehive* and summoning meetings of the L.W.M.A. and the metropolitan trades to hear delegates from Sheffield and to organise financial assistance.

The lock-out attracted nation-wide notice and in April the Wolverhampton Trades Council passed a resolution urging that 'the time has arrived when the trades of the United Kingdom ought to take action conjointly to rebut the lock-out system now so prevalent with the capitalists; and the dispute and lock-out in the Sheffield file trade affords an excellent opportunity for carrying this into effect'. They therefore urged 'that a conference of trades' delegates of the United Kingdom should be held in Sheffield.'[38] The London Trades Council was rather lukewarm in support of this proposal, but agreed, 'without committing itself to the principle involved', to send a delegate to such a conference if summoned. Potter and the L.W.M.A., on the other hand, were enthusiastic. In an article in the *Beehive* on May 12, Potter pointed out that he had frequently urged the necessity for 'a better organisation of Labour', and suggested that the whole of the trades in every town in the kingdom should be 'amalgamated into one great body, with a responsible and ruling head; and that the whole of these amalgamated trades, divided into five districts ... shall be represented in district Labour Parliaments, assembling quarterly, and that these district Parliaments should then be represented in one Labour Parliament, to meet annually'. The main purpose of this organisation would be to raise district and national funds to assist in any lock-outs or strikes.

The Wolverhampton proposal met with a favourable response from trades councils and trade societies all over the country, and

the Sheffield Association of Organised Trades therefore decided
to summon 'a conference of trades' delegates' in Sheffield, to
establish 'a national organisation among the trades of the United
Kingdom, for the purpose of effectually resisting all lock-outs'.
A circular was therefore issued 'to all national trades and trades'
councils of the country'.[39] Had Sheffield not done so, Potter and
the L.W.M.A. were preparing to summon such a national conference.

The leading figure in the Sheffield Association of Organised
Trades was its secretary, William Dronfield, who was to play an
important part in originating the idea of an annual Trades Union
Congress. Dronfield, a journeyman compositor, was secretary of
the Sheffield Typographical Society, he was also a member of the
executive and for three years (1852-5) president of the Provincial
Typographical Association, which had its headquarters in Sheffield
until 1865.[40] He was largely responsible for the establishment of the
Sheffield Association of Organised Trades, which originated out
of a strike at the *Sheffield Times* office in 1858,[41] and of which he
was secretary for nine years. Dronfield strongly supported the
policy of political agitation for legislative reform and had attended
the London trades' conference on the Master and Servant Law in
1864, where he had also urged united action to secure the legislative
establishment of Courts of Conciliation and Arbitration. It was he
who now wrote out and distributed the invitation to the Conference
of Trades' Delegates, which was held in Sheffield in July 1866, and
of which he was appointed secretary.[42]

This conference, attended by 138 delegates, representing nearly
200,000 members, was 'one of the largest of the trades that ever
assembled',[43] and, so Dronfield later claimed, 'laid the foundations
of the annual trades congresses'.[44] A large number of societies were
represented, including the trades councils of London, Sheffield,
Preston, Hyde, Derby, Bristol, Halifax, Nottingham, Liverpool,
Warrington, and Wolverhampton, many national unions, such as
the Carpenters and Joiners, Ironworkers, Boilermakers and Iron
Shipbuilders, Ironfounders, Tailors, Coopers, Painters, and Plasterers, many provincial or regional societies of miners, power-loom
weavers, spinners, printers, and potters, as well as a large number
of local societies. Potter was not there, but George Troup represented the L.W.M.A., and several other metropolitan societies also
sent delegates, while George Odger came from the London Trades
Council. The conference was composed predominantly, however,
of representatives from the Midlands and North, the Junta being
rather lukewarm towards it, because of the enthusiastic support

given to it by Potter and their distrust of the militant attitude of many provincial societies.

The chief outcome of this conference was the establishment of the 'United Kingdom Alliance of Organised Trades'—another attempt at a national association or federation of trades—for mutual support in lock-outs. The conference also advocated Courts of Conciliation and Arbitration, demanded amendment of the Master and Servant Law, and supported the principles of co-operation. The headquarters of the new Alliance were established in Sheffield: its executive was elected by the Sheffield trades and Dronfield was its secretary. It proved, however, no more successful than its predecessors. The Junta and the London trades generally held aloof,[45] and so did many important provincial societies. Further conferences were held in 1867 in Manchester (January) and Preston (September), but membership of the Alliance fell rapidly, due to internal dissensions, numerous strikes, trade depression, and inadequate funds,[46] and the Alliance, though lingering on for several years, soon ceased to be of any real importance.

There was another cause for its failure—the occurrence of the notorious trade union 'outrages' in Sheffield, where the Alliance had its headquarters. Non-unionists in certain trades were not only subjected to such persecution as the pilfering or destruction of their tools, with the object of forcing them to join a trade society and obey its regulations, but were also violently attacked and even, in a few instances, murdered.[47] The climax to these 'rattening' outrages (which were not confined to Sheffield) came in October 1866, when a can of gunpowder was exploded in the house of a non-unionist saw-grinder in New Hereford Street, Sheffield. This was merely one of a succession of similar outrages, but in the state of public irritation against trade unionism, which had been growing during the past few years of lock-outs and strikes, it served to precipitate events. There was a loud outcry against trade unions and a strong demand for a public inquiry. This was supported by most of the unions themselves, which were anxious to be dissociated from criminal acts, to secure the punishment of those responsible, and to prove the necessity, usefulness, and moderation of the great majority of trade societies. The London Trades Council, for example, sent representatives to Sheffield and Nottingham to inquire into the outrages, strongly condemned 'the abominable practice of rattening', and arranged a joint deputation of the London and Sheffield trades to the Home Secretary to urge the appointment of a Commission of Inquiry.[48] The United Kingdom Alliance also denounced the outrages, but it was eventually discovered (June 1867) that William Broadhead, its treasurer, was the ringleader.

This disclosure naturally exposed the Alliance to great hostility from the press and from employers, while moderate trade unionists were shocked into abstention or desertion.

It was while trade unionism stood thus on the defensive, under attack for the outrages and strikes for which it was held responsible, that another blow fell, in the shape of a decision by the Court of Queen's Bench of crucial importance in trade union history. Since the Act of 1825—repealing the Combination Laws and excluding combined action in regard to wages and hours of labour from prosecution for conspiracy, except in so far as 'threatening', 'violence', 'molestation', 'intimidation', or 'obstruction' were involved —trade unions had ceased to be unlawful, but had not yet acquired any legal corporate status. They had, however, secured the insertion of a clause in the Friendly Societies Act of 1855, which had enabled those trade societies which deposited their rules with the Registrar to proceed against defaulting officials, thus, it was thought, securing legal protection for their funds. Now, however, in the famous case of *Hornby* v. *Close*, concerning embezzlement by the treasurer of the Bradford branch of the Boilermakers' Society, the Court of Queen's Bench decided (January 16, 1867) that trade unions were not within the scope of the 1855 Act. Furthermore, the Lord Chief Justice declared that although, since 1825, trade unions were not actually criminal, they were yet so far 'in restraint of trade' as to be illegal.[49] Thus not only were they bereft of legal status and protection for their funds, but the limited legal recognition of 1825 looked like being withdrawn, in view of the current outcry against trade unions. The threat became really serious when the Government decided early in February 1867 to appoint a Royal Commission of Inquiry into trade unions.

Trade unions everywhere rose in their own defence, but their agitation, though vigorous, was lacking in unity. The Junta sought to maintain their leadership by establishing a 'Conference of Amalgamated Trades' in London—which, in reality, was simply themselves under another name—with the object of securing full legal recognition for trade unions and protection for their funds, and defeating the employers in their efforts to utilise the Royal Commission for the suppression of trade unionism.[50] They formed a 'permanent conference', able 'to attend regularly, and at the shortest possible notice to this work'. It was considered 'essential that a number of men should be appointed who would not [have to] leave their employers' work in the daytime', and so the conference was 'composed of secretaries of the various large societies'.[51] It represented, in fact, only the national amalgamated societies of Engineers, Carpenters and Joiners, and Ironfounders, together with a few London societies such as the Bricklayers, Ladies' Shoemakers, and Vellum Binders. It had about a dozen members, of whom the chief were Allan, Applegarth, Guile, Coulson, and Odger.

The Junta's leadership, however, was still strongly challenged by Potter and the L.W.M.A., supported by many of the small metropolitan societies. Rival deputations waited upon the Home Secretary in February 1867, and rival trades' meetings were held in London. There was practically no difference in policy—both parties wanted legislation to give security to trade union funds, working-class representation on the Royal Commission, and attendance of trade union representatives during its sittings. The differences—apart from those between the centralised amalgamated unions and the small local societies—were almost entirely personal. Potter was detested by the Junta as a 'mischievous meddler' who printed 'false and vicious statements' in the *Beehive*,[52] while Potter, though no doubt egotistical and fond of the limelight, was strongly opposed to the attempt by 'the Clique' to dominate the whole trade union movement. He was anxious 'to let bygones be bygones' and to secure 'unity of action', but the Junta would have none of him and rejected his overtures.[53]

While the Junta sought to retain close control in London, at the head of the trade union movement, convinced of their own wisdom and ability to see the crisis through, Potter sought to give a wider and more representative basis to the agitation. Immediately after the Queen's Bench decision in the *Hornby* v. *Close* case, a meeting of the L.W.M.A. decided to summon 'a conference of delegates from all the trade societies and trades councils of the United Kingdom to assemble in London' on March 5.[54] The necessity for such a conference was strongly confirmed soon afterwards by the Government's decision to appoint a Royal Commission of Inquiry into trade unions.[55] The Junta and London Trades Council, however, refused to participate. They considered that 'as the Commission ... has been appointed and agreed to by the House of Commons,[56] and the trades' council has, in conjunction with the Amalgamated Engineers, Iron Founders, Amalgamated Carpenters, Bricklayers, Bootmakers, etc., etc., had frequent interviews with members of Parliament, including Mr. Neate, regarding his bill now before the House to give protection to the funds of trade societies, and also having obtained from Mr. Walpole, Home Secretary, an opinion in favour of a representative of each society being present during the examination ... a conference is at the present time premature'.[57] Their underlying motive, however, was hatred of Potter and his associates.[58] They considered 'that the time for calling a conference will be when the Royal Commission present their report. Then we shall certainly do it, and hope that the societies generally will respond to the call.'[59]

Despite their opposition, however, the conference met in St. Martin's Hall, London, early in March 1867, and was attended by about 140 delegates representing nearly 200,000 members.[60] Nine trades councils—Edinburgh, Glasgow, Sheffield, Liverpool, Manchester and Salford, Wolverhampton, Preston, Halifax, and Nottingham—were represented, together with most of the important trade unions in the Midlands and North, including the Boilermakers and Iron Shipbuilders, Ironworkers, Miners, Stonemasons, Cotton Spinners and Weavers, Tailors, Plasterers, and Flint Glass Makers, as well as many local societies. There were also representatives from about seventy London societies, mostly small, but including some larger ones, such as the compositors, tailors, bakers, brass finishers, painters, steam-engine makers, and shipwrights. Such an attendance was indeed evidence of 'the general conviction of the desirability of such a conference, and of the urgency of the occasion for it', despite the expressed opinion of the Junta in the London Trades Council. It was, as the *Beehive* stated, 'one of the most numerous and influential ever known in the annals of trade unionists; it may truly be called a Parliament of Labour'. An effort, however, by the provincial delegates to settle the differences between the London Trades Council and the L.W.M.A. and secure unity of action resulted in failure, due to the Junta's personal dislike and jealousy of Potter, and both the London Trades Council and the Conference of Amalgamated Trades refused to join in the conference.[61]

The conference lasted four days, from March 5 to 8. Its two chief demands were, firstly, legislation to give protection to trade union funds, and, secondly, permission for representatives to attend the sittings of the Royal Commission, to conduct the trade union case. A committee was elected to try to achieve these objects. Its members were Potter (L.W.M.A.), Proudfoot (Glasgow Trades Council), Wood (Manchester and Salford Trades Council), Macdonald (Miners' National Association), Kane (Ironworkers), Leigh (Cotton Operatives), Connolly (Stonemasons), Allen (Boilermakers and Iron Shipbuilders), Holmes (West Yorkshire Miners), and Leicester (Flint Glass Makers). The conference also urged that local trades' committees should be appointed, to collect evidence, summon public meetings, forward petitions, and generally assist the conference committee in putting the trade union case before the Royal Commission.

Thus there were now two rival bodies—the Conference of Amalgamated Trades, dominated by the Junta, and the St. Martin's

Hall Conference Committee—each claiming to represent the trade unions of the country in negotiations with the Royal Commission. Rival deputations put forward similar requests in March and both parties were eventually allowed to have representatives at the sittings of the Royal Commission. Robert Applegarth attended on behalf of the Junta, and Thomas Connolly, president of the Operative Stonemasons, represented the Conference Committee. The Junta, however, aided by their middle-class friends on the Royal Commission, soon succeeded in elbowing the Conference Committee out of the way. An indiscreet speech by Connolly at a meeting of London trades' delegates on June 26, 1867, reflecting on J. A. Roebuck, one of the Commissioners, quickly led to his exclusion, and after that the Conference Committee ceased to take much interest in the proceedings of the Commission.[62] Neither did it take very active measures regarding agitation for the Bill which the conference had drawn up, to obtain the same legal security for trade union funds as was possessed by friendly societies. Its members, drawn from all parts of the country, could not, for lack of funds and for domestic and other reasons, remain continuously in London. The committee, therefore, soon faded out of existence. Reports of its activities ceased to appear in the *Beehive*, which stated in March 1868 that it had 'not been called together for some months past' and was practically defunct.[63] Later on it was stated that it 'came to grief through apathy', because of divisions among the trade union leaders, whereby 'both interest and confidence had been shaken', and because the societies failed to give adequate financial support, and 'the executive themselves lost heart'. 'After several well-intended meetings the lack of sympathy and the decline of funds necessitated a sort of break-up, and for months nothing has been done.'[64] The Junta or Conference of Amalgamated Trades, therefore, consisting of full-time union secretaries, resident in London, and backed by substantial funds, retained their leadership of the trade union movement and management of the trade union case before the Royal Commission, their representative, Robert Applegarth, being allowed to remain throughout its proceedings.[65]

Nevertheless, the St. Martin's Hall Conference of March 1867 is important as 'the immediate forerunner' of the T.U.C.[66] It is evidence of the growing desire for some representative body to voice general trade union opinion, and of dissatisfaction with the narrow control of the Junta, on the part not only of Potter and his metropolitan associates, but also of many provincial societies. The Conference Committee, which was a very representative body, strongly denounced the Junta's attempted domination of the movement and their refusal, for reasons 'wholly and solely party and personal', to join in a united front.[67] The Junta's reasons for refusing to do so, however, were not entirely personal. The amalgamated societies, as we have seen, were more pacific in trade affairs and more concerned with friendly benefits than those in Potter's following, which were more disposed to strike action. The Junta, anxious to put the moderate, conciliatory, friendly-society aspect of trade unionism before the Royal Commission, distrusted what they regarded as the 'wild men' in some of the London and provincial societies. Professor Cole has also suggested that the Junta's legislative claims were more limited than those of Potter and his allies: that they were mainly concerned with getting a legal status and protection for their friendly society funds, and not so much with securing legal recognition of picketing and strike action generally, which they were anxious to deprecate.[68] There was undoubtedly something to support this suggestion at first. In September 1867, for example, the Conference of Amalgamated Trades was of opinion that it 'should confine its efforts to the promotion of such Bills as would ensure trades societies the full right to combine and to attach sick and other benefits to their trade benefits, to obtain legal protection for their funds and the right to invest such part of them as any society might ... determine (in land and buildings)'.[69] Many societies outside the Conference, however, were equally if not more concerned with securing legalisation of the right to strike and take other coercive action. It was this difference in policy which caused disagreement over Professor Neate's Bill in March 1867,[70] and which was to cause similar disagreement over the Junta's Trade Societies' Bill in 1868. Eventually, however, as we shall see, as a result of the growing threat to trade unionism from further judicial decisions, the disagreement disappeared and the two parties united in their legislative demands.

Following on the *Hornby* v. *Close* case, the position of trade unions was made even more precarious by a series of legal decisions which almost crippled their power to strike and picket. One of the most notorious of these was that in *R.* v. *Druitt* (1867), resulting from an action brought by the London master tailors, following a strike, against the officers of the journeymen's trade society, whereby even 'black looks' could be interpreted as 'threatening', 'intimidation', or 'molestation'. It was followed by several similar decisions, which seemed to make almost any trade action by a union liable to prosecution for criminal conspiracy, despite the repeal of the Combination Laws in 1825.[71] There was an obvious need for united trade union action in the face of these threatening developments. The Junta, therefore, took the lead with a vigorous policy to secure legislative remedy for these injustices and to acquire for trade unions a secure legal position. At first, as we have seen, their main aim was simply to obtain legal protection for trade union funds, and they therefore supported Professor Neate's Bill, but this fell through.[72] Then, with the advice and assistance of Professor Beesley, Henry Crompton, Frederic Harrison, and other legal and parliamentary friends, a Trade Societies' Bill was drawn up, which was intended to put the legality of trade unions beyond doubt, prevent them from being prosecuted under the law of conspiracy, and give them legal protection for their funds. This Bill they eventually got Sir Thomas Fowell Buxton to introduce into the House of Commons in July 1868.[73] By that time, however, the session was nearly over[74] and no further progress could be made. The Conference of Amalgamated Trades decided, in fact, 'that before any decided course could be taken the Conference would have to wait the issue of the Report of the Commission'.[75] but the Bill, which the Conference had circulated to trade societies throughout the country, still remained the basis of trade-union demands. Trade unionists were urged to use their newly-won political power under the 1867 Reform Act to press the Bill upon Parliamentary candidates when elections for the new Parliament were held.

2 THE FIRST CONGRESS, MANCHESTER, 1868

The collapse of the committee appointed by the St. Martin's Hall Conference in March 1867 had left a clear field for the Junta. The only other organisation that was representative of trade unions generally was the United Kingdom Alliance of Organised Trades. This body made an attempt at its Preston conference, in September 1867, to get united action with the object of obtaining legal security for trade union funds and alteration of the common law of conspiracy as applied to trade unions. The executive were instructed 'to communicate with the trades' councils and other organised bodies' for this purpose, and a circular was to be issued 'inviting the co-operation of the whole of the trades of the country', while the executive were also 'to inaugurate public meetings for the purpose of diffusing information amongst the operatives and other classes'.[76] By that time, however, the Alliance had dwindled almost into insignificance[77] and its appeal appears to have had little if any response. The trade union leadership remained in the hands of the Junta.

Nevertheless, there was still a strong feeling among trade unionists for more united action and for a national trades' conference to voice their demands. Even the Junta felt it, but they were in no hurry to summon such a conference. In a report which they issued to the trade unionists of the United Kingdom in September 1867, they described the actions which they had taken following the *Hornby* v. *Close* decision and the appointment of the Royal Commission, and stated that they would 'follow up the work we have been so much engaged in until the Royal Commission has completed its labours, and make known the result to the trades from time to time, or call a conference of the trades generally, should it be found necessary'.[78] In a later circular, of February 1868, the Conference of Amalgamated Trades and the London Trades Council stated that they would be prepared for 'calling a national conference on the situation of trades unions as soon as the Royal Commission presented their report or a [Government] Bill were introduced to parliament on the subject'.[79]

Potter and the L.W.M.A., however, and the provincial trades councils and trade societies were not prepared to wait indefinitely for another national conference. Early in March 1868, therefore, we find the L.W.M.A. putting forward a proposal for 'the convening of a National Labour Parliament in London' in the following May.[80] The L.W.M.A., however, unknown to itself, had been preceded by the Manchester and Salford Trades Council, which, about a fortnight previously, had put forward a similar proposal, for a national trades' congress in Manchester early in May.[81] When the L.W.M.A. heard of this, it at once decided to shelve its own scheme and gave its blessing to the proposed trades' congress.[82]

The proposal of the Manchester and Salford Trades Council was not for a national trades' conference to meet in a particular emergency, like those in 1864, 1866, and 1867, but for regular annual Trades Union Congresses, which would permanently represent and voice the opinions of the whole of the trades of the United Kingdom on all questions of general trade union interest. It was a natural development, of course, from the local trades' councils and the previous national trades' conferences, but someone had to suggest the idea. We know that the Manchester and Salford Trades Council issued the circular summoning the Congress, but who thought of it and what prompted it?

It originated out of the experience of William Dronfield, secretary of the Sheffield Typographical Society and also of the Sheffield Association and the United Kingdom Alliance of Organised Trades. Dronfield was a very intelligent and enlightened trade unionist, who, as we have seen, had played a leading part in the agitation for amendment of the Master and Servant Law and for the establishment of Courts of Conciliation and Arbitration.[83] It was he who had been mainly responsible for the summoning of the national trades' conference in Sheffield in July 1866, to deal with the question of lock-outs, and he had been elected secretary of the resulting United Kingdom Alliance. He had also been prominent at the St. Martin's Hall Conference in March 1867. He was energetic in the working-class movement for the franchise and for national education. He was a moderate, peace-loving man, strongly condemnatory of the 'rattening' outrages in Sheffield and determined to show that such crimes were limited to a few of the old-fashioned societies of degraded workers; for this reason he became secretary of the Sheffield Trades' Defence Committee and gave evidence before the Royal Commission.

It was to defend trade societies from the attacks being made upon them in the press that he had previously, in October 1865, attended and spoken before the Ninth Annual Congress of the National Association for the Promotion of Social Science (more briefly, the Social Science Association), which was held that year in Sheffield. This Association had displayed considerable interest in trade unionism, as evidenced by its very thorough report on *Trade Societies and Strikes*, in 1860, and the subject naturally came up for discussion in Sheffield, where it was then attracting so much publicity. A paper was read before the Department of Economy and Trade by one John Wilson, with the title, 'What are the best means of establishing a system of Authoritative Arbitration between Employers and Employed in cases of Strikes and Lock-outs?'[84] Wilson, a pen-knife blade-grinder employed by Messrs. Joseph Rodgers & Sons, of Sheffield, was a strong anti-unionist.[85] He stated that he had 'stood aloof from trades' unions ... being a believer in free competition' and detesting 'interference with any man's labour'. He strongly denounced the policies of trade unions—their attempts at restricting the number of apprentices, their coercion of non-members, their 'ignorance of economical science', and their failure in strikes. Moreover, he belied the title of his paper by condemning the proposed Courts of Conciliation and Arbitration as futile, believing in 'the doctrine of non-intervention', i.e. in 'leaving masters and men to settle their disputes between themselves ... without the intervention of third parties'.

Dronfield followed him with a paper in defence of trade unions, but this was omitted from the Association's report, which merely states that 'in addition to the paper by Mr. Wilson ... Mr. Dronfield read a paper pointing out the advantages of trades' unions'.[86] There follows in the report a summary of the discussion upon this question, including speeches by Frederic Harrison, Professor Fawcett, and Thomas Hughes, generally in favour of arbitration, in order to avoid strikes and lock-outs, and also of voluntary combinations of workmen, but critical of trade union abuses— their extreme wage demands, coercion of non-members, and physical violence.

Dronfield was highly incensed at the unfairly biased attitude of the Social Science Association. Not only was his paper omitted from its *Transactions*, while his opponent was given several pages, but in the report of the ensuing discussion, in which a number of Sheffield trades' representatives took part, 'not a word they said is recorded'.[87] What was the use, then, of working men attending such meetings, 'if we cannot get justice done to us—if we cannot get our views represented—if when we express ourselves, either by writing papers, or in attempting to reply to the attacks made upon us, we are ignored in the official documents of the Society?' Since such middle and upper-class bodies denied them a fair hearing and report, trade unionists must rely on their own organisation to defend themselves. It was partly, no doubt, with this in mind that Dronfield summoned the national trades' conference at Sheffield in 1886.

Dronfield's experience and his conclusions made a great impression on two of the leading officials of the Manchester and Salford Trades Council, Samuel Caldwell Nicholson, president, and William Henry Wood, secretary. Both these men were, like Dronfield, journeymen compositors, being treasurer and secretary respectively of the Manchester Typographical Society. They knew Dronfield well, having met him several times both on printing and on general trade union affairs. Wood had been the more prominent of the two, having attended and taken a leading part in the national trades' conferences in 1866 (Sheffield) and 1867 (London). It was Nicholson, however, who suggested the idea of an annual Trades Union Congress. The way in which it occurred to him is described in his obituary in the *Typographical Circular* of February 1891. Having heard of Dronfield's experience with the Social Science Association's Annual Congress at Sheffield, 'Mr. Nicholson remarked, "Why not have a congress of our own?" and he at once, along with a few of his colleagues, set about to organise the first congress'. The need for such a meeting was obvious in the present position of trade unions—deprived of legal protection for their funds, prosecuted as illegal conspiracies, threatened by the Royal Commission, and blackened by prejudiced and ignorant attacks in the public press and elsewhere. There was no national body in existence properly representative of trade unions and able to

PROPOSED CONGRESS OF TRADES COUNCILS

AND OTHER

Federations of Trades Societies.

————◦◦◦◦◦————

MANCHESTER, FEBRUARY 21st, 1868.

FELLOW-UNIONISTS,

The Manchester and Salford Trades Council having recently taken into their serious consideration the present aspect of Trades Unions, and the profound ignorance which prevails in the public mind with reference to their operations and principles, together with the probability of an attempt being made by the Legislature, during the present session of Parliament, to introduce a measure detrimental to the interests of such Societies, beg most respectfully to suggest the propriety of holding in Manchester, as the main centre of industry in the provinces, a Congress of the Representatives of Trades Councils and other similar Federations of Trades Societies. By confining the Congress to such bodies it is conceived that a deal of expense will be saved, as Trades will thus be represented collectively; whilst there will be a better opportunity afforded of selecting the most intelligent and efficient exponents of our principles.

It is proposed that the Congress shall assume the character of the annual meetings of the British Association for the Advancement of Science and the Social Science Association, in the transactions of which Societies the artizan class are almost entirely excluded; and that papers, previously carefully prepared, shall be laid before the Congress on the various subjects which at the present time affect Trades Societies, each paper to be followed by discussion upon the points advanced, with a view of the merits and demerits of each question being thoroughly ventilated through the medium of the public press. It is further suggested that the subjects treated upon shall include the following :—

1.—Trades Unions an absolute necessity.
2.—Trades Unions and Political Economy.
3.—The Effect of Trades Unions on Foreign Competition.
4.—Regulation of the Hours of Labour.
5.—Limitation of Apprentices.
6.—Technical Education.
7.—Arbitration and Courts of Conciliation.
8.—Co-operation.
9.—The present Inequality of the Law in regard to Conspiracy, Intimidation, Picketing, Coercion, &c.
10.—Factory Acts Extension Bill, 1867: the necessity of Compulsory Inspection, and its application to all places where Women and Children are employed.
11.—The present Royal Commission on Trades Unions : how far worthy of the confidence of the Trades Union interest.
12.—The necessity of an Annual Congress of Trade Representatives from the various centres of industry.

All Trades Councils and other Federations of Trades are respectfully solicited to intimate their adhesion to this project on or before the 6th of April next, together with a notification of the subject of the paper that each body will undertake to prepare; after which date all information as to place of meeting, &c., will be supplied.

It is also proposed that the Congress be held on the 4th of May next, and that all liabilities in connection therewith shall not extend beyond its sittings.

Communications to be addressed to MR. W. H. WOOD, Typographical Institute, 29, Water Street, Manchester.

By order of the Manchester and Salford Trades Council,

S. C. NICHOLSON, PRESIDENT.
W. H. WOOD, SECRETARY.

speak and act for the whole movement, to direct and focus trade union opinion and lend strength to union demands. The Conference of Amalgamated Trades in London was doing good work, but it was a cliquish and dictatorial body, by no means representative of the whole trade union movement.

So the Manchester and Salford Trades Council issued a circular summoning the first annual Trades Union Congress. This summons, the Webbs have informed us, was dated April 16, 1868, and was only preserved by the fortunate fact that it was reprinted in the *Ironworkers' Journal* of May 1868, no original copy having survived; for which reason they reprinted it again in an appendix to their *History of Trade Unionism*, from which it has been reproduced by later writers. It is quite clear, however, from the *Beehive* and other sources, that this was not, in fact, a copy of the original summons, but of a second and revised one. The first summons was reprinted in the *Beehive* on March 21, 1868, and was evidently issued towards the end of February.[88] The present author therefore searched the records of the Manchester Typographical Society and in 1955 fortunately discovered an actual copy, dated February 21, 1868, proposing a 'Congress of Trades Councils and other Federations of Trades Societies'. (This document was subsequently donated by the Manchester Typographical Society to the Trades Union Congress.)

'The Manchester and Salford Trades Council,' this circular began, having recently taken into their serious consideration the present aspect of Trades Unions, and the profound ignorance which prevails in the public mind with reference to their operations and principles, together with the probability of an attempt being made by the Legislature, during the present session of Parliament, to introduce a measure detrimental to the interests of such Societies, beg most respectfully to suggest the propriety of holding in Manchester, as the main centre of industry in the provinces, a Congress of the Representatives of Trades Councils and other similar Federations of Trades Societies. By confining the Congress to such bodies it is conceived that a deal of expense will be saved, as Trades will thus be represented collectively; whilst there will be a better opportunity afforded of selecting the most intelligent and efficient exponents of our principles.' No invitation, in other words, was sent to individual trade societies in this first circular, but only to 'Trades Councils and other similar Federations of Trades Societies'.

The name 'Congress' for the proposed meeting had sometimes been applied to earlier trades' conferences, but it is fairly certain that in 1868 it was derived from the 'Annual Congresses' of the

Social Science Association. Indeed, not only was the name borrowed, but the same conference procedure was to be adopted. It was proposed that the Trades Union Congress should 'assume the character of the annual meetings of the British Association for the Advancement of Science and the Social Science Association,[89] in the transactions of which societies the artizan class are almost entirely excluded; and that papers, previously carefully prepared, shall be laid before the Congress on the various subjects which at the present time affect Trades Societies, each paper to be followed by discussion upon the points advanced, with a view of the merits and demerits of each question being thoroughly ventilated through the medium of the public press'.

It was suggested that the following subjects should be brought before the Congress:

'1. Trades Unions an absolute necessity.
2. Trades Unions and Political Economy.
3. The Effect of Trades Unions on Foreign Competition.
4. Regulation of the Hours of Labour.
5. Limitation of Apprentices.
6. Technical Education.
7. Arbitration and Courts of Conciliation.
8. Co-operation.
9. The present Inequality of the Law in regard to Conspiracy, Intimidation, Picketing, Coercion, &c.
10. Factory Acts Extension Bill, 1867: the necessity of Compulsory Inspection, and its application to all places where Women and Children are employed.
11. The present Royal Commission on Trades Unions: how far worthy of the confidence of the Trades Union interest.
12. The necessity of an Annual Congress of Trade Representatives from the various centres of industry.'

'All Trades Councils and other Federations of Trades' were 'respectfully solicited to intimate their adhesion to this project on or before the 6th of April next, together with a notification of the subject of the paper that each body will undertake to prepare'. It was proposed 'that the Congress be held on the 4th of May next, and that all liabilities in connection therewith shall not extend beyond its sittings'. Communications were to be addressed to Mr. W. H. Wood, Typographical Institute, 29 Water Street, Manchester. The circular was signed, by order of the Manchester and Salford Trades Council, S. C. Nicholson, president, and W. H. Wood, secretary.

The reprint of this circular in the *Beehive* differed on one or two points from this original document, which may possibly have been a proof copy, to which minor alterations and additions were later made. These referred particularly to the expected trade-union legislation, 'which might prove detrimental' to their interests, it was emphasised, 'unless some prompt and decisive action be taken by the working classes themselves'. The list of proposed topics for discussion, moreover, included an additional item on the 'Legalisation of trade societies', to follow the debate on the Royal Commission. The duration of the Congress, it was also added, was 'not to exceed six days'. The other alterations were merely slight verbal ones.

At the quarterly meeting of the Manchester and Salford Trades Council on April 16, however, it was decided to postpone the Congress until June 2, in Whit-week, 'in order to afford sufficient time for all the various trade organisations to send delegates and prepare papers.'[90] It was also decided 'that all trades feeling inclined to send delegates should be at liberty to do so'; in other words, the invitation to the Congress was now extended to include individual societies as well as trades councils and other federations. It seems probable that this decision was made owing to lack of support for the Congress as originally planned, or else to make it a more impressive gathering.

Another circular, therefore, was immediately prepared, dated April 16, 1868, and issued to 'Trades Councils, Federations of Trades, and Trade Societies Generally'. It was this which was printed in the *Ironworkers' Journal* of May 1868, and which the Webbs have reprinted. It was also, unnoticed by the Webbs and apparently by all later trade union historians, printed in the *Beehive* of April 25, 1868. Except for the revisions mentioned, it was very little different from the original circular.

There was, as George Howell has pointed out, an important difference between these proposed annual Congresses and earlier schemes like that of the United Kingdom Alliance of Organised Trades. In the latter organisations 'the main object ... was some form of amalgamation or federation. The promoters and founders of Trade Union Congresses had no such ambition. Their object was to confer annually, upon urgent questions affecting workmen and labour associations, whether the result of legislation or otherwise ... to promote co-operation in respect of general questions affecting labour, and watch over its interests in Parliament. The Congress would in no way affect the existing organisation and independence of trade unions or interfere in the legitimate work of trade unions.'[91] It might therefore be expected to secure more general support than the earlier schemes involving federation or amalgamation.

The Junta, however, appear to have regarded the proposed Trades Union Congress with disfavour, as a rival to their own authority,[92] and only two metropolitan representatives, George Potter and a delegate from the small London Pressmen's Society, attended it. Provincial trades councils were strongly represented —Manchester and Salford, Liverpool, Sheffield, Birmingham, Bradford, Preston, Bolton, Warrington, Nottingham, Dundee, and Dublin. The only provincial trade unions of any importance to send delegates were the Amalgamated Ironworkers (John Kane), the Amalgamated Tailors (Peter Shorrocks and J. Adamson), the Ironfounders (A. Ridge), the Masons (T. Davies), the Amalgamated Joiners (F. Booker), the Boilermakers and Iron Shipbuilders (C. Hutchinson), and the Flint Glass Makers (T. J. Wilkinson). Moreover, most of these men were from Lancashire towns and may not, in fact, have been sent by their national executives. The other delegates were from local societies or branches of bricklayers, painters, printers, and dyers in Manchester, Liverpool, and a few other Lancashire towns, with one or two from small societies farther afield, like the Yorkshire Glass Bottle Makers. Altogether there were thirty-four delegates, who claimed to represent 118,367 members.[93]

The Congress was held in the Mechanics' Institute, David Street, Manchester, during Whit-week, from Tuesday, June 2, to Saturday, June 6, 1868.[94] Samuel Nicholson, president of the Manchester and Salford Trades Council and originator of the Congress, should have presided, but he had to attend the Annual Moveable Delegation of the Order of Druids (of which he was general secretary), which was being held in Derby that same week.[95] In his absence, W. H. Wood, secretary of the Trades Council, was elected president.[96] Papers were read, followed by discussion, on all the various subjects listed in the summons to the Congress. The most important were naturally those concerning the Royal Commission and the legal position of trade unions. On these, despite the aloof attitude of the Junta, resolutions were passed, largely through John Kane's influence, supporting the policy and action of the Conference of Amalgamated Trades in London. The Congress expressed the 'suspicion and disfavour' with which the great majority of trade unions regarded the Royal Commission, 'both in regard to the unfair composition and also to its one-sided, and to a great extent secret, proceedings'. It pledged itself, in the name of the societies represented, 'to aid the London Committee of Amalgamated Trades in their laudable effort to secure the legal protection of trade societies' funds', and declared 'its firm determination to continue the agitation, and to make the support of this measure a condition with candidates for parliamentary honours before we give any pledge of support or vote at the ensuing election'. It also resolved 'that the influence of this Congress shall be directed to aiding the London Conference of Amalgamated Trades in their endeavours to alter the third section of the act of the 6th of George IV [1825], cap. 129, the object being to amend the law in regard to conspiracy, intimidation, picketing, coercion, &c., which is ... capable of such misconstructions that it is utterly impossible that justice can be done'.

Thus the trade union leadership was still left in the hands of the Junta, the Congress making no attempt to appoint a permanent committee of its own. The Congress does not appear to have excited very much notice or to have had much influence on the course of events. John Pullon, secretary of the Nottingham Typographical Society and Trades Council, stated in a paper which he prepared for the second Congress in Birmingham, on 'What means are the best to make the Congresses permanently successful?',[97] stated that, 'regarding my own immediate neighbourhood, a knowledge of the business of that Congress [the first one, in Manchester] and acquaintance with the papers read, has been obtained by the working class community only so far as the delegate was able to give his report to the trades' council, and only so far as the ephemeral daily sheets of news have thought well to give their epitomised reports. And where now is the influence sent abroad and evoked by the papers and discussions which characterised that meeting? Echo says, "Where?".' This, he considered, was because a Congress committee had not been appointed 'to meet between Congress and Congress' and 'carry out the views adopted by the Congress, and give them wider scope and influence among our fellow men'.

The first Congress, in fact, as George Howell later pointed out, was of a 'preliminary character.... The delegates attending it were but feeling their way to a more permanent organisation.'[98] Indeed, 'it was hardly expected even by the most sanguine of the promoters of the gathering that the one then being held would really constitute the first of a continuous series, though that was the dream and the hope of the originators of the movement'.[99] The Congress did, however, pass a resolution 'That it is highly desirable that the trades of the United Kingdom should hold an annual congress, for the purpose of bringing the trades into closer alliance, and to take action in all Parliamentary matters pertaining to the general interests of the working classes'. It was therefore decided 'that the next congress should be held at Birmingham, the time to be left to the Birmingham Trades' Council'.[100]

3 THE T.U.C. BECOMES AN ESTABLISHED NATIONAL ORGANISATION

The Conference of Amalgamated Trades in London seems to have paid scant attention to the Manchester Congress. The next month, in fact, it was itself proposing to summon a national conference, as previously promised: this it would do 'at the most fitting time, which, probably, will be at the beginning of the Session of the new Parliament'.[101] The Junta had by now greatly strengthened their position in London, and Potter and his allies were finding it increasingly difficult to oppose them. The circulation of the *Beehive* had been seriously affected by the Junta's enmity, and the Trades' Newspaper Company had fallen into debt and was unable to pay any dividend to its shareholders, while many of its shares remained unsold.[102] Potter was therefore forced into dropping his hostility to the Junta and making repeated appeals for trade union unity and support. The *Beehive* would, in future, 'endeavour to draw in one united body all those labouring in the ranks of industry; to heal those unhappy differences which have so long existed amongst the representatives of the working classes. . . . This can only be done by mutual forbearance and conciliation; and we trust that all those in our ranks who, from whatever cause, may have differed from us, will cordially unite in our support. . . . As one means to the above end, all personalities will be excluded from our columns.'[103]

This change of heart, coupled with the growing threat to trade unionism from successive judicial decisions, brought about a reconciliation between the Junta and their opponents, and on August 22, 1868, it was reported in the *Beehive* that 'the leaders of the large trade societies in the metropolis have at last awakened to a sense of danger, and are taking active measures for calling together a conference of delegates from every trade society in the metropolitan district, for the purpose of considering what measures shall be adopted to meet the present crisis; and, what is still more important, that the two parties into which the union leaders of London are unhappily divided, will on this occasion—and we trust always in future—act in concert together, and that the circular convening the delegates will bear the signatures of the leading members of the Amalgamated Conference Trades, the Trades' Council, and the Working Men's Association'. In the next number

(August 29), however, it was regretted that 'the arrangement has fallen through', and the L.W.M.A. therefore expressed its intention of summoning a trades' conference on its own responsibility. But the differences were eventually removed and a circular was issued summoning a delegate meeting of the whole of the London trades at the Bell Inn, Old Bailey, on Wednesday, October 14, 1868. The signatories included Allan, Applegarth, Guile, Odger, Coulson, Potter, Dunning, Howell, Shipton, and Leicester. As the *Beehive* said, 'It is a long time since those names appeared in unison together; and ... it shows the gravity of the crisis which has brought about the union.'[104]

The main purpose of this meeting was to consider the Trade Societies' Bill, promoted by the Junta, which had been introduced into the Commons at the end of the last session. There was sharp difference of opinion on the third clause, defining criminal action by trade unions, but, after several adjourned meetings, the Bill was eventually adopted.[105] In March 1869, however, the reports of the Royal Commission on trades' unions were presented to Parliament, and, since the Government declined to take immediate legislative action, Frederic Harrison drew up a new Bill, based on the minority report.[106] This Bill would get rid of the objectionable third clause in the old Bill by abolishing all special criminal legislation in regard to trade unions and bringing them under the common law, while it would also enable trade unions, by registering under the Friendly Societies' Acts, to secure legal protection for their funds. It was therefore adopted by the Conference of Amalgamated Trades in place of the old Bill, and arrangements were made for summoning another delegate meeting of the London trades at the Sussex Hotel, Bouverie Street, on April 28.[107]

The Junta did not, it is to be noticed, fulfil their previous promises to summon a national trades' conference. They decided merely to issue another circular 'to the trades societies of the United Kingdom ... explaining the intentions of the Conference with reference to the Bill now before the House'.[108] It was also evident that the rift in the London trades had not been completely closed, for the L.W.M.A. also summoned delegate meetings of the London trades at the Bell Inn, Old Bailey, on April 13 and 20.[109] The delegates at these meetings 'represented [London] societies at the large conference held at St. Martin's Hall in 1867'.[110] The *Beehive* deplored the continuing disunity in the London trades, and at the same time Frederic Harrison and other legal advisers of the Junta urged the necessity for united trades' action. The result was that the Conference of Amalgamated Trades invited the delegates of the other trades to their meeting on April 28.[111]

Here, at last, unity was achieved.[112] A resolution was unanimously adopted in favour of the Bill, which had been introduced into the Commons by Messrs. Hughes and Mundella on April 10, and it was decided to hold a great aggregate meeting of the London trades in its support; meanwhile, M.P.s would have to be lobbied and a political campaign organised. To carry out this work a committee was appointed, consisting of Potter, Howell, Druitt, Dunning, and Broadhurst, to act with the committee of the Conference of Amalgamated Trades, comprising Allan, Applegarth, Odger, Guile, and Coulson.[113]

The London trades' meeting was held in Exeter Hall on June 22, when it was decided to send a deputation to Mr. Bruce, the Home Secretary, 'to solicit the support of the Government to this Bill'.[114] The new Parliament, elected under the 1867 Reform Act in November 1868, contained a large Liberal majority, and trade unionists had high hopes of favourable treatment from the new Ministry of Mr. Gladstone. The Government, however, wished to give further consideration to the question of trade union legislation, and eventually Messrs. Hughes and Mundella agreed to drop their Bill, after a formal second reading on July 7, on the understanding that the Government would at once pass a temporary measure giving legal protection to trade union funds and would introduce a complete trade union Bill next session.[115]

Meanwhile, the Birmingham Trades Council, in accordance with the decision of the first Trades Union Congress in Manchester, was making preparation for the second annual Congress to be held in Birmingham.[116] The circular summoning it was issued at the end of March or early in April 1869, stating that it would meet on June 21.[117] The response, however, does not appear to have been very encouraging, while many societies which did reply asked for more time, so a second circular was sent out in May announcing postponement of the Congress to August 23.[118] Other reasons for the postponement were that 'important questions affecting the trade unions were pending in the legislature',[119] and that the Trades Council wished 'to avoid collision with a gathering in London of a similar character',[120] that of the London trades on June 22.

The Congress met in Birmingham, in the Oddfellows' Hall, Temple Street, on August 23–28, 1869.[121] It was a more representative assembly than the first one in Manchester. There were forty-seven delegates present, representing forty societies with a total membership of 250,000. The London Trades Council sent George Odger, and George Howell got himself elected by the Paddington lodge of the Bricklayers' Society, considering that it would be 'a disgrace not to have our Society represented there'.[122] William Cremer and William Harry attended as representatives of the Marylebone and Chelsea Working Men's Associations, and Thomas Connolly, of the Stonemasons, also came from London. Apart from these, however, and George Potter, the Congress was again a mainly provincial affair. There were delegates from the trades councils of Birmingham, Manchester, Nottingham, Preston, the Potteries, and Dublin, and also from a number of important national trade unions, including the Ironworkers, Miners, Stonemasons, Tailors, and Flint Glass Makers, and from several smaller and local societies, while representatives were admitted from other working class bodies such as the Co-operative Movement, the Labour Representation League, and the National Education and Emigration Leagues.

The main subject of discussion at the Congress, of course, was the Royal Commission's report and proposed trade union legislation. A resolution was again passed, proposed by George Howell, in support of the policy of the Conference of Amalgamated Trades, demanding 'that in any attempt at legislation with regard to trades' unions, the following principles shall be distinctly recognised: 1. Entire repeal of the combination laws. 2. Complete protection of funds. 3. No interference with, nor attempt to separate, benefit from trade funds. 4. That in respect of the recommendation of the Commission to compel registration of trade rules and open accounts, this Congress would be against any exceptional clause in this respect from that enforced in regard to other legal societies of the country.' It was also decided 'to appoint a committee to prepare a statement, in accordance with this and other resolutions, to go out to the world, to the trades' unions and legislators, as to the reasons why we hold the opinions therein contained'. This committee was to consist of the Congress officers (Wilkinson, Flint Glass Makers, president; Kane, Amalgamated Ironworkers, vice-president; and McRae, Birmingham Trades Council, secretary), together with Horrocks (Amalgamated Tailors), Owen (Potteries Trade Council), Howell (Operative Bricklayers), Clare (Dublin Association of Trades), and Bailey (Preston Trades Council). William Cremer had strongly urged the appointment of a Congress committee 'to watch legislation next year', since it 'would far better represent the national will than a committee sitting in London'; but the Congress resolution did not go so far. Davis states in his *History of the British Trades Union Congress* (p. 9) that this Congress appointed the first 'Parliamentary Committee', the forerunner of the modern General Council, with a central office which was to be in London, in order to watch and promote labour legislation, by drafting Bills, lobbying M.P.s, interviewing Ministers, and generally assuming 'authority for voicing the opinion of the organised trades for the body politic of trade unionists'. It is clear, however, that the resolution which the Congress actually passed, though appointing a sort of embryo 'Parliamentary Committee', did not go anything like so far as Davis asserts. It only established a temporary committee 'to prepare a statement' after the Congress, publicising and explaining the resolutions which had been passed. Nevertheless, George Odger appears to have considered that such a committee might become a rival to the Conference of Amalgamated Trades and he therefore declined to serve upon it. There is no evidence, however, of this committee holding any meetings in the interval between the Birmingham Congress and the next one.

Other subjects of general trade union interest which were discussed at the Congress, and upon which resolutions were passed, included 'Justification of Trade Unions', 'Trade Unions, Political Economy, and Foreign Competition', reduction of the hours of labour, apprentice limitation, strikes and lock-outs, factory legislation, co-operative production, primary education, the necessity of working-class newspapers, and 'Labour Representation' in the House of Commons.

According to the *Beehive* report, it was decided that the next Congress should be held in London and that the summoning and arrangements for it 'should be left in the hands of the London Trades Council'. In fact, a committee was appointed consisting of the London delegates, Potter, Howell, Cremer, Harry, and Odger, 'to co-operate with the London Trades Council' in making arrangements for the Congress.[123] The decision to hold the Congress in London was 'on account of the opportunities it would afford (the Congress being held during the session) of waiting upon Members of Parliament'.[124] No date was fixed, but the Congress would be arranged to coincide with the introduction into Parliament of the Government's promised Trade Union Bill.[125]

There was nothing, in fact, that the trade unions could now do but await this Bill, and the Conference of Amalgamated Trades therefore held no meetings between April 1869 (when it completed preparations for the London trades' meeting on June 22) and February 1870. In the interim, however, the Junta finally got Potter and his associates under their thumb by acquiring control of the *Beehive*.[126] This achievement was given the appearance of an alliance. All differences, it was stated, had disappeared and 'the leaders of the various organised sections of working men now stand together to do battle, side by side, for the benefit of their class'. A joint committee representing the whole of the London trades had, as we have seen, been appointed at the delegate meeting on April 28, 1869, and when the Conference of Amalgamated Trades met again in February 1870, its membership was extended to include the delegates of the other London trades appointed at that meeting, including Potter, Howell, Broadhurst, Dunning, and a number of others. But Potter had by this time been completely muzzled. The *Beehive*, which had been running at a loss, had now been brought under the control of a new management committee, including the leading members of the Junta—Allan, Applegarth, Odger, and Guile—together with others such as Howell, Cremer, and R. M. Latham, President of the Labour Representation League, while Potter had been made secretary instead of manager. To increase the paper's circulation, it was decided to reduce its price from twopence to a penny and to alter its form and contents. This would necessitate £10,000 of new capital, which was to be provided by the large trade unions, the Labour Representation League, and the Co-operative Societies. Potter was to be 'assisted' in the editorial work by the Rev. Henry Solly, nominee of the Junta, best known for his foundation of Trades' Halls and Working Men's Clubs and Institutes, and once an adherent of the middle-class wing of the Chartist Movement.[127] It seems, in fact, from the change in the tone and contents of the *Beehive* from now on, that Potter had actually been superseded by that reverend gentleman, and though he continued for a few years to stand among the trade union leaders the real power now rested almost unchallenged in the hands of the Junta.

The trade union world anxiously awaited in 1870 the introduction of the Trade Union Bill promised by the Government, but the Parliamentary session passed and no such Bill appeared. Early in August, therefore, the Conference of Amalgamated Trades sent a deputation to the Home Secretary, who informed them that a Bill would be brought in at the beginning of the next session, and that meanwhile the temporary Act for the protection of trade union funds would be renewed. The Conference therefore adjourned 'until such time as it was necessary to hold a meeting'.[128]

Meanwhile, however, the provincial trades councils and trade societies were getting impatient for the summoning of the annual Congress to be held that year in London, and the committee appointed at Birmingham therefore issued a circular in August announcing that the Congress would meet on October 24.[129] When October arrived, however, another circular was issued stating that, 'after a more matured determination with the representatives of the large societies on the subject', the committee had decided to postpone the Congress until 'the first Monday after the Bill is before Parliament'.[130] The reason for this decision was that, if they waited until the Bill was introduced into Parliament the following session, the Congress could be held concurrently with the second reading and the delegates would be able, if necessary, to lobby M.P.s and make representations to the Home Secretary. To hold a Congress now would involve useless expense and might militate against the success of the one which would certainly have to be held soon afterwards, when the Bill was brought in.

The Government Trade Union Bill was at last introduced in February 1871.[131] It was a disappointing measure, fulfilling trade union fears and dashing most of their hopes. It would, it is true, grant full legal recognition to trade unions and enable them to secure protection for their funds by registration under the Friendly Societies Act; but, by its third clause, it would still leave trade unionists liable to criminal prosecution for such vague, undefined acts as 'molesting', 'obstructing', 'threatening', 'intimidating', and so on, as under the ambiguous 1825 Act and later judicial decisions. A storm of indignation, therefore, immediately rose in the trade union world against the criminal section of the Bill, and to give nation-wide expression to this feeling and bring pressure upon Parliament the third Trades Union Congress was now summoned to meet in London, in the Portland Rooms, Foley Street, Marylebone, on Monday, March 6, to coincide with the second reading of the Bill.[132] This Congress was the first really national one, being attended, despite the very short notice, by delegates from forty-nine societies, representing 289,430 members.[133] The unions represented included most of the important ones—Engineers, Miners, Ironworkers, Ironfounders, Boilermakers and Iron Shipbuilders, Cotton Spinners, Carpenters and Joiners, Stonemasons, Bricklayers, Tailors, Shoemakers, and Flint Glass Makers—and there were also representatives from the trades councils in London, Manchester, Leeds, Nottingham, Preston, Oldham, the Potteries, and Maidstone. The Conference of Amalgamated Trades, now combining almost all the London trades, was strongly represented, and many of the leading provincial unionists were also there.

The main, almost exclusive, concern of the Congress was the Government Bill, the criminal section of which was strongly denounced. A deputation was appointed to wait on the Home Secretary, but got no satisfaction, so it was decided to appoint a committee 'to work with the committee of the Amalgamated Trades' in organising political agitation against the Bill. Thus was established the first permanent committee—the 'Parliamentary Committee'—of the Trades Union Congress. It was to consist of Alexander Macdonald, of the Miners' National Association, Lloyd Jones, representing the Manchester Fustian Cutters, and Joseph Leicester, of the Flint Glass Makers' Society, together with George Potter (chairman) and George Howell (secretary).

The committee at once drew up and distributed to M.P.s a printed circular asking for rejection of the criminal provisions of the Trades Union Bill. Their prompt action 'gave dissatisfaction to some members of the Conference of Amalgamated Trades', with whom they had been instructed to co-operate, but agreement was eventually reached between the two bodies,[134] the Conference of Amalgamated Trades instructing its committee and officers 'to act with the Congress committee and to take such steps as might seem necessary to improve the Government Bill as far as possible'.[135] The utmost concession that could be obtained, however, was division of the Bill into two, the 'Trades Union Bill' and the 'Criminal Law Amendment Bill', the latter containing the criminal clauses to which trade unionists objected so strongly. All the efforts of the joint committee failed to prevent the Criminal Law Amendment Act from being passed, but trade unions did at least, by the other Act, secure full legal recognition and protection for their funds.

Immediately after the passing of this legislation, the Conference of Amalgamated Trades dissolved itself, considering that it had 'discharged the duties for which it was organised'.[136] As the Webbs point out, 'The Secretaries of the Amalgamated Societies, especially Allan and Applegarth, had, indeed, attained the object which they personally had most at heart. . . . The wider issue which remained to be fought required a more representative organisation'.[137] This was provided by the Trades Union Congress, now established as a national 'Labour Parliament', meeting annually, with a permanent Parliamentary Committee to provide representative leadership for the whole trade union movement. Under its leadership was waged the vigorous agitation which finally resulted in 1875 in the repeal of the obnoxious Criminal Law Amendment Act.[138] Trade unions, to use George Howell's words, were now 'liberated from the last vestige of the criminal laws specially appertaining to labour'. This resounding triumph was the first in the long list of achievements of the Trades Union Congress down to the present day.

NOTES

1. *Manchester Guardian*, 14 and 15 Sept. 1882.
2. Webb, S. and B., *History of Trade Unionism* (1920), p. 280, n. 1.

3. Cole, G. D. H., 'Some Notes on British Trade Unionism in the Third Quarter of the Nineteenth Century', *International Review for Social History*, Vol. II (1937), reprinted in E. M. Carus-Wilson (ed.), *Essays in Economic History*, Vol. III (1962).
4. Webb, S. and B., *op. cit.*, pp. 113–68. Cole, G. D. H., *Attempts at General Union*, 1818–34 (1953).
5. *Poor Man's Guardian*, Oct. 19, 1833.
6. For which, see Holyoake, G. J., *History of Co-operation in England* (1906), vol. i, pp. 120–5.
7. Webb, S. and B., *op. cit.*, pp. 170–3.
8. *Ibid.*, pp. 186–95.
9. George Odger stated in 1866 that 'though there is a remnant of it, it is a perfect myth, so far as its recognition by societies at large is concerned'. (*Report of Conference of Trades' Delegates*, Sheffield, July 1866). George Howell stated that it 'continued to exist until 1867'. (*Labour Legislation, Labour Movements and Labour Leaders*, 1905, vol. i, p. 95. Cf. his statement in the *Contemporary Review*, Sept. 1889, that it 'continued in existence down to 1861'.)
10. Webb, S. and B., *op. cit.*, p. 195.
11. *Manchester Guardian*, Nov. 23, 1853, and March 8, 1854, containing reports of meetings in Manchester. A full account of the movement is to be found in the *People's Paper* published by Jones.
12. Karl Marx and Louis Blanc were elected honorary delegates, but did not attend the conference. Marx, however, sent a letter in its support.
13. *Address from the Delegates of the Metropolitan Trades to the Trades of the United Kingdom* (1854). See also the report on *Trades' Societies and Strikes* (pp. 220 and 260–3) issued by the National Association for the Promotion of Social Science (1860).
14. Webb, S. and B., *op cit.*, p. 228. *Trades' Societies and Strikes* (1860), pp. 53–76. Howell, G., *Labour Legislation, Labour Movements and Labour Leaders* (1905), vol. i, pp. 128–35. Postgate, R., *The Builders' History* (1923), pp. 167–79. Anon., *The London Trades Council, 1860–1950* (1950), pp. 3–5.
15. Webb, S. and B., *op. cit.*, pp. 242–3. Richards, C., *A History of Trades Councils from 1860 to 1875* (1920).
16. *Op. cit.*, pp. 245 and 247. See also Anon., *The London Trades Council, 1860–1950* (1950), pp. 9 and 15–16.
17. 1861 Rules.
18. See Humphrey, A. W., *History of Labour Representation* (1912), p. 10, Gillespie, F. E., *Labor and Politics in England from 1850 to 1867* (1927), pp. 203–34, and Brand, C. F., 'The Conversion of the British Trade-Unions to Political Action', in the *American Historical Review*, Jan. 1925.
19. Gillespie, *op. cit.*, p. 227.
20. *Operative Bricklayers' Society's Trade Circular*, Oct. 1861.
21. *Reynold's Newspaper*, Nov. 10, 1861.
22. See the works by Gillespie and Brand previously cited.
23. *Report of Conference on the Law of Masters and Workmen ... Held in London on 30th and 31st May, and 1st and 2nd June, 1864* (Glasgow, 1864). See also Webb, S. and B., *op cit.*, pp. 249–53.
24. L.T.C. Sixth Annual Report (1864–5).
25. See Webb, S. and B., *op. cit.*, pp. 254–5, Postgate, *op. cit.*, pp. 181–218, Richards, *op. cit.*, pp. 20–2, Anon., *The London Trades Council,*

1860–1950 (1950), pp. 13–14 and 20–3. See also S. W. Coltham, 'George Potter, the Junta, and the *Beehive*', *Int. Rev. of Soc. Hist.,* Vols. IX (1964) and X (1965).

26. Postgate, *op. cit.,* p. 169.
27. *Op cit..* pp. 254–5 and 298, n. 1.
28. He was also an important figure in the labour political movement. See Humphrey, *op cit.,* p. 10, n. 1, and Gillespie, *op cit.,* pp 210–11. 230–1, and 258–9.
29. See the *Beehive* and the L.T.C. Sixth Annual Report (1864–5).
30. Printed report, *Mr. Potter and the London Trades Council* (March 1865).
31. L.T.C. minutes, Aug. and Sept. 1865.
32. Hansard's Parliamentary Debates, Third Series, vol. clxxiii, Feb.–Mar. 1864, p. 1577. See also Humphrey, A. W., *The Life of Robert Applegarth* (1915), pp. 52–5.
33. L.T.C. minutes, April 1865.
34. L.T.C. Annual Delegate Meeting Report, Aug. 1865. The memory of this incident still rankled in 1867 (*Beehive*, March 9, 1867, statement by George Odger).
35. The L.W.M.A. was opposed not only by the Trades Council, but also by the Reform League (which was supported by the L.T.C.), as being a rival organisation in the working-class movement for political reform. It was, in fact, a political rather than a trade union organisation. See Humphrey, *op. cit.,* pp. 10–21, Gillespie, *op. cit.,* pp. 255–6 and 258–9, Brand, *op. cit.,* pp. 261–2, and Cole, *op. cit.,* p. 15.
36. Detailed reports were given in the *Beehive* and in the Sheffield newspapers.
37. L.T.C. minutes, March 22 and May 10, 1866.
38. *Ibid.,* May 1866. *Beehive*, April 28 and May 12, 1866.
39. *Beehive,* May 19, 1866.
40. There is a short biography of Dronfield by W. H. G. Armytage in *Notes and Queries,* vol. cxciii (1948), pp. 145–8, in which, however, there are some inaccuracies regarding his official career in the Provincial Typographical Association. Brief biographical sketches are also to be found in the *Typographical Circular,* Sept. 1891 and Sept. 1894, and in the *Sheffield Independent,* Aug. 28, 1894.
41. P.T.A. Half-Yearly Reports, 1858–9. *Typographical Societies' Monthly Circular,* 1858–9. *London Press Journal and General Trades' Advocate,* 1858–9. Lengthy accounts are also to be found in the Sheffield newspapers. The Webbs wrongly date the establishment of the Association in 1857 (*op cit.,* p. 243, footnote).
42. *Report of the Conference of Trades' Delegates of the United Kingdom, held in … Sheffield, on July 17th, 1866, and four following days* (Sheffield, 1866). The Webbs wrongly date this conference in June (*op. cit.,* p. 257). It was originally planned for that month, but the date was later altered.
43. *Ibid.,* p. 40.
44. Typographical Association, 1877 Delegate Meeting Report, p. 12.
45. The London Trades Council would not even pay its share of the conference expenses (L.T.C. Eighth Annual Report, 1866–7. *Beehive,* Jan. 5 and 12, 1867). Cole, *op cit.,* p. 14, states that the Sheffield conference 'proposed that a further general Conference should be held in the following year, and that the London Trades Council …

should be requested to call it. To this request the London Trades Council appears to have paid no attention.' There seems, however, to be no evidence for this statement. There was some discussion at the 1866 conference as to whether the next one should be held in London or Manchester, but the decision was in favour of the latter (*Report*, pp. 67–8). There is no doubt, however, that the Junta were lukewarm towards the Sheffield conference and opposed in 1867 to the summoning of another. See below, pp. 35–6.

46. See the conference reports, reports in the *Beehive*, and also Webb, S. and B., *op. cit.*, pp. 258–9. The Preston conference was attended by delegates from only thirteen societies and there were then only forty-seven small societies, with a total membership of 23,500, in the Alliance.

47. Webb, S. and B., *op. cit.*, pp. 256–7 and 259–60. S. Pollard, *The Sheffield Outrages* (1971).

48. L.T.C. minutes and reports.

49. Webb, S. and B., *op. cit.*, pp. 261–2. Hedges, R. Y., and Winterbottom, A., *The Legal History of Trade Unionism* (1930), pp. 52–7. Full accounts appeared in the *Beehive* and in the public press generally.

50. MS. Minutes of the Conference of Amalgamated Trades, 1867–71 Webb Trade Union Collection, British Library of Political and Economic Science). L.T.C. minutes and annual report, 1866–7, *Report on the Varios Proceedings taken by the London Trades Council and the Conference of Amalgamated Trades in reference to the Royal Commission on Trades' Unions and other Subjects in connection therewith* (London, Sept. 1867). The conference held its first meeting on January 28, 1867.

51. L.T.C. Annual Report, 1872–3.

52. L.T.C. Eighth Annual Report (1866–7).

53. *Beehive*, Feb. 2 and March 9, 1867.

54. *Beehive*, Feb. 2, 1867.

55. *Ibid.*, Feb. 9, 1867. See also the First Annual Repport of the L.W.M.A. (*Beehive*, April 20, 1867), in which Potter criticised the London Trades Council for its failure to summon a national conference.

56. The trade union deputations had been unable to get working-class representation on the Commission, but the L.W.M.A. had secured the inclusion of the barrister, Frederic Harrison, who supported their case.

57. L.T.C. minutes, March 4, 1867.

58. *Beehive*, March 9, 1867.

59. L.T.C. Eighth Annual Report (1866–7).

60. *Report of the Trades' Conference held at St. Martin's Hall on March 5, 6, 7 and 8, 1867* (London, 1867). This report is reprinted in an appendix to Davis, W. J., *History of the British Trades Union Congress* (1910). See also the *Beehive*, March 9, 1867, and Webb, S. and B., *op. cit.*, pp. 272–3. Professor Cole's 'full list of societies represented' (*op. cit.*, pp. 15 and 23) is far from complete.

61. *Beehive*, March 9, 1867. When a deputation of provincial delegates met the Conference of Amalgamated Trades, the latter denounced Potter and his followers as 'meddlers in trade matters and traders on the misfortunes of the working class'. The L.W.M.A. was said to contain 'anti-unionists', who were not members of a trade society, and to be composed mostly of 'systematic political agitators'. (Minutes of Conf. of Amalg. Trades, March 8, 1867). Many of the provincial delegates were not aware of the split in the metropolitan trades until they arrived in London.

62. *Beehive*, June 29, July 6, 13, 20, 27, Aug. 3, 10, and Nov. 23, 1867. See also the statement by Potter to the first T.U.C., in the *Manchester Guardian*, June 4, 1868.
63. *Beehive*, March 28, 1868.
64. *Ibid.*, Jan. 30, 1869.
65. See Webb, S. and B., *op. cit.*, pp. 263 ff.
66. Davis, *op. cit.*, p. 138.
67. Address of the Conference Committee 'To the Operative Classes of the United Kingdom', appended to the printed report of the St. Martin's Hall Conference. See also the *Beehive*, March 16 and 23, 1867. The Manchester and Salford Trades Council passed a resolution regretting 'that the London Trades' Council have allowed their individual feelings to interfere with the performance of their public duties in preventing their constituents from being represented at the conference of trades' unions at London'. (*Beehive*, April 20, 1867).
68. *Op. cit.*, pp. 16–18.
69. Minutes, Sept. 30, 1867.
70. Report of St. Martin's Hall Conference. *Beehive*, March 16, 1867.
71. See Webb, S. and B., *op. cit.*, pp. 278–9, and Hedges and Winterbottom, *op. cit.*, pp. 45–51.
72. Minutes of Conference of Amalgamated Trades, Feb. 14 and 21, and March 1, 1867. L.T.C. minutes, Feb. 20, 1867, and Annual Report, 1866–7. *Report of the Various Proceedings taken by the London Trades Council and the Conference of Amalgamated Trades* (Sept. 1867).
73. Minutes of Conference of Amalgamated Trades, Sept. 1867–July 1868. *Beehive*, Nov. 23 and 30, 1867, and July 4 and 18, 1868. Circulars issued by Conference of Amalgamated Trades 'to the Members of the Trade Societies of the United Kingdom', Feb. and July, 1868.
74. The Webbs state (*op. cit.*, p. 265, *n.* 1) that this Bill was introduced early in the 1868 session, whereas, in actual fact, it was not read a first time until July 7, 1868, shortly before Parliament was prorogued.
75. Minutes, Sept. 11, 1868. Protection for trade union funds, however, was incidentally provided by Russell Gurney's Act, dealing with larceny or embezzlement of a co-partnership's funds by any of its members. *Beehive*, Dec. 26, 1868. Webb, S. and B., *op. cit.*, p. 275, *n.* 4. Hedges and Winterbottom, *op. cit.*, p. 57.
76. *United Kingdom Alliance of Organised Trades. Minutes of Conference held in the Spinners' and Minders' Institute, Preston, on Tuesday, September 24th, 1867, and the two following days.* An address 'To the Trades of the Alliance and the Country Generally' was appended to this report.
77. See above, p. 33.
78. *Reports on the various Proceedings taken by the London Trades Council and the Conference of Amalgamated Trades in reference to the Royal Commission on Trades' Unions and other subjects in connection therewith* (Sept. 1867). Minutes of the Conference of Amalgamated Trades, Sept. 2, 1867.
79. L.T.C. minutes, Jan. 10 and 21, and Feb. 18, 1868. Minutes of the Conference of Amalgamated Trades, Jan. 10, 1868.
80. *Beehive*, March 7, 1868, reporting on L.W.M.A. meeting of March 3.
81. *Ibid.*, March 21 and 28, 1868.
82. *Ibid.*, April 11, 1868.

83. See above, p. 32.

84. National Association for the Promotion of Social Science, *Transactions*, 1865 (Report of the Ninth Annual Meeting, at Sheffield, Oct. 4–11, 1865), pp. 476–80.

85. He had been at one time a collector and committee member of the Pen-knife Blade-grinders' Society in Sheffield, but, so it was stated at the end of 1866, 'for years past, both in public and private, [he] has been one of the most determined opponents of the doings of the Sheffield Trades' Unions'. (Report of L.T.C. deputation to investigate the Sheffield 'outrages', Nov. 1866.)

86. Armytage, W. H. G., *A. J. Mundella, 1825–1897: the Liberal Background to the Labour Movement* (1951), p. 49, states wrongly that Dronfield was forbidden to read a paper which he had prepared in defence of the unions'. Cf. his article on Dronfield in *Notes and Queries*, 1948.

87. Statement by Dronfield in the *Report of the Conference of Trades' Delegates of the United Kingdom* (Sheffield, July 1866), pp. 69–70.

88. The reprint in the *Beehive* is undated. The *Beehive* did not get news of the circular until two or three weeks after it was issued. Hartwell stated at the second annual meeting of the L.W.M.A. in April that the Manchester and Salford Trades Council called a Trades Union Congress a fortnight before the L.W.M.A. decided, on March 3, to summon a 'National Labour Parliament'. (*Beehive*, April 11, 1868.) The circular was read to the Conference of Amalgamated Trades on March 16, 1868 (Minutes).

89. There seems to be no very clear reason why the British Association for the Advancement of Science was mentioned in this circular, along with the Social Science Association. Trade unionists appear neither to have had nor to have desired any part in its proceedings. In the second, revised circular only the Social Science Association was referred to.

90. *Beehive*, April 18, 1868.

91. Howell, G., *Labour Legislation, Labour Movements and Labour Leaders* (1905), vol. i, p. 177. See also his article in the *Manchester Guardian*, Sept. 14, 1882.

92. When the Manchester and Salford Trades Council's circular was read to the Conference of Amalgamated Trades, 'the Secretary was instructed to write for further information respecting it' (Minutes, March 16, 1868), but there is nothing more about it in the minutes. There is no mention whatever of the Congress in the minutes of the London Trades Council.

93. William Dronfield, representing the Sheffield Association of Organised Trades, was one of the most prominent delegates.

94. Detailed reports of its proceedings are to be found in the *Manchester Guardian* and *Courier* and in the *Beehive*.

95. *Manchester Courier*, June 2, 1868. Davis (*op. cit.*, p. 2) lists him, wrongly, among the delegates at the Congress.

96. Sadly, it must be recorded that some years later Wood was expelled from the Typographical Association, after it was discovered that he had been systematically embezzling union funds over a long period.

97. *Beehive*, Jan. 1, 1870. The paper was not, however, read at the Congress.

98 'Trades Union Congress and Social Legislation', *Contemporary Review*, Sept. 1889, p. 405.

99. *Manchester Guardian*, Sept. 14, 1882.
100. *Beehive*, June 13, 1868.
101. Circular of July 1868.
102. *Beehive*, June 20, 1868.
103. *Ibid.*, July 1868.
104. *Beehive*, Sept. 26 and Oct. 3, 1868.
105. *Ibid.*, Oct. 17, 24, and 31, 1868.
106. *Ibid.*, April 17, 1869. Webb, S. and B., *op. cit.*, pp. 274–5.
107. Minutes, April 1869.
108. Minutes, April 19, 1869.
109. *Beehive*, April 17 and 24, 1869.
110. Earlier on Potter had proposed another national conference like that of 1867, to consider the Royal Commission's report (*Beehive*, Jan. 30, 1869), but his proposal had fallen flat.
111. *Beehive*, April 24, 1869. Minutes of Conference of Amalgamated Trades, April 19, 1869.
112. *Beehive*, May 1, 1869.
113. Note that this establishment of trade union unity was accompanied by a similar consolidation in the working class political movement, with the establishment in Aug. 1869 of the Labour Representation League, 'a central association embodying all sections of the London working men, to secure the return of practical working to Parliament'. The League's executive committee included Allan, Applegarth, Connolly, Coulson, Cremer, Guile, Harry, Howell, Newton, Odger, and Potter. *Beehive*, Aug. 7 and 21, 1869. Humphrey, *History of Labour Representation* (1912), p. 32.
114. *Beehive*, June 26, 1869.
115. *Ibid.*, July 3 and 10, 1869. Webb, S. and B., *op. cit.*, p. 275. A temporary Trades' Unions (Protection of Funds) Act was immediately passed. *Beehive*, Aug. 7, 1869. Hedges and Winterbottom, *op. cit.*, pp. 57–9.
116. *Beehive*, Feb. 13, 1869.
117. Circular summoning the 'Second Annual Congress of Trades' Councils and Trade Societies Generally' (Birmingham, March 25, 1869). *Beehive*, April 24, 1869.
118. *Beehive*, May 29 and July 24, 1869.
119. Report of Congress by R. S. Kirk.
120. Report of Congress in *Beehive*, Aug. 28, 1869.
121. *The Second Annual Congress of Trades' Unions, held on August 23, 24, 25, 26, 27 and 28, 1869, in the Odd Fellows' Hall, Upper Temple Street, Birmingham. Specially reported by R. S. Kirk* (Birmingham, 1869). Lengthy reports are also to be found in the *Beehive* and the local press.
122. The Bricklayers' executive had refused to appoint him as 'the expence [would be] too much'. Howell paid all his own expenses, except for his railway fare. Howell Letters (Bishopsgate Institute), July 20, 26, 27, and 31, and Aug. 9, 1869.
123. Circulars distributed by the committee in Aug. and Oct. 1870. See also Howell's article in the *Contemporary Review*, Sept. 1889, p. 406.
124. *Beehive*, Sept. 4, 1869.
125. L.T.C. minutes, March 12, 1870.
126. *Beehive*, Dec. 11, 1869.
127. *Beehive*, Feb. 12, 1870.

128. Minutes, Aug. 3, 1870.
129. Circular dated Aug. 11, 1870. *Beehive*, Aug. 13, 1870.
130. Circular dated Oct. 2, 1870. *Beehive*, Oct. 22, 1870.
131. *Beehive*, Feb. and March, 1870. Webb, S. and B., *op. cit.*, pp. 276–80.
132. Undated circular, probably issued at the end of Feb. 1871. *Beehive*, March 4, 1871.
133. The MS. Minute Book of the Congress is in the George Howell Collection (Bishopsgate Institute), Howell being its secretary. Detailed reports appeared in the *Beehive* and there were accounts in many other newspapers.
134. Report of the Parliamentary Committee to the Fourth T.U.C., at Nottingham, Jan. 8, 1872.
135. Minutes, March 24, 1871.
136. Minutes, Sept. 1, 1871.
137. *Op. cit.*, pp. 282–3.
138. *Ibid.*, pp. 283–92.

Chapter 4

TRENDS IN MODERN TRADE UNIONISM*

MODERN trade-union organisation and attitudes are tenaciously rooted in the past. Products of a slow and often painful evolutionary process, trade unions continue, even in this era of rapid social change, to cling stubbornly to traditional policies and modes of action. Thus when the present writer's history of trade unionism in the printing industry was published in 1954, A. P. Wadsworth, editor of the *Manchester Guardian* and himself a profoundly knowledgeable historian, was led to write:

> No reader ... will be left in any doubt that trade unions are almost the most conservative force in the country. Those eager reformers who think they can change the atmosphere of industry overnight had better restrain their optimism.

It is true, as we shall see, that considerable changes, both in organisation and policies, have occurred since the late nineteenth century, but these changes have been very gradual and a cynic might say, *plus ça change, plus c'est la même chose.* One can see this in the deep-rooted sectionalism which still persists in 'trade' affairs, the continued occurrence of 'demarcation' disputes, the strong opposition to any centralised T.U.C. negotiations on national incomes policy, the insistence still on established free-bargaining procedures, and deep distrust and fears of any legislative controls, whether by a Labour or Conservative Government. The T.U.C. summed up this attitude of resistance to change and of faith in traditional methods, in evidence to the Donovan Commission on trade unions in the late 1960s, pointing out that

> trade unionists show no great enthusiasm for sweeping away the forms of collective bargaining which have stood them in good stead over the years ... Insofar as successs [in securing a national incomes policy] depends on changing people's attitudes, progress must neces-

---

*This previously unpublished paper, originally composed in the 1950s, drew not only upon the author's own researches, but also upon those of others, notably B. C. Roberts, A. Flanders and H. A. Clegg, and J. H. Richardson. It has required only slight subsequent revision.

..ly be relatively slow ... The complexity of trade-union structure in Britain will always remain.[2]

It is impossible, therefore, to understand the structure, policies and problems of modern British trade unions without knowledge of their historical evolution. In their early years, in the eighteenth and nineteenth centuries, trade unions had to fight long and bitter struggles against legal and economic repression. They could be prosecuted as common-law conspiracies or under parliamentary statutes such as the Combination Laws. Even after these laws were abolished, in 1825, it was many years before trade unions succeeded in acquiring full legal recognition. Legislation in the early 1870s gave them an apparently assured status, but in 1901 the famous Taff Vale case again threatened their position, which was not securely established till the Trade Disputes Act in 1906. Today, by contrast, it is often argued that trade unions have become too powerful and need subjecting to tighter legislative control. But memories of the past still haunt trade-union minds, and attempts to reimpose such control arouse fierce opposition.[3]

While struggling for legal recognition, the trade unions fought continually to obtain for their members a fairer standard of living, through increased wages, reduced working hours, etc.; there was gross inequality in the distribution of wealth and income. In serious trade depressions unionists suffered severely, experiencing heavy unemployment and wages cuts. It was only in the years just before the First World War that the foundations of the modern Welfare State began to be laid, with the establishment of unemployment and sickness insurance, labour exchanges, old-age pensions, etc. Until then the unions had borne heavy burdens in the form of unemployment, sickness, superannuation and funeral benefits to their members; such payments far exceeded those on strikes, and they continued to do so for some years, most unions still continuing them as supplements to State benefits.

The memory of this past history—of legal oppression, social inequality, unemployment, strikes and bitterness in relations with employers—still exercises a profound influence upon modern trade unions, even though most of these evils have by now been removed. Even though unions are now a well-recognised part of the machinery of industrial administration, freely negotiating agreements on wages and working conditions, though they are nowadays brought into consultation by Government on major economic and social issues, though standards of living have risen substantially, there are still fears and distrusts—fears of mechanisation and labour redundancy, for example, and distrust of 'the bosses'; there is still the confrontation of capital and labour, still deep class division; and trade-union objectives therefore remain basically unaltered, to safeguard and improve the living and working standards of their members.

But although the basic attitudes and aims remain the same, considerable changes have occurred in trade-union structure and organisation since the late nineteenth century. There has been a gradual consolidation or concentration, as shown by the decline in the number of unions and increase in their size, as a result of amalgamation, federation, and the growth of 'industrial' and 'general' unions. This has been accompanied by greater centralisation of government and centralised bargaining with employers' national organisations. These developments have greatly increased union strength, but they have also created serious problems.

Early trade societies were purely local, established in individual trades in particular towns or districts. The members were in direct touch with society affairs, the general meeting of members being the governing body, their amateur officials working alongside them at bench or forge or loom. They were composed of skilled craftsmen, a 'labour aristocracy', much better paid than the mass of unskilled and semi-skilled workers, who remained unorganised, excluded from these craft societies.

The resources of these small local societies, however, were generally insufficient against the power of employers, and so during the nineteenth century there gradually developed regional or national unions of workers in particular trades, though small local societies still remained numerous. There were even occasional attempts at wider 'general union' or trades' federation, none of them successful, e.g. Doherty's National Association and Owen's Grand National. The Trades Union Congress, however, established in 1868, did provide national leadership for the whole labour movement; but it was a mainly political body and did not interfere with the jealously guarded autonomy of individual unions in trade affairs.

The growth of national unions brought with it constitutional problems: the creation of a national executive and national rules, relations between executive and branches, union finance, strike control, etc. The tendency was towards government by an elected central executive, controlled by periodic delegate meetings with legislative functions. In some industries, such as cotton and coal, the local or district organisations remained very strong and refused to endow the national executive with very wide powers. In most national unions, however, the national executive and officials (now full-time professionals) tended to gain increasing control and by the late nineteenth and early twentieth century they were negotiating national agreements in some trades. At the same time, national strikes were becoming a dangerous possibility, though the bargaining power and negotiating skill of the national officials had the result of greatly reducing the number of petty disputes and average annual strike payments.

These unions were still, until the late nineteenth century, almost all craft societies of skilled workers, but the surge of 'New Unionism' from the 'eighties onwards resulted in the formation of many unions of unskilled and semi-skilled workers, such as those of the dockers, gas-stokers, agricultural and general labourers, recruited by mass enrolments, with low subscriptions—products of mass agitation and Socialist leavening, more aggressive and more political in their policies. In the past, such outbursts had proved ephemeral, collapsing under employers' attacks and trade depression, but these new unions of the late nineteenth century did not generally break up. They were aided in their beginnings by officials of the craft societies—a mark of the widening 'brotherhood' or solidarity of labour—and they were gradually to develop in organisational strength and finances until today such unions as the Transport and General Workers' Union and the National Union of General and Municipal Workers are amongst the most powerful in the country.

At the time when the Webbs produced the first edition of their history, however, in 1894, the new unions were in their infancy and had not begun to federate extensively and enrol workers in many trades; as yet they were mostly restricted to workers in separate occupations, e.g. dockers, gas-stokers, etc., though there were some general labourers' unions. The Webbs considered that the trade union of the future would be 'co-extensive with its craft' and would not 'spread beyond the boundaries of a single occupation'. They recognised, however, that 'the selfish spirit of exclusiveness which often marked the relatively well-paid engineer, carpenter, or boiler-maker' in earlier times was giving place to 'a more generous recognition of the essential solidarity of the wage-earning class', as illustrated by their helping labourers to form unions and by the revision of the rules of the Amalgamated Society of Engineers in 1892, whereby the ranks of 'this most aristocratic of unions' was opened to 'practically all the mechanics in the innumerable branches of the engineering trade'. Thus, while recognising the continuing strength of occupational sectionalism, the Webbs did anticipate that the scope of union membership would be broadened. They also recognised that whilst boundaries between sectional unions would be maintained, unions would increasingly tend to collaborate on broader economic, social and political issues, with tendencies towards federation if not amalgamation.

This, then, was the position in 1894. There were at that time, according to the Labour Department of the Board of Trade, 1,314 trade unions with a total membership of 1,530,000. By the end of 1951 the number of unions had fallen to 704, but total membership had soared to 9,480,000. Thus average union membership had risen from 1,160 in 1894 to 13,452 in 1951. There has clearly been a consolidation in trade unionism: the number of unions has been reduced by amalgamations and the average union is much bigger. In actual fact, the concentration has become much greater than these broad general figures indicate: detailed figures show that in 1951 seventeen unions, each with a membership of more than 100,000, had a combined total of 6,305,000 members; these few unions, that is, comprised about two-thirds of total membership. On the other hand, although trade-union membership is highly concentrated, many small societies still survive and trade unionism is spread through a far wider range of industries and occupations than it was in the 1890s.

It is also clear that the Webbs' opinion regarding the limitation of individual trade-union membership to a single craft or oc-cupation has not proved entirely correct. Craft and occupation, it is true, are still of fundamental importance in the pattern of trade-union organisation, but their importance has been diminished by the progress of mechanisation, which has reduced the significance of craft skills and blurred craft distinctions; moreover, two World Wars have also resulted in 'dilution'. Old craft unions have therefore been obliged, firstly, to widen their membership to include semi-skilled workers and 'labourers', as the engineers have done, and secondly, to amalgamate or federate with other unions in the same industry, so as to overcome problems of demarcation, as well as to acquire increased strength. This is a process which has gone on gradually and piecemeal over many years and is still not complete. At the same time, however, other unions have developed which are more deliberately and consciously based on the idea of 'indus-trial unionism', combining together all workers in a particular industry, as in railways, coal-mines, textiles, etc., that is in industries where the great majority of workers are non-craft, semi-skilled and labourers, in industries devoid of any apprenticeship system and not generally requiring any prolonged period of technical training. These unions, however, still possess a strong occupational sense and cohesion. Much more novel was the development, from the late nineteenth century onwards, of 'general' unions, not confined to any particular industry, but recruiting their membership from a wider range of 'general workers' or labourers in different industries and occupations, though usually with some concentration in two or three.

The idea of 'industrial unionism' developed very strongly between the period when the Webbs produced their first edition and the First World War. It was strongly influenced by the growing Socialist emphasis on workers' solidarity in the face of capitalist concentration and processes of mechanisation, which, firstly, presented trade unions with much stronger opposition, secondly, was tending to produce an undifferentiated industrial 'proletariat', without craft distinctions, and thirdly, was threatening wider labour redundancy; the associated notion of 'gild socialism' or 'syndicalism' also exercised some influence, with its idea of replacing capitalist organisation with workers' industrial control.

The Webbs considered syndicalism impracticable, believing rather in progress towards Socialism by social-democratic political means, by a gradual, constitutional process, rather than by the violent overthrow of capitalism. But they came to realise the strength of the movement towards 'industrial unionism', of which the most outstanding example was the establishment of the National Union of Railwaymen in 1913. In the revised edition of their history in 1920, therefore, they recognised that this would be the 'new model' of future trade-union organisation, just as they considered the engineers' amalgamated craft union had earlier been; indeed, the engineers themselves had been moving further towards this broader form of industrial organisation, as signalised by the formation of the Amalgamated Engineering Union in 1920.

Subsequent history, however, has demonstrated that the Webbs perhaps too easily changed their opinion on future trade-union development, and that they were right in their original emphasis on the strength of craft or occupational sectionalism. This, certainly, has by no means withered away. Despite modern technological changes, blurring or destroying such distinctions, workers do not generally regard themselves as members of a homogeneous proletariat, but still as belonging to a particular craft or industry or occupation, and, as such, they still have strong sectional interests: they are not simply 'workers', comprising the 'masses', but still engineers, printers, cotton-spinners, plumbers, locomotive drivers, dockers, lorry or bus drivers, etc., and they still expect their union, above all, to safeguard their particular interests, often viewed very narrowly. There is a limit, therefore, to the extent to which a 'general' union can spread—apart from the demarcation problem— without losing basic loyalties and cohesion. Moreover, even the more limited 'industrial unionism' has not carried all before it.

There are still distinctive groups within particular industries, with deep-rooted craft, status, and wages differentials. Thus the National Union of Railwaymen, which aimed on its establishment 'to secure the complete organisation of all workers employed on or in connection with any railway in the United Kingdom', has failed to absorb the separate organisations of the engine-drivers and firemen and the salaried staff; indeed there has occasionally been considerable hostility between them, the engine drivers, for example, objecting strongly to narrowing of wage differentials. Another example is the conflict which sometimes occurs between the National Amalgamated Stevedores and Dockers and the Transport and General Workers' Union. Similarly in the printing industry, not only does craft sectionalism still survive—between craft and chaft (as between letterpress and lithographic printers), as well as between craft and non-craft—but geographical sectionalism still existed until very recently between London, the provinces, and Scotland in letterpress printing (before the recent formation of the National Graphical Association). In the shipbuilding industry likewise, demarcation disputes have been rife. Moreover, in the newer 'professional' unions similar differences are institutionalised, as in the separate organisations for teachers in secondary modern, grammar, technical, teacher-training and university institutions, associated with differences in academic qualifications, status, and salaries. In fact it would appear that the spread of trade unionism among 'white collar' workers, in banks, civil service, local government, and teaching, and also among technical and supervisory staff, has strengthened the old sectional characteristics.

Trade unions, for all the talk of 'brotherhood', are still largely dominated by the spirit of selfish sectionalism. Each is mainly concerned with getting as large a slice from the national cake as possible and with maintaining the relative position of its membership in the established industrial or occupational hierarchy as defined by wages or salaries and recognised status. Nor do they shrink from using their economic power not merely against their employers, but in such a way as may injure other groups of workers (by throwing them out of work, for example) and seriously inconvenience the general public by depriving them of essential goods and services; indeed, they often rely mainly on this wider dislocation to force employers or Government to give way.

Sectionalism, therefore, has been a great stumbing-block in the way of trade-union amalgamation. For although amalgamation has undoubtedly made considerable progress during the past sixty years, many unions, especially craft unions, still cling to their autonomy, disliking the loss of individuality and levelling down which amalgamation may bring, while official rivalries and jealousies have also played some part. Where amalgamation has proved impossible, however, unions have been prepared to participate in federal arrangements, now a widespread feature of British trade unionism. The Webbs, as we have mentioned, had already discerned this tendency in the 1890s; it was associated with the development of collective bargaining at national level, for when national negotiations were being conducted simultaneously by several unions in the same industry, there was naturally a tendency for national officers and executives to come together, either to present employers with a united front, or, very often, under pressure from employers themselves, to prevent complicated piecemeal bargaining and 'leapfrogging' by individual unions. It proved comparatively easy to get general collaboration in regard to hours of work, working conditions, holidays, etc., which tended to be standardised, but much more difficulty has been experienced in combined wages negotiations, because of the problems of differentials; even here, however, in several industries, successful efforts have been made to devise a 'wages structure'.

In these ways, without going as far as 'industrial unionism', without losing individual union identity, though inevitably with some sacrifice of autonomy, unions have been able to produce order out of chaos by such industry-wide agreements. In some industries such collaboration has led to the establishment of federations, with their own rules, offices, and staff, as in the case of the Confederation of Shipbuilding and Engineering Unions, the Printing and Kindred Trades Federation, and the National Federation of Building Trades Operatives. In other cases, developments have been less formal: unions have acted together on joint industrial councils and wages councils, or on T.U.C. committees where the interests of several unions have been involved.

In several instances federations have led on to the formation of amalgamated unions. Thus the Transport and General Workers' Union developed from the Transport Workers' Federation; the National Union of Mineworkers succeeded the Mineworkers' Federation; and the Union of Post Office Workers grew out of an amalgamation of the Postmen's Federation and several other post office unions. The two latter, of course, demonstrate the continued tendency towards 'industrial unionism', whilst the T. & G.W.U., despite Ernest Bevin's triumphant achievement of a powerful centralised organisation, is rooted mainly among dockers and road transport workers, and its constitution recognises the strength of these group interests by sectional arrangements.

It has frequently been demonstrated, in fact, that such general unions do not have the centralised strength and cohesion of the older amalgamated craft societies or some more recent occupational ones, such as the Electrical Trades Union. The powers of the T. & G.W.U. executive and general secretary, for example, cannot overrule the interests of the different sections, each of which has its own sectional officials and carries on sectional bargaining. At times severe differences, even conflicts, have arisen between these sections and the union—as well as internal differences within each section—and have simetimes threatened to result in breakaways. The monolithic public appearance of the T. & G.W.U. is very misleading; sheer size of membership is not necessarily to be equated with union strength; and the powers of its general secretary have often been exaggerated, for in a union of this kind, sectional interests prevent any kind of centralised dictatorial control.

General unions are inevitably prone to such problems. But even in the more unitary 'industrial' unions, there are limits to centralisation. One can still see within them, in fact, strong survivals not only of craft or occupational sectionalism, but also of old geographical divisions and loyalties. The miners, for example, throughout the nineteenth and into the twentieth century were organised primarily on the basis of strong district unions, in Durham, South Wales, Lancashire, etc., and only loosely combined in federal organisations, such as the Mineworkers' Federation and previous bodies. Thus, despite the early growth among them of the idea of industrial unionism, it was not until 1945 that the National Union of Miners was finally formed. And even this unitary organisation still retains strong federal features: the various districts still possess considerable strength and still retain their traditionally distinct organisations; the powers of the national executive and officials are still limited and the districts cannot be overruled from the centre; although national agreements are negotiated on wages, etc., these have to be ratified by district delegate conferences.

The National Union of Railwaymen, on the other hand, is subject to sectional pressures of a different sort. Not only has it failed to absorb the separate organisations of the locomotive drivers and salaried staff, but within the union itself there are sectional or grade pressures by signalmen, clerks, maintenance men, and porters. All railwaymen are clearly not equal, or at any rate do not so regard themselves.

Another long-familiar effect of trade-union sectionalism has been the occurrence of disputes about 'demarcation' and 'poaching'. These had long existed between different though related crafts, with overlapping areas of work, and they were increased in the late nineteenth century by the development of general unions, sprawling across traditional industrial boundaries. The problems were made more acute by the progress of mechanisation, leading to semi-skilled 'labourers' or 'machine-minders' doing work traditionally performed by skilled craftsmen; such workers, excluded from the old craft societies, came eventually to form unions of their own, or were absorbed into general unions, causing inevitable inter-union conflict. Demarcation disputes, however, have become much fewer and less serious as a result of several factors. Some unions, as we have seen, like the Amalgamated Engineering Union, have extended their membership to include non-craft workers, members being enrolled into separate sections. Amalgamation and federation and the reduction in the number of unions have also greatly reduced the problem of overlapping. At the same time, unions have negotiated agreements in regard to these boundary disputes, allocating types of work and agreeing on which union should organise particular groups of workers. A general agreement on these problems was reached at the Trades Union Congress at Bridlington in 1939, when the principles of 'good trade union practice' were agreed and a policy on enrolment and spheres of influence was established. This has by no means ended demarcation disputes, but the importance of those which do occasionally occur has been greatly exaggerated in the press.

Sectionalism, then, though still a powerful force—resisting the development of industrial unionism and of amalgamation, and at the same time creating stresses within as well as between unions, especially in general unions—has not prevented the gradual concentration of trade-union membership into an ever smaller number of increasingly big unions.[4] The growth in the size of unions has resulted partly from the spread of trade unions among previously unorganised workers, especially among 'white collar' or professional groups: the percentage of the total working population organised in trade unions has steadily increased, though still by no means a majority.[5] The process of amalgamation has also, of course, greatly contributed to the growth of large unions. Trade unionists have become increasingly aware of the advantages to be achieved by large-scale organisation, not only in confronting employers—themselves becoming steadily more organised and powerful—but also in administrative efficiency, with the growth in number and expertise of full-time professional secretaries, organisers, and office staff. As a result of increased financial strength, bargaining power and negotiating skills, national agreements have been secured providing industry-wide agreements and achieving substantial improvements in wages, hours, and working conditions. At the same time, large modern unions have been able to provide legal, research, and educational facilities beyond the resources of small unions (just as the national amalgamated unions of the nineteenth century were able to finance a wider range of friendly benefits); they have also been enabled to finance trade-union M.P.s and to take more effective political action.

Large-scale organisation, however, has also given rise to serious problems. The most fundamental is that of combining efficient centralised administration with the maintenance of democratic interest and control. In the early days of trade unionism, as we have seen, the members were able to play an active part and have a direct interest in the affairs of their local societies. But with the growth of large national unions and the development of centralised bargaining, the individual member feels remote from union affairs, branches having been reduced to petty routine matters. The national executive and officials seem to run the show. It is true that branches do discuss wages and working conditions, but for the most part these matters are determined by national negotiations, wages councils, and arbitration tribunals. Machinery of democratic government has, of course, been created: in addition to branch meetings, there are district and national delegate meetings and voting papers to give the membership opportunities of expressing their views and controlling union government, while the national executive and officials are elected by and responsible to the membership, and there is no doubt that they are sensitive to the demands of their members and that pressures from below do make themselves felt. But there is inevitably some loss of direct contact with the rank and file, while union machinery is apt to be bureaucratic and slow-moving, open to manipulation by executive and officials, who, in practice, have permanent tenure of power.

The union branch has suffered a serious decline. Meetings are usually held monthly, but are mostly dull and formal, with little active participation except by two or three officers; attendance averages no more than 5 to 10 per cent of branch membership. On the other hand, the workshop machinery and the power of the shop steward have developed considerably, especially in the large works of the engineering and motor industry, where control is largely in the hands of shop stewards' committees and works conveners. Whereas branch meetings are thinly attended, members display much more interest in workshop affairs, since these are of direct and immediate concern and there is a corporate sense among the workers. Shop stewards are in constant touch with the members, they are able to intervene immediately in any works disputes, or to deal with any grievances; they also often negotiate workshop agreements giving improvements over and above nationally negotiated agreements.

It may therefore be misleading to conclude that concentration of power in the hands of central executives and officials has resulted in apathy among the great majority of union members.[6] This is certainly suggested by attendance figures at branch meetings and voting figures in national ballots, but against this must be set the widespread evidence of membership participation at the workplace, leading often to 'unofficial' action and sometimes to the formation of 'splinter' groups. These developments show that apathy is by no means general, that interest can be and often is aroused among the rank-and-file, that members can and often do take matters into their own hands if the national machinery is too slow-moving or unresponsive. On the other hand, the increasing power of shop stewards is an indication that national executives and officials are in danger of losing control of their membership, who have comparatively little interest in general union affairs.

Such apathy, displayed in meagre attendances at branch meetings and in the small numbers who vote in election of officers or on policy issues, has its dangers. It gives opportunity to zealous minorities to seize control and exploit the unions for their own ends, e.g. Communists exert an influence within the trade-union movement out of all proportion to their members. In some unions, indeed, they have been able to seize national power, as general secretaries and presidents and executive numbers.[7] In other unions where they have failed to secure central power, they can cause continual disruptions locally, by seizure of control over branches and workshops. On the other hand, Communist influence is often exaggerated, or is made an excuse for official union shortcomings— 'unofficial' disputes usually have a basis of genuine grievance, and men do not usually come out on strike for nothing.

Nevertheless, strikes, both official and unofficial, are a cause of serious concern. It is sometimes said that the growth of the Welfare State—greatly improving social conditions for the mass of people— has, paradoxically, made trade unions more prone to use their strength in strikes, or in threatening strikes. In the nineteenth century trade unions were also friendly societies and much the greater part of their funds was devoted to relief of their members in unemployment, sickness, and old age; they were therefore loath to pour away their resources in strike payments, if strikes could possibily be avoided. Moreover, when strikes did occur, the burden of supporting strikers' wives and children fell mainly on the union, or on the savings of their members. For these reasons, unions sought not only to avoid strikes, but also to limit the area of strikes if they occurred, so that strikers could be supported by those still in work, upon whom levies were often imposed. Nowadays, however, not only have unions been relieved by the Welfare State of having to provide friendly benefits for their members, and have thus been able to amass larger strike funds, but they have also been relieved, very largely, of the burden of supporting strikers' dependents. Thus the financial restrictions on strike action have been greatly reduced. At the present day, therefore, despite the enormous improvement in living standards compared with the nineteenth century, and even in a semi-socialist society, there are threats, and occasional occurrences, of strikes on a much greater scale than in the earlier period.

These arguments, however, are open to some strong objections. Firstly, there has always been a great deal of exaggeration of the 'irresponsible power' and strike-proneness of trade unions; comments of this kind could be culled just as abundantly from nineteenth-century newspapers as from those of today. Secondly, although nineteenth-century trade unions certainly did try to avoid strikes if possible, nevertheless strikes constantly occurred and were often very prolonged, sometimes with widespread violence, destruction of property, and occasionally loss of life; financial restraints, before the establishment of the Welfare State, certainly did not prevent strikes being endemic. Nor is there any evidence that since the Welfare State has been established strikes have become more numerous; in fact the evidence goes the other way. It should also be pointed out that Britain until recent years has had a pretty good record in regard to the number of 'days lost' through strikes, by comparison with most other industrial countries. State benefits for strikers' dependants, together with the greater financial resources of the unions, certainly do prevent the severe distress that accompanied nineteenth-century strikes, but there seems to be little evidence that they have made unions more strike-prone.

Strikes, however, when they do occur today, especially those by powerful national unions controlling vital areas of the national economy, can have disastrous effects and are cause for serious concern. Nationalisation was for long regarded by trade unions as a panacea for all industrial ills, but we have seen this notion exploded: disputes have certainly not disappeared from mines, railways and post office. In nationalised and private industries alike, organised workers now as in the past are determined to maintain their own sectional interests, if need be against the public interest. The policies of the Labour Governments in 1945–51[8] placed the unions in a dilemma, but most unions would not or could not exercise restraint for long and insisted on trade-union freedom in collective bargaining. They dislike authoritarian Government control and fear loss of trade-union liberties so hard-won over so many years; this might happen if Government were to fix incomes and prices and control trade-union activities by leglislation. On the other hand, however, there is a growing body of public opinion which considers that the traditional role of trade unions must alter with the changing structure of society, and that the weapons forged in the days of unrestrained capitalist exploitation, individualism and 'self-help' are no longer appropriate in an age of social democracy, and many people would like to see legislative controls imposed and union participation in shaping a national incomes policy.

It is doubtful, however, whether such controls could be enforced, at any rate in a free society.[9] Trade unions, with their long memories of past history and their deep-rooted sectionalism, might well defy laws and Government. The best hope of further improvement in industrial relations would seem to lie, as the T.U.C. has maintained, in the continuance of earlier trends, in the gradual reshaping of organisation and policies, within a changing social framework— in a process, that is, of evolutionary, voluntary change without legislative compulsion.

This conclusion appears to have been justified by recent experience of the present Conservative Government's Industrial Relations Act.[10] Perhaps A. P. Wadsworth is smiling posthumously at the eager and over-optimistic efforts of Mr. Heath 'to change the atmosphere of industry overnight'.[11] But this legislation, supported by a considerable weight of public opinion, may at least convince trade unions that they must move more quickly towards co-operation with Government and employers in working out a national incomes policy, instead of a nineteenth-century free-for-all.

NOTES

1. *Manchester Guardian*, 25 June 1954, reviewing Musson, *op. cit.*
2. *Royal Commission on Trade Unions and Employers' Associations, Selected Written Evidence* (1968), T.U.C. Evidence, pp. 130, 148, 210.
3. This has been fully confirmed by the recent experiences of both Labour and Conservative Governments.
4. This trend has continued since this paper was originally written. Thus in 1967 the total number of unions had fallen to 555, with total membership of about 10 millions (cf. above, p. 69). There are still a considerable number of small unions—294 at that date, each with less than a thousand members—but these tiny unions, though comprising 42 per cent of the total number of unions, account for less than one per cent of total membership, whereas the nine biggest each with over a quarter of a million members and a combined figure of 5.4 millions, comprise just over 54 per cent of total membership.

5. About a half of all manual workers are unionised, but only about a third of 'white collar' workers and about a quarter of all women workers. In some particular industries, such as printing, on the other hand, there is nearly 100 per cent union membership.

6. It is interesting to note that similar complaints of apathy were made even in early nineteenth-century local societies: see below, p. 85.

7. Since this paper was originally written, the most notorious example has been the scandalous vote-rigging, etc. in the Electrical Trades Union.

8. And again in the 1960s.

9. This penultimate paragraph was added in 1968, after the Donovan Report, when the paper was read at the University of Bradford. This was the Royal Commission's view.

10. This last paragraph, of course, was only recently added, in September 1972.

11. See above, p. 65.

Chapter 5

EARLY TRADE UNIONISM IN THE PRINTING INDUSTRY*

The Webbs defined trade unions as 'continuous associations of wage-earners', but continuous trade-union records have rarely survived from the years before the mid-nineteenth century. Minutebooks, reports and accounts, even if kept, have mostly disappeared, so that trade union histories have had to be constructed from scrappy information in newspapers and periodicals, parliamentary reports, Home Office papers, the Place MSS., and other sources. The trade societies in the printing industry form the most notable exception: in London, Manchester and elsewhere substantial records have survived of early local societies and also of the first district and national unions when these emerged. Mr. Ellic Howe was therefore able to produce, in the late 1940s, well-documented accounts of trade unionism in the metropolitan printing trade, and the present writer was subsequently encouraged to make a similar investigation in the provinces. The available material made it possible to construct an account of early craft unionism in the printing industry more detailed than in any other trade. For this reason, the early part of the history originally published in 1954 is reprinted here, to complement the previous surveys of general trade-union development. This is particularly necessary because in the nineteenth century trade unionism was predominantly a matter of local, district and national societies in particular trades or industries. The better-known episodes in general trade-union history, such as Owen's 'Grand National', were comparatively brief and ephemeral, and even the Trades Union Congress in the second half of the century was of practically no importance in trade affairs, as distinct from political. To understand the fundamental concerns and methods of trade unionism, it is necessary to examine the organisation and activities of local trade clubs and unions in particular industries. The printing trade provides an excellent opportunity of doing so.

* This chapter is constructed from Part I of A. E. Musson, *The Typographical Association: Origins and History up to 1949* (Oxford University Press, 1954).

I THE DEVELOPMENT OF TRADE UNIONISM IN THE PROVINCIAL PRINTING INDUSTRY UP TO 1830

T H E expansion of the printing industry in the second half of the eighteenth century and the breakdown of State and gild regulations brought a threat to the journeymen's customary standard of life. Hitherto, wage rates and apprenticeship regulations had been enforced by Statute or by the Stationers' Company; there was even an authoritarian control over details of manufacture and working conditions. Now the journeymen were left unprotected, at a critical period in the industry. It is true that there had been a body of permanent journeymen, excluded by the gild oligarchy from participation in the government of the Company; that there had been complaints against this exclusiveness, against 'small wages' and the increase of apprentices as early as the sixteenth century, complaints which had been echoed right down to the present period; and that there had long been a tendency towards separate organisation by the journeymen. But it was not, apparently, until the Industrial Revolution, with the accompanying expansion of the printing industry, growth of competition, and rapid influx of apprentices, that the journeymen began to form their own organisations. Another factor which figures prominently in the trade documents of the period, was the sharp rise in the cost of living during the Revolutionary and Napoleonic Wars.

The earliest information we possess of trade unionism among journeymen printers comes from London. It appears that 'there is no evidence pointing to the existence of a London compositors' trade union until the end of the eighteenth century'.[1] But from 1785, if not earlier, the journeymen formed an organisation, though probably not continuous, to secure wage advances, regulate working hours, and enforce the customary apprenticeship regulations. Agitation on these questions went on throughout the war years, 1793–1815, and has left a considerable amount of documentary evidence.

There is no such detailed information with regard to early unionism among provincial printers, but it is clear that during the war years journeymen in the larger provincial towns were imitating their metropolitan brethren in establishing trade societies for mutual protection and to secure increased wages. The rise in the cost of living and the other factors which led to the establishment of the London Society had similar effects in the provinces, where, moreover, the journeymen frequently justified their demands by reference to the London advances. When, for example, the Edinburgh compositors memorialised their employers for an advance in 1803, they pointed out that wage increases had already been granted to the London men 'in consequence of the continual variations in the price of provisions and the rate of living'.[2] Similarly, when the journeymen printers of Manchester memorialised their employers for increased wages in 1810, they pointed out 'that a material advance has taken place, for some time, in London, Dublin, Liverpool, Bristol, and other leading towns throughout the United Kingdom'.[3] They requested an increase which would give 'stab hands 35s. per week, with overtime payment of 7d. per hour; compositors on piece-work, 6d. per 1,000 ens; and pressmen, 6½d. per hour. These demands, however, must have been either refused or modified, or there were post-war reductions, for in 1825 the Manchester Society had not yet established a regular piece-scale, while the 'stab wages of the town were only 30s. per week. This was not, apparently, the first time the Manchester men had taken such action, for they pointed out 'that there is no instance on record of the Master Printers giving to the Journeymen a rise unsolicited', having, it would seem, had to ask for advances in the past.

There was, quite definitely, a printers' trade society in Manchester at this time. The earliest rule book extant in 1897, dated 1825, bore on its title page the words 'Instituted November, 1797',[4] and in the *Compositors' Chronicle* for March 1843 there is a letter from R. Roberts, one of the actual founders of the Manchester Society and for many years its secretary, stating that it 'was established in the year 1797, for the protection of journeymen's rights'. The Manchester Society was one of the earliest, if not the earliest, of provincial typographical societies. It was 'the oldest society in the Northern Union' (established 1830), older, that is, than those in Liverpool, Leeds, Sheffield, and the other forty-odd branches.[5]

The minutes and half-yearly reports of the Manchester Society are almost the sole source of information for the early development of trade unionism in the provincial printing industry; but, unfortunately, there are none of these in existence prior to 1825. Two resolutions, passed in 1826 and 1827 respectively, provide evidence as to the number of societies then in existence. The first was, 'that . . . the allowance to Tramps with tickets from old established societies, be four, instead of five shillings; and those from minor Societies, such as Preston, Wigan, Warrington, Bolton, Rochdale, Blackburn, Macclesfield, and Hanley, to receive 2/6'. The second laid down 'that hereafter, the Allowances to Tramps with Tickets from the undermentioned places shall be as follows: Those from Dublin, Glasgow, Liverpool, Leeds, Sheffield and Bristol [doubtless the "old established societies" of the first resolution] to receive 4s. Those with tickets from every other part of the United Kingdom, 2/6.'

It is clear that by 1826 'old established' typographical societies existed in nearly all the chief cities of the United Kingdom and that even in the smaller towns, particularly in Lancashire, journeymen printers were organised. These societies, moreover, were linked together by a tramp-relief system. 'Tickets' or 'tramp cards' were given to unemployed or strike members who desired to leave town in search of employment. It was also customary to give such members 'travelling money' or 'relief allowed upon leaving town', which they had to refund in the event of their returning within a certain specified period. In Manchester, this travelling allowance varied in the early years, but was fixed in 1839 at 10s. for a single and 15s. for a married man. No relief, other than purely voluntary assistance, was given to a member's wife and family while he was 'on the road'.

On arrival in another society town, travellers presented their cards to the local secretary, who would give them 'tramp allowance'—enough for bed and breakfast in the 'society house'. Assistance to secure employment was also given, while tramps were warned against entry into any 'unfair' offices. If the tramp found work he had to return the allowance given him, but if no employment was to be had he moved on to the next town, since he could secure relief only once in each town within twelve months, all payments being entered on his card. After this period had elapsed his card had to be renewed, often at a lower rate of relief. Tramp relief was confined to 'fair' trade society members. Discrimination in Manchester between the amount paid to tramps from large cities and those from 'minor societies' was due to the fact that the latter could afford to give only a very small allowance and their tramps, consequently, were not paid the full rate of relief in Manchester. In some places tramps received as little as 9d. or 1s.

This tramp-relief system obviously forged links between the various societies. Many journeymen printers, at some time in their life, took to the road—sometimes of necessity, sometimes to widen their experience—and thus became familiar with men and customs in other towns. The system also gave rise to correspondence with regard to cards and admission of members. The former were apt to be forged, to have dates and names altered, or payments erased, and it was often necessary to write to other towns to check their authenticity, Moreover, tramps often went into 'unfair' houses or were otherwise suspect, and it was necessary to warn other societies and to check up on tramps before their admission. Warnings of strikes were also sent to other towns in order to secure the co-operation of their members and mutual assistance was often given in periods of trade depression. This co-operation between individual societies was to lead to the formation of the Northern Union (1830) and the National Typographical Association (1844).[6]

The Manchester minutes provide a clear picture of the principles and functioning of an individual typographical society in this period. It may be more than a coincidence that the earliest minutes extant date from July 1825, just after the repeal of the Combination Laws: the Society may possibly have kept no minutes prior to that date and conducted its affairs on somewhat underground lines. In that year, however, it springs full-grown into view, with its Committee of Management, its monthly, quarterly, and special General Meetings, its President, Secretary, and Treasurer, as well as minor officers, such as Beer Stewards and Door-keepers. These officials, together with the Committee, were elected every quarter. There was, however, no great scrambling for office, which involved arduous and poorly paid duties.[7] Members often refused, in fact, to accept office and were fined in consequence. It proved so difficult to get volunteers for election to the Committee that a resolution had to be passed in 1826 that all members should 'serve on the Committee, in rotation', on pain of being fined sixpence. This system proved so distasteful, however, that the Society eventually reverted to the elective system.

Obviously, there must have been a great deal of apathy among members of the Society, or at least an unwillingness to participate actively in trade affairs. Voting figures show that rarely more than one-fifth, and often as few as one-tenth, of the members attended monthly meetings. The constant arrears of subscriptions tell a similar story of indifference. We find certain men, of undoubted zeal and ability, continually elected to office and becoming almost permanent officials. Robert Roberts, for example was secretary of the Manchester Society from 1825 at least, perhaps from the establishment of the Society in 1797, until 1834.

These men performed their amateur, part-time duties in the evenings, in a public-house. The landlord would provide a room for Society meetings and reaped his profit from the beer consumed, if he was not paid a rent. The 'society house' was often changed, usually on account of 'the badness of the ale', a frequent source of complaint. Members were permitted a regular allowance of ale on monthly nights, which gave rise to one of the largest items in the Society's expenditure. There must have been a few hectic interludes at these meetings, for, in spite of rules against threatening and abusive language, fighting, and drunkenness, brawls often occurred and offending members had to be thrown out. The minutes reflect, as a rule, considerable dignity and decorum, but it must have been difficult at times to transact Society business.

The main trade principles of the Manchester Society were enforcement of the seven years' servitude, exclusion of 'foreigners', apprentice restriction, regulation of wages and hours, and punishment of 'rats' or 'unfair' hands. The Committee adopted a very autocratic tone towards erring members, who were summoned before the Committee and ordered to correct their behaviour, or were heavily fined, or even expelled from the Society.

A rigorous control was exercised over admission to the Society. Those who had not served a full seven years' apprenticeship to letterpress printing were automatically excluded, and there are numerous instances of members being ordered to give notice unless certain 'foreigners' were dismissed, or being fined for working with men who had 'no recognised right to the trade'. All legitimate printers, however, were expected to join the Society soon after arrival in town or on completion of their apprenticeship, and those who 'held aloof' longer than three months were fined. Members were not, apparently, allowed to work with non-members, though this rule was frequently infringed.

The Society also tried to restrict the number of apprentices. In 1828, for example, numerous committee meetings were held to consider what action should be taken against employers who were taking 'an unlimited number of Apprentices' and often employing no journeymen. Several restrictive regulations were suggested, but the time was considered unpropitious for their enforcement and no fixed rule was established until after the foundation of the Northern Union. Instead, chapels were urged to protest, 'in a respectful and suitable manner', against the introduction of extra apprentices and to point out the injurious consequences of boy labour to both employer and employed. Many masters, apparently, agreed with the journeymen, but the evil persisted, especially in the smaller offices. In 1829, therefore, it was decided that members should refuse to take employment 'in any office where no men are regularly employed, and the number of Apprentices is more than two'. During the early thirties the Society began to award monetary compensation to members refusing work in such houses, while those who went in were expelled as 'rats'.

The Society also attempted, as we have seen, to regulate wage rates.[8] Most Manchester offices were on 'stab and 'the establishment of the town' in 1825 was 30s. per week. The *Manchester Gazette,* however, was on piece work, which was strongly condemned by the Society 'as eminently calculated to engender rancour and bad feeling amongst the workmen; to reduce the number of hands that should be employed . . . and in every sense detrimental to the interests of the profession'. The Society decided, therefore, to procure its abolition, or at least to resist its introduction into other news offices. The men on the *Gazette* refused to obey the Society and were consequently expelled, but in spite of the Society's opposition piece-work was introduced on several papers. The Society therefore attempted to regulate piece rates, deciding that 6*d*. per 1,000 ens should be the price for minion and 7*d*. for non-pareil, though it is not clear whether these rates were successfully enforced.

Steady opposition to the piece system was manifested by the Manchester Society throughout the nineteenth century, Manchester being notorious as a staunch 'stab town. A number of other towns, however, preferred piece-work to 'stab and there was a continual conflict of opinion in regard to the respective merits and demerits of the two systems.

No journeyman was admitted into the Manchester Society unless he was receiving the established wages of the town. The Society also kept a constant check on wages paid in the various offices. Those paying less than the recognised rate were condemned as 'unfair' and the men in them as 'rats'.

Hours were also subject to Society regulation. It is not clear what the working hours were in Manchester at this time, but in Leeds, according to the local scale of 1826, the 'stab hours were 'twelve hours a day, including meal hours (that is, half an hour for breakfast, one hour dinner, and half an hour for tea). . . . All overhours to be paid sixpence per hour.' At York, in 1836, the 'stab hours were 'from 7 to 7 o'clock, with 6*d*. per hour overhours'.[9] A 12-hour working day, with 2 hours for meals, or 59 working hours per week, seems to have been the custom in most towns. Some of the larger societies were also attempting to secure a 'fixed and defined' working day, with extra payment for all overtime.

Typographical societies almost invariably adopted a moderate and conciliatory attitude towards employers in disputes and relations between masters and men were, on the whole, fairly good. In 1841, for example, the Manchester secretary spoke of 'the feeling of respect and good-will shown towards us by our employers', due to the fact that 'in every dispute we have had with them, it has ever been our study to adopt a course of quiet, respectful, but determined conduct. Reason and justice have prevailed, where threatening and intimidation would have failed.'[10] In the event of failure to settle a dispute by deputation and argument, the men were merely withdrawn after a fortnight's notice. The house was then 'closed' and no Society man was to accept work in such an 'unfair' office, on pain of being heavily fined or even expelled.

These strikes were petty affairs, rarely involving more than one office. Employers very seldom combined against the men, owing to the barriers of competition, and the only large-scale 'turn-out' during the whole of this period was that in Edinburgh in 1847, when thirty-eight employers combined to 'lock-out' 200 men.[11] Nevertheless, these petty strikes caused considerable hardship to the few men involved and it was only fair to see that members did not suffer unduly for having made 'a sacrifice in the interests of the profession'. We therefore find in the minutes of the Manchester Society early references to strike payments. At first these were not systematic, but it eventually became the rule to pay 30s. per week, full 'stab wages, to strike hands.

Other large societies also adopted the system of weekly strike payments, but the more usual course was to 'back' the tramp-cards of strike hands, that is, to write the circumstances of their sacrifice on the back, so that other societies would give them additional, usually double, relief in the event of their having to leave town in search of employment.

Efforts were also made by the Manchester Society to relieve its out-of-work members. Tramp relief was the normal method, but in periods of widespread unemployment it broke down and additional assistance became necessary. At first emergency funds were raised, but in 1844 a permanent relief or out-of-work fund was established, with a subscription of 3d. per week from fully employed members, to provide the out-of-work with 7s. per week.

Relief, however, was a mere palliative. What the unemployed wanted was more work. The restriction of apprentices and exclusion of 'foreigners' were mainly intended to secure work for qualified journeymen. The Society also tried to prevent 'strangers' working in the town when any members were out of employment. 'Smooting' was also forbidden and the Society attempted to reduce 'systematic' overtime in order to secure work for more hands.

The Manchester Society was 'not a trade society alone, but a benefit society as well.'[12] In addition to unemployment relief, it had established sick and burial funds, the former providing weekly payments to members off work through illness, together with 'the medicine and professional attendance of a respectable surgeon', the latter, lump sums on the death of members or their wives.

These various benefits were common to most large societies.[13] In Dublin, for example, in the 1830s, strike, unemployed, tramp and funeral allowances were being paid.[14] In addition, the Dublin

Society had an emigration fund, the earliest of which the present writer has found trace, providing allowances of £4 for emigrants to England and £8 to America. Emigration was frequently advocated in the trade periodicals of the 1840s as a means of equating the supply of labour to the demand, but few other typographical societies seem to have actually established a fund for the purpose until the 'fifties.

London provided additional benefits. In 1827, for example, there was established in the metropolis a 'Printers' Pension Society' for superannuated members, while in the forties a 'Printers' Asylum, or 'Almshouse' was founded for the aged poor. Liverpool appears to have been the only other city with a printers' pension society.[15]

Typographical societies do not appear to have suffered much from the prevailing system of repressive legislation against trade unions. George White, clerk to Hume's Committee on the Combination Laws in 1824, asserted that the Act of 1800 had 'been in general a dead letter upon those artisans upon whom it was intended to have an effect—namely, the shoemakers, printers, papermakers, shipbuilders, tailors, etc., who have had their regular societies and houses of call, as though no such Act was in existence'.[16] Our examination into the activities of printers' societies in the first quarter of the nineteenth century amply confirms his opinion as regards this particular trade. Journeymen printers in this period formed societies in practically all the large cities and in many of the lesser towns, and seem to have negotiated quite openly with their employers on matters of wages, hours, and apprentices. This was due partly, no doubt, to the tradition of such corporate action which existed among skilled handicraftsmen, and to the fact that there was, in the majority of instances, little difference of social status between masters and men, the former usually having served their apprenticeship among the journeymen and most offices being small. It was also due to the fact that 'in the skilled handicrafts . . . we find even under repressive laws, no unlawful oaths, seditious emblems, or other common paraphernalia, of secret societies'.[17] Journeymen printers usually adopted a 'correct' attitude of respect and moderation towards their employers. They also restricted themselves exclusively to trade matters and had no air of political or social conspiracy about them.

Nevertheless, there were a few instances of prosecution against printers' trade societies in this period, like that of the London pressmen in 1798[18] and of *The Times* compositors in 1810,[19] in each case for 'conspiracy', the accused men being found guilty and imprisoned. These were the martyrs of trade unionism in the printing industry. There may possibly have been other prosecutions, which might account for the paucity of information prior to 1825, societies being driven underground until after the repeal of the Combination Laws. But when the great increase in the number of societies and the known instances of wages negotiations are taken into consideration, it seems that, on the whole, typographical societies suffered little from the law.

II. The Northern Typographical Union, 1830–44

We have seen in the previous section how, early in the nineteenth century, typographical societies in the various towns all over the country were linked together by the tramp-relief system, how they were all actuated by certain common principles, and how they assisted each other in the event of serious dispute or distress. These connexions, this association in the pursuit of common objects, led naturally to the establishment of the Northern Typographical Union in 1830, a Union which eventually came to comprise over forty towns, mainly in the north of England, particularly in Lancashire and Yorkshire, but also extending as far south as Gloucester and Monmouth.

The movement towards 'greater unionism'—towards national unions of workers in particular trades—was general in the late 'twenties and early 'thirties in the nineteenth century, particularly among the Lancashire and Yorkshire textile and building operatives. In 1829, for example, the National Union of Cotton Spinners was established, in 1830 the Potters' Union, and in 1832 the Builders' Union. Journeymen printers shared in this movement, which, so far as their particular trade is concerned, began in the early months of 1830 and centred in Lancashire.[20] It 'arose from the inadequacy of the isolated efforts of single societies . . . to stem the continued encroachments of employers and to prevent the reduction of wages'. There was at that time 'no limitation to the number of apprentices and men were working for whatever remuneration they could obtain'. Robert Roberts, therefore, and other leading members of the Manchester Society, 'seeing the necessity of union', decided to communicate with other societies 'in Lancashire and its neighbourhood' with regard to a meeting. Favourable replies were received from Liverpool, Preston, Sheffield, and one or two other towns and a meeting was therefore held in Manchester on 13 September 1830, attended by seven representatives, who drew up rules for the establishment of a Northern Typographical Union.

The Northern Union, then, started in a small way, with a mere handful of societies. Little more than an agreement on general principles would seem to have been reached in 1830, for it was not until late in the next year, at a second Delegate Meeting in Manchester, that the Union received a financial basis. It was then decided that each member should contribute sixpence 'towards defraying the expenses incurred during the past year by the Northern Typographical Union' and that, in future, a regular sub-scription of twopence per member per month should be paid into the central fund of the Union.[21] It seems to have taken two or three years to get the Union firmly on its feet, years in which the Manchester Society and its veteran Secretary, Robert Roberts, played a leading part. The Union's headquarters, however, were in Liverpool, where the Committee of Management and the General Secretary, John Backhouse, remained until late in 1844, when the Northern Union was merged into the National Typographical Association.

The union survived the first few critical years and, as trade and trade unionism boomed in the years 1832–6, its membership grew. By 1834 it had thirty-six branches and 628 members, by 1837 forty-three branches and 783 members.[22] During the next seven years, however, years of trade depression, when unemployment figures rose and many national unions collapsed, provincial printers had a hard struggle to maintain their organisation. The cost of tramp relief rose rapidly, strikes became more frequent, and expenditure began to exceed income. Subscriptions had to be increased and levies imposed, yet deficits continued. Many members deserted the Union or refused to pay their subscriptions, while others 'ratted' and a number of the smaller societies collapsed. Nevertheless, the Union kept its head above water and even increased its membership slightly. The following figures illustrate its progress up to 1840:

Date	Branches	Members	Income			Expenditure			Strike allowance		
			£	s.	d.	£	s.	d.	£	s.	d.
1834	36	628	64	7	2	42	3	2	22	10	0
1837	43	783	104	15	6	62	10	8	13	3	0
1838	40	893	144	6	2½	82	15	2	42	7	6
1839	42	942	131	10	6	225	10	2	120	19	6
1840	44	984	200	14	6	209	19	3	110	1	3

It is difficult to estimate accurately what proportion of provincial journeymen printers joined the Northern Union. Its operations were restricted to the English provinces, particularly the north. Scotland and Ireland established their own unions in 1836—the Scottish Typographical Association and the Irish Typographical Union—on principles very similar to those of the Northern Union. London also remained independent. The Union did not, moreover, include all English provincial societies. The *Printer* estimated in June 1844 that, apart from the four big typographical unions (the Northern Union, London Union of Compositors, Scottish Association, and Irish Union), there were about twenty 'recognised societies', while the London 'Report on the National Typographical Association' of September 1844 stated that these 'independent or unconnected societies' numbered twenty-six.

According to statistics laid before the Northern Union Delegate Meeting of 1842, there were at that time 978 members and 248 'non-society men' in towns connected with the Union.[23] Thus it is clear that at least one-quarter to one-third of journeymen printers in Northern Union branches were non-members. There were, in fact, scores of 'unfair' houses in these towns: it was stated in 1844 that 'in only fourteen towns in the Northern Union, there are no less than fifty-three prohibited or unfair houses'.[24] Even in 'fair' houses, moreover, non-unionists were frequently employed. Furthermore, in a great many English provincial towns the Northern Union had no branches. It is doubtful, therefore, whether the Union included a half of provincial compositors.

We will now examine the Northern Union's structure, policy, and achievements under the following heads: (1) Government. (2) Regulation of hours and wages. (3) Apprentice restriction. (4) Attitude towards machinery. (5) Strikes. (6) Tramp relief.

(1) *Government of the Northern Union*

The Northern Union was presented with the problem of combining central control with local autonomy. Although local societies were prepared to surrender a certain amount of sovereignty, in order to secure general co-operation in apprentice restriction and maintenance of wage rates, with the backing of a central fund, they still preserved a strong spirit of independence in local affairs. It was a continual difficulty, therefore, to decide what were local matters and what the concern of the central executive.

Typographical societies had always recognised the democratic principle that all members had equal rights, that all should have an equal voice in society affairs, that 'what concerned all should be decided by all'. This principle found practical expression in rule by general meeting. But it was obviously impossible to frame laws for the scattered branches of a federal union by general meeting of the trade. Resort was therefore had to Delegate Meetings. Initiative, however, still remained with the individual members and branches : any member could put forward proposals, which were discussed at special branch meetings and, if adopted, placed on the Delegate Meeting agenda. Delegates were also instructed how to vote : branch members merely delegated their collective voice to an elected representative.

The Northern Union had been established by a Delegate Meeting in 1830. Another was held in 1831, but the next was not until 1836. A gap of four years also followed before the next in 1840, but it was then decided 'that a meeting of delegates take place not later than once in two years'. In accordance with this rule, Delegate Meetings were held in 1842 and 1844. Such an assembly held supreme legislative power.

It was necessary, however, to have some central body to administer the rules established by Delegate Meeting, to receive Union subscriptions and dispense the funds, to investigate disputes and award strike pay, to report 'closed' houses and 'rats', and exercise a general supervision over tramp relief. This executive power was placed in the hands of a 'governing branch', chosen by Delegate Meeting. The Union could not support the expense of a representative central committee, which would, moreover, at a time when the first railways were only just being built, have been very difficult to convene and slow to act. Liverpool was the governing branch of the Northern Union throughout the period 1830–44. The central executive consisted of a General Secretary, Treasurer, and Committee of Management, composed of nine members. The Secretary was chosen by Delegate Meeting, the Treasurer and Committee elected annually 'by the society where the Secretary resides'. The Union, like the local societies, did not possess a staff of professional officials. Even the General Secretary was an amateur, a working journeyman and part-time official, who received only £26 per annum in 1840 and probably a good deal less in earlier years. He was distinct, however, from the local secretary, though it is probable that the local treasurer and committee were also Treasurer and Committee of the Union. The Union officials, like those in the branches, were more or less permanent, or at least continuously elected to office : John Backhouse was Secretary for the whole fourteen years of the Union's existence. The same names also recur on the Committee.

The Union subscription was, as we have seen, 2d. per member per month in the early years, but was later increased to 3d. and finally, in 1840, to 4d. per month.[25] The Executive were also empowered in 1842 to impose levies in case of emergency.

In spite of Delegate Meetings, Committee of Management, Union rules and subscriptions, local societies still to a great extent managed their own affairs. They made their own local rules, had their own officials, committee, and general meetings, decided their own rates of subscription and tramp relief, and administered their own unemployment, sick, and burial funds.[26] Railways and the penny post undoubtedly aided centralised organisation, but in a Union composed of scattered towns and myriads of small offices a considerable degree of local autonomy was inevitable. Moreover, as we have seen, there was not as yet the financial basis or experience for a professional central administration.

Local independence, however, made it difficult to secure united action and obedience to the decisions of the Union Committee and Delegate Meetings. The larger branches, particularly Manchester, strongly objected to any interference in what they considered to be local affairs. The Union possessed certain general regulations regarding wages, hours, and apprentices and had also a central fund for strike payments, but the powers of the Executive Committee were very limited, amounting to little more than general supervision over trade affairs. The Union was, in many ways, little more than a tramping society. It was stated, in fact, in 1844, that the Northern Union was such 'only in name', comprising 'some thirty or forty societies united together without any general principles or laws for their government, but each society acting as it thinks best. Even on those points on which they profess to be guided by the committee of management, some of the larger societies claim to act independently of such authority.'[27]

The 'chapel', of course, with its 'father' and 'clerk' and its workshop rules, still remained the basic cell of typographical trade unionism.

(2) *Regulation of Hours and Wages*

We have already seen individual societies trying to regulate the hours of labour. These isolated attempts do not appear to have been very successful, 'many employers requiring their men to work an indefinite number of hours without any remuneration whatever beyond their regular wages'.[28] The Northern Union Delegate Meeting of 1836 therefore decided to establish a general rule 'that fifty-nine hours' labour per week be the standard for the members of the Union; and if employed on the Sunday, the mode of charge to be the same as the London scale; and if required to work after ten o'clock in the evening, or before five in the morning, one shilling extra to be charged; and if required to labour a greater number of hours than fifty-nine, sixpence per hour for such overtime shall be charged'. Thus the Union attempted to establish a standard working *week*, with overtime payment for all hours over fifty-nine. There was also a suggestion, in the 'night shilling', of a 'normal' working *day*, with extra payment for all time worked before or after defined daily hours.

There seem to have been relatively few differences between masters and men with regard to hours of labour in this period, though it is evident that abuses did exist. There is an interesting article in the *Typographical Gazette* (August 1846) on 'Hours of labour in the printing profession', from which it appears that the hours of piece hands were almost completely unregulated, fluctuating 'according to the briskness or depression of business', and that the defined hours of 'stab hands were merely 'nominal', as many as 20 or 30 hours often being worked at a stretch, particularly on the publication nights of weekly newspapers or to complete rush orders in jobbing offices. The writer maintained that 'long hours, night labour, and, too often, ill-ventilated work rooms' caused ill health and premature debility among printers, a statement confirmed by later medical evidence.

For this reason and also to secure work for unemployed hands, many unionists sought to restrict the amount of overtime worked. It was proposed at the Delegate Meeting of 1842 'that a strict inquiry should be instituted into ... working out of time, as many are known to work from three to four, and some even five to six hours' overtime per day, whilst numbers of unemployed men are walking the streets'. But the meeting considered that it was 'quite impossible' to curtail or abolish overtime. 'Doubtless it was desirable to equalise employment, but it was not practicable', owing to fluctuations in the printing trade.[29]

By 1830, when the Northern Union was established, a number of individual societies had secured 'established' wages and piece-work scales, but there was extraordinary variation from town to town. It was not until the Delegate Meeting of 1836 that an attempt was made not only to secure a definite minimum rate in each town, but also to reduce the existing variation to a certain uniformity. The Committee of Management were then instructed 'to divide the Northern Union into four districts for piece and establishment work' and try to secure uniform wage rates for each. The attempt, however, proved a complete failure; in fact the Committee never seriously persisted in it. In their Sixth Annual Report (December 1836) they pointed out the 'almost interminable correspondence' that would be required and that the Union funds could not stand the strain of the inevitable wage disputes, in which they would almost certainly be defeated owing to the large numbers of tramps and 'rats'. The idea of wages districts, they considered, was 'premature'. They would 'attempt no more at present than to assist the societies in those towns in which wages are much too low, to raise them to a reasonable rate'.

The four districts still existed at the end of 1840, but had proved 'entirely useless'.[30] The Union continued, however, its attempt to secure 'established' wage rates in each town. In estimating the degree of success or failure attending its efforts we are faced by conflicting evidence. In 1841 Robert Roberts of Manchester maintained that, since the formation of the Northern Union, 'we have been enabled to receive a pretty adequate remuneration for our labour'.[31] The General Secretary of the Northern Union also stated at the end of 1840 that 'within the last three or four years ... an increase has been obtained in the rate of wages'.[32] It was further pointed out, in 1842, 'that in those towns where union prevails, and men are associated in defence of their labour—there and there alone is the rate of wages such as will procure a decent maintenance; whilst in every other part, where no associations exist, printers have but a beggarly allowance, varying from £1 to 12s., and some few instances might be found where men do not receive more than 1s. or 1s. 6d. per day'.[33]

Numerous instances could be quoted from the trade periodicals of the 'forties in support of this statement. There is no doubt that the minimum 'stab rates and piece scales of the various towns were established as a result of agitation by the trade societies, which acted as a bulwark against wages reductions and succeeded, on the whole, in maintaining 'war-time' rates during the years 1815–50 and even, here and there, securing small increases. There is no doubt, also, that wages were highest in the large industrial cities, where unionism was strong, and lowest in the country towns, where it was weak or non-existent. But there is also good ground for believing that printers' rates owed as much to 'natural' economic forces as to trade-union action. Composition was a skilled art, requiring reasonably educated and intelligent workmen, of whom there was a limited supply in the first half of the nineteenth century, but for whom there was an increasing demand, owing to the expansion of the industry. The variation in wage rates between the large cities and small towns was largely due to variation in the cost of living. The quantity and pressure of work were also less in small country towns and usually of a kind requiring less skill. Neither the Northern Union nor any succeeding typographical association, down to the present day, has ever been able to establish a uniform standard of wages for the whole country. Moreover, the 'established' wage rates of the Northern Union were not paid in hundreds of non-society houses, while cheap apprentice labour was everywhere rife.

There was a good deal of controversy in this period over the relative merits of the establishment, or 'stab, and piece-work systems. A few societies in the Northern Union had piece-work scales, but most provincial towns were on the 'stab system. 'The "piece" is confined to the metropolis and a few other large towns', it was stated in 1846, 'while country offices but rarely adopt the system'.[34] Both 'stab and piece came in for considerable criticism.[35] The chief objection against the 'stab system, the payment of standard weekly wages, was that it placed the idle, incompetent journeyman on a level with the skilful and conscientious—that it was unfair both to superior workmen and to employers, since it required 'equal remuneration for all', regardless of ability or effort. The piece system, on the other hand, its advocates pointed out, gave 'remuneration according to the amount of work actually performed .... Each man is paid the amount he earns, and every grade of ability or skill has its full reward.' Under the 'stab system employers tended to 'weed out' indifferent workmen and impose 'task-work', to secure the maximum output for the minimum wages. Less skilful workmen, therefore, were often unemployed and either became a burden on the union funds or went into 'unfair' houses at less than the established wages. High 'stab rates, in fact, caused many employers to make their offices non-society and to employ cheap apprentice-labour.

That many master printers were opposed to minimum 'stab rates is clear from the evidence given before the Select Committee on Combinations in 1838. While prepared to pay good wages to competent workmen, they strongly objected to 'the same rate of wages for all', preferring to pay a man 'what he was worth'.

To these objections the Northern Union gave the following answer: 'First, that we do not seek to force any man on an employer, and, consequently, if the employer be not satisfied, he has always his remedy by discharging the individual, or placing him upon piece-work; and, secondly, that we do not insist upon a maximum, but a minimum standard: we do not say an employer shall not give more than a certain sum, but that he shall not give less.'[36] There is, undoubtedly, much to be said for establishing a reasonable minimum standard of living, which has always been the aim of all trade unions. Unfortunately, this minimum tends to become a maximum: employers refuse to pay more than the established rates and workmen are jealous of any of their fellows who get more than they do. Moreover, the fact that an employer can discharge an incompetent workman leaves unions with the

problem of such 'rejects', who are unable to get work at established
wages and therefore tend to enter 'unfair' houses at lower rates.

Disputes, however, were just as frequent over piece prices as
over 'stab wages, and there were endless differences in regard to
the innumerable 'extras' for difficult matter and as to what was
the 'property' of house or piece hands. There were also petty
jealousies and bickerings among the men about division of the 'fat'.
Piece hands suffered from the system of 'mixed' offices, in which
both 'stab and piece hands were employed, the former getting most
of the 'fat'; or, alternatively, hands might be switched from piece
to 'stab, or vice versa, according to the class of work, whether 'fat'
or 'lean'.[37] The 'stab system had the great merit of being uniform
and simple and much less liable to produce friction and disputes.
The hours of piece hands, moreover, were often undefined and
there was a great deal of 'standing for copy'. There was also a
tendency on piece-work for quality to be sacrificed to quantity and
for the men to produce 'scamped' work. Piece-work tended to make
men greedy for high pay packets and thus to work at high speed
and all hours, regardless of the fact that they were putting others
out of a job. It was far more likely, in fact, to create unemployment
than the 'stab system.

(3) *Apprentice Restriction*

The 'apprentice problem' was one of the greatest facing the
Northern Union. Many employers exploited cheap apprentice
labour: it was not at all unusual to find offices with as many as
half a dozen or more apprentices and only two or three journeymen; in many there were no journeymen at all, merely the master
and a few apprentices. Moreover, many men working as journeymen
printers had never 'served their time' to the trade, or had not been
properly bound apprentices, or had served less than seven years.

To oppose these evils the Northern Union tried to limit the
number of apprentices in each office, to enforce a seven years'
servitude and legal binding, and to exclude 'foreigners'.

The Manchester Society, which had previously been unable to
establish a fixed rule for the limitation of apprentices, decided in
1834 'that ... no Office in this town shall be deemed fair, where
there are a greater number of Apprentices than two, unless in those
Offices where they are in the habit of employing four Journeymen
regularly, when the number of Apprentices may be increased to
three, but on no account to have more. Where more are now bound,
the introduction of others shall be resisted till the number be
brought to the prescribed limits.'[38] This resolution was adopted
by the Northern Union Delegate Meeting of 1836. Its restrictions

were to be applied in all towns belonging to the Union. Hitherto, few, if any, societies had succeeded in their isolated efforts at apprentice limitation. It was now hoped that associated strength and the Union fund would secure the enforcement of a general rule.

The policy of apprentice restriction was justified in an 'Address to the Printers of Wales' in 1841.[39] This 'Address' pointed out that 'there are at present a vast number of printers more than the wants of the community require; the consequence of which is, that many have but partial, and many more no employment'. This 'super-abundance of hands' also resulted in lowered wage rates, 'ratting', and other evils. 'Self-preservation' was therefore the motive and justification of their restrictive policy. But restriction was also for the good of the apprentices themselves, who, in the present state of the trade, were likely to find themselves, at the expiration of their seven years' servitude, thrown badly trained into an over-stocked market. The Union also pointed out to employers that journeymen 'execute more work in a given space of time, damage much less type, and cause the employer less expense and trouble' than apprentices; that boy labour tended to produce incompetent workmen, and that it was but a cheap form of competition, which 'honourable' employers should assist the journeymen to stamp out. Similar arguments could be multiplied, for apprentice restriction was an endless topic throughout this period.

The Union placed equal emphasis on the seven years' servitude: no one was to be admitted unless he could produce a legal indenture. Strikes often occurred against the employment of 'foreigners' or 'illegal men'. The Union also tried to deal with the problem of 'runaway apprentices' or 'turnovers'. Apprentices became fairly proficient after two or three years' training and many, instead of serving out their time on a small pittance, preferred to 'run away' to another master, where they could earn higher wages. They would 'traverse the trade in search of the most profitable employment' and might, in a few years, change masters half a dozen times.[40] In each case there was no legal 'turnover' from one master to the next and the runaways were not, therefore, bound to any employer. They might carry on like this, underworking legally qualified journeymen, until they were as much as twenty-six years of age. The Union legislated against the practice, but without much apparent success.

At a Delegate Meeting in 1842 the Manchester Society proposed a stiffening of the apprentice restriction rule in small offices.[41] The ensuing discussion is interesting as illustrating the results of the previous policy and general feeling on the subject at the time. The

Manchester delegates declared that their society had on the whole been successful in applying the present restriction, 'except in small offices'; these were the bane of the Union, the cause of the existing unemployment. It was true that 'the returns they had received of the number of men and boys in the various towns, proved that the proportion of lads was greater upon the whole than the regulations of the Northern Union allowed. Still, ... a great good had been effected, and it was worthy of consideration whether something more might not be done.'

The general feeling of the meeting, however, was against further restriction, which 'they had not the power to carry out'. It was considered that 'the old rule should be enforced before they thought of a new one ... there was a town in connection with the Union, in which there were 41 men and 61 boys. ... In Leeds five apprentices were allowed.... In York and Doncaster, the present principle was not carried out.... In Derby, too, the same laxity prevailed.' Most of the 'unfair' offices were caused by the present rule and further restriction would increase their number. It would cause numerous strikes, which would be disastrous in the existing unemployment and bankrupt state of the Union funds. The proposition was therefore rejected.

It is obvious that the attempt at apprentice-restriction was not proving very successful, particularly in the smaller towns and offices. This state of affairs is confirmed by other evidence, though conflicting statements were often made. It was stated in 1840 that 'there are still in many places a disproportionate number of apprentices',[42] and at the end of 1841 John Backhouse confessed 'that there are at this time nearly as many apprentices in our business as there are journeymen in regular employment.... The want of a due limitation in a great portion of the United Kingdom is woefully apparent at the present period.'[43] The chief blame, he asserted, lay on Scotland, London, and Wales, where there was practically no restriction on the number of apprentices—a fact which rendered the Northern Union's efforts at limitation futile. The situation remained the same at the end of 1842, when it was stated that 'the malady of the apprenticeship system is still in full vigour ... notwithstanding all the efforts ... which have been made'.[44] Scores of instances could be cited from the trade reports and periodicals in support of these general statements.

There are various reasons for this failure. Apprentice-restriction led to numerous strikes, the 'closing' of offices to Union members, and the influx of 'rat' labour. Many felt it a hardship to sacrifice their situations on that account, particularly in times of unemployment, and therefore acquiesced in violation of the rule. The basic cause of failure, however, was that restriction simply could not be enforced in the face of expanding industry and commercial competition.

Many employers sympathised with the men. Master printers giving evidence before the Select Committee on Combinations in 1838 considered 'there was some necessity to protect the men in a fair way' and 'not to have such a number of apprentices trained', so that 'men, having got a good education, and having served seven years, should not be obliged to hunt the world for employment'. They also approved of restriction because it helped to 'keep up the respectability of the business' and kept out 'those of an inferior grade'. Many 'respectable' employers disapproved of small masters who were using apprentices as 'cheap labour' and thereby 'overstocking the trade'. But they strongly opposed arbitrary regulation by the journeymen.

Members of the Select Committee, advocates of a 'free labour' policy, suggested some telling arguments against restriction. Printers' wages, they considered, were maintained by a 'monopoly', while other workers were earning low wages or were unemployed. Education and technical ability would provide automatic limitation on entry without trade society barriers. All who could learn the trade should be permitted entry, if a demand for their labour existed. There should be none but 'natural checks against overstocking the market, instead of persons associating to exclude their fellow-beings'.

There is no doubt that the Union's apprentice rule was restrictive, more suited to a static economy than to the rapidly expanding and competitive industry of the nineteenth century. It was, in fact, a heritage from the craft gilds, with their medieval, monopolistic outlook. Nevertheless, we can hardly blame the Union for its attempt to maintain a traditional standard of life in a time of fierce undercutting competition and trade fluctuations, which often brought widespread unemployment and distress.

(4) *Attitude towards Machinery*

At the time when steam-power was first applied to printing, a very strong feeling existed in the minds of the working classes against the introduction of machinery, which it was felt, tended merely to benefit the capitalist and deprived the working man of his right to labour by throwing him out of employment. Pressmen naturally shared with other handicraftsmen this fear and hatred of mechanical innovations. John Walter II had, for this reason, erected Koenig's printing machine secretly in a separate building adjoining *The Times* office, for fear that the pressmen might, like the 'Luddites' in the textile trade, smash the offensive machinery. The London pressmen maintained for many years a stubborn but vain opposition to steam printing. Their intransigence merely brought in 'irregular' labour, mechanics and others who had never served an apprenticeship to printing. There was thus created a new class called 'machinemen', 'machine minders', or 'machine managers', who eventually (1839) established their own organisation, the London Printing Machine Managers' Trade Society.

Printing machinery was introduced several years later into the provincial trade and there is evidence of similar opposition. We hear, for example, in 1842, that the Manchester Society had 'engaged in useless strikes—ruinous, ridiculous, and unjust contests against the employment of machinery'.[45] There is, however, no evidence of violent opposition or machine breaking. Although the machines gradually displaced hand pressmen, they created added employment for hand compositors. Opposition was futile, in any case, and typographical societies were forced to modify their attitude so as to maintain control over the press department. The Manchester Society required the machines to be worked by its members and even passed a rule that 'on any printing machine used ... none but journeymen or apprentices shall be employed in *feeding* the machine'.[46] But this rule was expunged in 1847, the committee considering it 'hardship and injustice that apprentices to the printing business should be compelled to waste their time in feeding machines'. Employers were therefore 'allowed to employ such persons as they may think proper to feed machines', but these people, labourers or unbound boys and girls, were 'not allowed to interfere in any other manner in connection with the machine, or in any other department of the printing business'.[47]

Even 'machine-minding' or 'managing' was regarded by journeymen printers as somewhat degrading and consequently some of the larger employers, using several machines, began to bind apprentices exclusively to that department, thus creating a specialised class of 'machinemen'. Specialisation was inevitable as the industry expanded, but throughout the second half of the century 'twicing' was common: the great majority of firms had only one or two machines, worked intermittently by compositors. 'Not till some time had elapsed after the introduction of machinery in the provinces did machine minders exist to any extent as a separate class.'[48]

The Northern Union followed the policy laid down by the Manchester Society in regard to printing machines. It was decided in 1840 'that no person attending a printing machine, who has not served a seven years' apprenticeship to either press or case, shall be admitted a member of any society of the union'. This rule did not attempt to confine the working of the machines to journeymen members, but merely excluded from the Union such 'machinemen' as were not 'legal' printers. Manchester attempted to maintain control over the machine department, but in most other towns the 'machinemen', where they existed, were unorganised and outside the society, regarded by the compositors as an inferior class of mere mechanics and labourers.

Composing machinery affected the printing trade hardly at all during the first half of the nineteenth century, but where composing machines were introduced hand compositors strongly opposed them. They were regarded as a 'much dreaded novelty', a 'mechanical spectre', and denounced as 'wretched abortions'. The *Compositors' Chronicle* made a bitter attack upon 'the introduction of machinery into those branches of labour which previously afforded sustenance to honest and honourable workmen', thereby causing unemployment, lowered wages, untold misery, and a spirit of discontent. It was feared that compositors might be reduced to the condition of the handloom weavers.[49] The *Printer* pointed out that composing machinery 'must, if successful, deprive the labouring man of his subsistence'.[50] There was also a fear that skilled labour would be ousted by cheaper women and boys. For this reason the Midland Board of the National Typographical Association (successor of the Northern Union) would only sanction the introduction of Rosenberg's machine at Hull 'provided the established wages of the town are paid and the legal limitation of apprentices observed'.[51] The trade-union periodicals gleefully reported the successive failures of composing machines.

(5) Strikes

Our survey of Union policy in regard to wages, hours, and apprentices has shown that there was fruitful ground for dispute between masters and men. Strikes were, in fact, frequent and the number of 'unfair' offices considerable. Many employers were strongly opposed to the 'tyranny' exercised by the printers' trade societies. The *Oxford Herald*, for example, declared that

among the various conspiracies by which the freedom of trade and freedom of labour have been resisted, few have been more vexatious or unreasonable than that of letter-press printers. The rate of wages, the proportion of apprentices, and every minute point in the management of the business, they pretend to regulate. They prohibit any distinction between the skilful and the bungler, the indolent and the industrious. A certain amount of wages must be paid to all alike. . . . Again, if a man, however excellent his character, or however valuable to his employer, becomes obnoxious to the conspirators, he must be hunted from the trade.... In short, their interference and dictation are perfectly intolerable to any employer of ordinary independence of feeling.[52]

Under the circumstances, it is not surprising that there were innumerable strikes.

The Northern Union committee cannot, however, justly be accused, as they were by some employers, of deliberately fostering disputes. They invariably adopted a cautious, conciliatory policy and were opposed to unjustifiable strikes. Thus it was resolved at Manchester in 1836 'that every means shall be adopted by the central commitee and local societies to prevent strikes, they being hereby declared to be generally injurious to the trade, and that all parties shall strive as much as possible (consistent with honour) to prevent such disagreeable consequences, and endeavour as speedily as possible to bring matters to a good understanding between employers and journeymen'. It was a rule of the Northern Union 'that, to avoid the injustice frequently arising from acting on *ex parte* statements, in all cases of dispute, wherever practicable, the society shall hear the statement of the employer on the subject'. The Union's aims, it was urged, 'can be most effectually accomplished by our always exhibiting peaceful conduct, and allowing justice, reason, and unanimity to preside in our counsels'.[53] There was nothing revolutionary or aggressive about the Northern Union. Its motto was 'United to protect, but not combined to injure'.

Nevertheless, when an important principle was involved it was often impossible to avoid a strike, in which case the Union sought to recompense members who 'sacrificed their situations in the interests of the profession'. This was, in fact, the main purpose of the central fund. The Union was to give added strength to local societies in 'resisting reductions of wage-rates, the taking a disproportionate number of apprentices', or other 'injustices'.[54] It seems likely that some sort of strike payment existed from the Union's foundation. In 1837 it was £2, increased in 1840 to £4, paid in instalments of from 15s. to £1 per week, or in one lump sum if the strike hand wished to leave town. In addition to this sum, strike hands were entitled to double relief on tramp. Secretaries were to 'state on the back of their cards the cause of leaving their situations, and request that every facility may be afforded them in getting employment'.

It was proposed by the Wolverhampton Society in 1837 that a 'sinking fund' should be established to provide weekly allowances to strike hands, instead of a lump sum and a 'backed' card, but the Union committee decided it would be too expensive.[55] Several of the larger branches, however, supplemented the Union strike allowance, or even established local strike funds to provide weekly allowances.

We have already noticed the friction which was apt to arise between the central committee and local societies. This was particularly visible in the question of strike decisions. The Executive strove constantly to maintain control, but found it difficult to curb local independence. Quite often societies started strikes 'upon trivial causes', swayed by local feeling, contrary to the declared policy of the Union. The Union rule was not clear as to where ultimate responsibility lay. It stated

> that whenever a dispute may arise between the employer and the employed ... respecting a reduction of wages, apprentices or any other matter involving the interests of the profession, the secretary of such society shall transmit to the secretary of this Union, a correct, clear, and full statement thereof; stating whether pecuniary aid is wanting, signed by the officers of the said society. The secretary of the Union shall then consult the committee of management on the case, and act as he may be advised.

This was liable to conflicting interpretations. The *Compositors' Chronicle*, for example, asserted in 1842 that 'the laws of the Northern Union do not forbid them [local societies] to strike without the consent of the committee of management—they only require that the particulars of a dispute should be sent to headquarters'. This lack of central control was 'productive of innumerable disputes'. Such an interpretation, however, was rebutted by the Halifax Society, which maintained 'that no local society could strike ... without having, whilst the matter was merely in dispute, consulted the Union secretary and the committee of management, and it is also certain that if they so acted they would not be granted the usual allowance in case of strike'.

This, it seems, was the more usual interpretation of the rule. Nevertheless, and despite the Union's declared policy, strikes were frequent, though mostly petty affairs, involving only one office and a few hands. The majority proved unsuccessful, owing to the influx of 'rats', especially tramps. The paltry strike allowance was insufficient compensation for the sacrifice of a situation and many men 'stayed in', while in periods of widespread unemployment and distress, such as 1836–43, tramp relief did little to relieve hardship and failed to prevent many men accepting situations in 'unfair' houses or entering those where strikes were going on.

The General Secretary issued a 'monthly Circular' giving details of strikes, the names of 'unfair' houses, non-members, and 'rats', information about tramps, &c. There are references to this Circular in the minutes of the Manchester Society as early as 1834, but no copy appears to have survived. It was the forerunner of the *Typographical Societies' Monthly Circular* established in 1852, which became the *Provincial Typographical Circular* in 1875 and the *Typographical Circular* in 1877.

(6) *Tramp Relief*

Tramp relief had linked typographical societies together long before the Northern Union was established. Relief was therefore given by Northern Union branches not only on each other's cards, but also on those of the London, Scottish, and Irish Unions and all other 'recognised' societies.

The amount of relief was individually determined by the various societies and varied from 9*d*. in the smallest to 5*s*. in the largest, the average being about 1*s*. 6*d*. No tramp was relieved twice in the same town within twelve months. Even so, tramp relief was a heavy burden on small societies. It was therefore decided in 1838 to establish a Reimbursement Fund in order 'to equalise the burden of relieving tramps'. Each member had to contribute a penny per month to this fund, from which small societies (with less than forty members) could claim reimbursement of all tramp-relief expendituer above 9*d*. per member per month.

The total amount of relief, however, was still trifling. It was stated in 1841 that 'if a tramp were to call upon the whole of our Societies, the utmost amount he would get is £2. 19*s*. for the first twelve months: if he should be so unfortunate as not to obtain one month's employment [the minimum period for acquiring membership] in a town where there is a Society during that period, and be obliged to travel a second year with the same card, he would not be able to obtain above half that sum'.[56]

Other trades had different tramp relief systems—'by the mile' or 'by the day'—and there was some argument among printers as to which method was best. The mileage system was discussed at the Delegate Meetings in 1840 and 1842, but rejected as impracticable.

The number of men on tramp varied with trade fluctuations. Even in periods of brisk business there was a good deal of tramping, but depression brought 'hordes' on the road. The number of tramps relieved by the Manchester Society varied from 110 in 1835 to 340 in 1841. They naturally made for cities such as Manchester and Liverpool, where the largest amount of relief was given and where there was most chance of work; but as only one allowance was to be had in each place tramps were forced to move from town to town in search of relief and employment. All societies, therefore, had their share of tramps. But the Northern Union area, comprising over forty societies in towns close together, was obviously a much better hunting ground for tramps than the south of England, where there were very few societies. Thus the Northern Union, with a smaller membership than that of the London Union, had to bear a far heavier burden of tramp relief—a great grievance among provincial printers. London, on the other hand, complained that the tramp system enabled the provinces to export their unemployed to the metropolis.

Tramp figures provide evidence of considerable mobility among journeymen printers in this period. It was not unusual for a tramp to perform a 'grand tour' of the three Kingdoms, particularly in periods of depression, when employment was nowhere to be found. This 'floating' labour force was of great importance in strikes. Tramp relief was intended not merely to relieve distress and help the unemployed to find work, but also to keep them faithful to the Union and out of 'unfair' houses. But the amount of relief was extremely small and a tramp might, in a bad period, be on the road for months, suffering considerable hardships, with no more than a few days' casual employment. Unfair houses presented great temptations to men so circumstanced: hence the influx of tramps which ruined so many strikes.

Tramp relief was open to considerable fraud and abuse. To prevent 'imposition of any kind by worthless members of the profession in search of employment', branch secretaries were to report cases of forged cards, erasures, neglect of work, or 'ratting' to the General Secretary, who would warn all known societies to stop further relief to the guilty parties.[57] The names of these 'worthless characters' were frequently printed in the Northern Union circulars and annual reports and in the trade periodicals. Tramps, in fact, acquired an almost proverbial reputation for being idle, dissolute, and inferior workmen. The system certainly tended to foster 'professional roadsters'. On the other hand, there were 'many instances of men who have tramped long and hard, and yet have never ... brought the least disgrace upon their own characters, or upon the profession'.[58] The misconduct of a few, no doubt, resulted in exaggerated statements about all tramps.

Apart from voluntary chapel aid and occasional branch relief funds, the tramp system was the only method of unemployed relief in this period, except in a few large towns, which, in the early 'forties, established their own systems of weekly allowances. Its inadequacy, however, became increasingly obvious in the trade depression of 1836-43. Not only was it open to many abuses, but also involved great hardships. A man had to tramp the country in

all weathers, hopelessly looking for work, suffering severe priv-
ations, often falling ill, degraded and demoralised in lodging houses,
while his family was left destitute at home to fall on parish relief.
No wonder, then, that men refused to come out on strike, or that
tramps often went into 'unfair' offices.

It was the problem of unemployment, the inadequacy of tramp
relief, and the closely connected failure of strikes that, more than
anything else, led to the attempts at reorganisation of printers'
unions in the early 'forties which finally resulted in the foundation
of the National Typographical Association.

III   EVENTS LEADING UP TO THE FOUNDATION OF THE NATIONAL TYPOGRAPHICAL ASSOCIATION

Throughout the first four decades of the nineteenth century
there was frequent co-operation between the various typographical
societies in the British Isles—in London, the English provinces,
Scotland, and Ireland. They were linked together by feelings of
brotherhood, common principles, and the tramp-relief system, and
often assisted each other in strikes or trade depression. Co-operation
became much closer after the establishment of the Northern Union
(1830), the London Union of Compositors (1834), and the Scottish
Association and Irish Union (1836). Not only was there frequent
correspondence between them, but their officials met at Northern
Union Delegate Meetings, to which representatives from all independent societies were invited.

The idea naturally arose, therefore, of a union of all printers in
the United Kingdom. This was suggested at least as early as 1840,
when the Northern Union put forward the following proposals:
firstly, 'that a general sinking fund for the United Kingdom ...
should be established', to provide assistance in strikes, and,
secondly, that the unions should 'consider whether it is not advisable
to connect the London, Irish, and Scotch Unions with the Northern
Union, and what steps are necessary for that purpose'.[59] Nothing,
however, came of these proposals.

Nearly all the following suggestions for reorganisation and more
extended union arose out of the failure to deal with the problem of
the unemployed—the breakdown of the tramp-relief system and
the failure of strikes. It was in vain that rules were passed against
'ratting', warnings were issued, names published, and tramp cards
detained. The paltry strike allowance and tramp relief were insufficient to retain the loyalty of out-of-work members.

These failures led 'A Northern Unionist', writing in the *Com-*

positor' Chronicle in 1841, to urge the abolition of tramping and the adoption in its stead of regular weekly allowances to the unemployed and strike hands in their own towns.[60] He pointed out that it was unreasonable and unjust to send a man on tramp from town to town, leaving his wife and family at home, when trade was so bad that there was no hope of finding work. Weekly out-of-work payments in their own towns would keep men true to the union, while haphazard tramping could be replaced by unemployment returns to headquarters and a system of labour direction. More effective safeguards and punishments could also be provided against fraud and neglect of work. The increased financial burden could be met by 'consolidation' of the separate unions into 'one body or association divided into districts, under a central executive, which would exercise stronger control over strike decisions'.

The *Compositors' Chronicle* strongly supported these proposals. John Backhouse, General Secretary of the Northern Union, also approved of them, but pointed out the great expense they would involve, especially in periods of trade depression.[61]

That some sort of reorganisation was necessary seemed clear from the Northern Union's annual report. The increased subscription of 4*d.* per month had proved insufficient, expenditure had exceeded income, funds were exhausted, and a levy had to be imposed. The number of tramps had been 'great, beyond all former example', almost every society had exhausted its funds in relief payments, and expenditure on reimbursement account was nearly twice the income, thus necessitating borrowing from the General Fund. Owing to the lack of funds and the number of unemployed and 'rat' hands, strikes had failed and apprentices multiplied. The Committee was well aware that trade depression was mainly responsible for these misfortunes, but felt that some improvement might be made by reorganisation.

The greatest objection to the new plan was that the proposed unemployed and strike allowances would be too costly and contributions too high. The industrious would have to support the idle and dissolute. Moreover, by restricting movement the proposed scheme would cause the unemployed to stagnate in their own towns without going out to find work. The new organisation would also be unwieldy and impracticable.

The Liverpool Society therefore put forward an alternative scheme, for a 'General Tramping Reimbursement Fund' including all the various unions.[62] Tramping should not be abolished: instead, its burdens should be more equally distributed. The provinces were spending far more in relieving London cards than London was in relieving theirs: London should bear its fair share of the expense, by contributing to a General Reimbursement Fund.

Here, then, were the two plans put forward to solve the present difficulties: one for a complete reorganisation by amalgamation and division into districts, with weekly out-of-work and strike payments; the other for reform of the tramping system only, by equalising the burdens of relief expenditure. Both were to be given a trial, the latter in 1842, when a General Reimbursement Fund was established, the former in 1844, with the foundation of the National Typographical Association. Both were to fail and in 1848 the streams of trade-union history in the printing trade were to return to their old channels.

The Liverpool scheme for a 'General Tramping Reimbursement Fund' was strongly supported at the Northern Union Delegate Meeting in June 1842, before representatives from all important typographical societies in the United Kingdom.[63] Statistics revealed the inequality of tramp-relief burdens borne by the London and Northern Unions. The Scottish and Irish Unions, however, were bearing their fair share of tramp relief and were therefore excluded from the plan. It was decided that Northern Union members should, as hitherto, contribute a penny, London members two-pence, to the Reimbursement Fund, in order to relieve the financial burden on small societies.

It is obvious that this plan would not solve the acute problems of the time. It might do something to relieve the financial burdens of the Northern Union; it might also succeed in raising slightly the amount of relief given to tramps; but it would not cope with the problems of the unemployed and 'ratting'. It merely re-enacted, more stringently, the old safeguards against fraud and entry into 'unfair' or 'strike' houses. Furthermore, it failed to secure the support of the London Union, which, in spite of the plenipotentiary powers given to its delegates, rejected the scheme on their return.

The trade's problems, therefore, remained unsolved. A suggestion had been put forward at the Delegate Meeting on the lines of the plan proposed by 'Northern Unionist', but seems hardly to have been considered, in view of the general feeling in favour of a reimbursement fund. Now, when the latter misfired, a number of remedies were suggested, all more or less variations upon the 'Northern Unionist' theme. Thus in the *Compositors' Chronicle* of November 1842, R. Davies, of Liverpool, a member of the Northern Union committee, put forward a scheme for 'General Union', a 'Proposed plan of sustaining Members of the Profession who have relinquished their situations in defence of Trade Principles, by the adoption of a Consolidated Fund, embracing the

London, Northern, Scotch, and Irish Unions'. He pointed out that £4 and a backed card were utterly inadequate compensation to strike hands and that larger societies in the Northern Union were already providing weekly strike pay. He did not, however, propose any radical reorganisation: the unions were to remain separate, but to assist each other in strikes by levies paid into a 'Consolidated Fund'.

Davies stated that 'the Secretary, Mr. Backhouse, and the Committee of Management ... have given their unqualified approval to the general principle of this plan'. The *Compositors' Chronicle* also approved of the idea, but considered the proposed means inadequate and also urged reform or abolition of the tramping system.

The Northern Union's Annual Report for 1842 further emphasised the need for new measures. The situation had worsened in the past year. The present subscription was 'totally inadequate'. The number of unemployed had resulted in reduced income, while expenditure had risen on tramp relief and strikes, so that there was a large deficit, in spite of a levy and a loan from the Dublin Society. Several small branches had collapsed. Obviously these were evils which no trade union could cure: they were caused neither by apprentice labour nor grasping employers, but by prolonged trade depression. Nevertheless, the journeymen sought salvation in reorganisation, in wider union.

The details of Davies's 'Proposed Plan' were clearly unsatisfactory, but its main principle of supporting strike hands by weekly allowances and his idea of a 'General Union' based on this principle secured wide support. Thomas Houghton, of the Preston Society, writing in the *Compositors' Chronicle* under the pen-name 'Argus', accepted these basic ideas, but himself propounded a much sounder scheme of reorganisation.[64] He maintained that 'a general union, to be effective, must be formed on the principle of a sinking fund', otherwise 'there would be no funds in hand when it was known a strike would take place'. Thus a fund raised by levies during strikes would be insufficient. Houghton also proposed the abolition of the tramp system and its replacement by weekly allowances to the unemployed, as well as to strike hands. An increased subscription would, of course, be necessary; a shilling a week he estimated.

The Northern Union's Annual Report for 1843 officially condemned the tramping system and supported this scheme. The whole question was to be discussed at the Delegate Meeting in the summer of 1844.

Before this meeting took place further plans were put forward in the *Printer*, all advocating 'General Union', abolition of tramping, and payment of weekly allowances to unemployed and strike hands. 'Our relative position and mutual dependence upon each other', it was urged, 'are no longer determinable by the claims of nationality, nor bounded by geographical limitation. Partial operations have hitherto failed from the want of concentrated force and the inability to maintain our principles from paucity of support.'[65] A 'General Union' or 'Amalgamation' of all typographical societies would bring success.

IV   THE NATIONAL TYPOGRAPHICAL ASSOCIATION, 1844–8

The 'Printers' Parliament' at Derby on Monday, 15 July 1844, was the largest Delegate Meeting of printers that had ever been held. After four days' discussion a plan of amalgamation was unanimously agreed on, to come into operation on 1 January 1845. Its basis was a proposition put forward by the Preston Society in which Thomas Houghton expanded his previous proposals for 'General Union'.[66]

It was decided 'that this Association be called the National Typographical Association, and shall consist of all typographical societies and printers (who have served a seven years' apprenticeship) of fair character in the United Kingdom; and that the principle upon which it shall be based be impartial justice to all with whom it may co-operate or oppose'. As one writer put it, 'This is a good title. ... It is not a "Union"—oh no! That term is offensive to ears polite: It is not sectional, nor provincial, but a "National" Association.'[67] Moreover, a union could not be maintained unless it did 'justice' to its members: weekly out-of-work and strike payments were therefore provided. The Association would also maintain 'justice' in its dealings with employers: non-aggression, moderation, and conciliation were to be its characteristics.

The objects of the Association were 'to advance the interests of the typographical profession, and to improve the social condition of its members'. The subscription was to be 6d. per week for the fully employed,[68] proportionately less for those partially employed, and nothing for the unemployed. New members were to pay an entrance-fee of 5s. and would also be fined if guilty of having 'held aloof' or of 'unfair' practices.

The Association was divided into five geographical districts. England was split into three—the South-eastern, South-western, and Midland Districts, while Scotland became the Northern and Ireland the Western District. These divisions were not, of course, new: the Northern and Western corresponded to the existing Scottish and Irish Unions, the Midland covered roughly the same area as the Northern Union, the South-eastern was dominated by London, while the South-western was the embodiment of previous hopes for a 'Western Union'.[69]

Each District was to be governed by a District Board, consisting of seven (later nine) members, 'elected from the society named for that purpose by a Delegate Meeting': each District, in other words, was to have its 'governing branch'. It was eventually decided that the district centres should be London (South-eastern), Bristol (South-western), Liverpool (Midland), Dublin (Western), and Edinburgh (Northern). Each District Board was to appoint its own secretary and treasurer. These were still working journeymen and only part-time officials, secretarial salaries varying from £8 to £20 per annum. They and the Board members had nearly all been active as officers or committee-men in their Unions or local societies. Thus there was no break in continuity of government.

Each Board was to be 'arbiter of every question affecting the interests of the Association' in its district, that is, of questions which were beyond the powers of branches to decide, such as threatened strikes. It was also to have control over the surplus money left over from Association subscriptions after branches had met such liabilities as unemployment and strike payments, salaries, &c. The aggregate amount accumulated in the various districts would be the Association's capital. District Boards would, in case of need, remit money to branches to meet claims for unemployed or strike payments. Should a District Board itself require funds, it was to apply to the General Secretary, who would communicate the fact to the other Boards.

Each Board was competent to decide 'questions affecting a district only'. Important matters, particularly strike decisions, had to be dealt with by the Executive. There was, however, no central Committee for the whole Association. The Executive consisted of the five District Boards, in whom, collectively, resided 'the whole judicial and executive power of the Association'. The Association was, in fact, a rather loose federation of districts which still preserved a good deal of their old independence and autonomy. Co-ordination was achieved by means of a General Corresponding Secretary, to whom all important questions requiring Executive decision were transmitted by the various District Boards. He submitted the facts to all the other Boards, who, after consideration, sent back to him their individual decisions. Each Board had one vote and a majority of such votes constituted the decision of the

Executive, which was made known to the District Board concerned by the General Secretary.

This organisation was extremely cumbersome, requiring a tremendous amount of postal communication, involving long delays and encouraging friction, not only between the various Boards, but also between them and the General Secretary. The latter was the king-pin of the whole organisation, a kind of one-man central office. He was meant to be a mere 'go-between', but inevitably acquired considerable influence and power, which aroused jealousies and suspicions and fears of dictatorial action. The office was held by our old friend John Backhouse, ex-Secretary of the Northern Union, at a salary of £25 per year. Even his was an amateur, spare-time office.

Obviously there was considerable feeling against centralisation. The different districts still retained their varying customs. Their policies in regard to apprentice restriction, for example, differed widely: the Midland District tried to maintain the old Northern Union rule, while in London there was no rule at all; no general regulation was made on the subject. Neither did the Association attempt to secure any uniformity in wage rates and hours. Nevertheless, it was a great step forward in harmonising the aims and co-ordinating the actions of the hitherto separate Unions.

Local societies still retained a good deal of independence. Each was to 'elect its own members, appoint its own officers, watch over the interests of the profession in its own town, and aid by all means in its power in carrying out the general objects of the Association'. The Midland Board decided 'to allow each Society to frame its own regulations, and that the printing of any General Local Rules is inadvisable'.[70] Local societies, therefore, still retained most of their old regulations. Their independence, however, was considerably curtailed by the control of the District Boards, especially over financial matters and threatened disputes.

The right of all members to a voice in Association affairs was preserved through the medium of Delegate Meetings, which were to 'make all laws for the general government of the Association'.

The Association funds would provide weekly out-of-work and strike payments. Amalgamation would secure 'concentration of the energies and resources of the trade in all cases of dispute', which would not only achieve greater success in strikes, but also enable more equitable strike allowances to be paid.[71] Strike hands would receive weekly three-fourths of the wages sacrificed for a period of six months (or, if they secured casual employment, would have their earnings made up to the wages of the town), and out-of-work allowance afterwards if still unemployed.

The Association did not, however, wish to encourage disputes. *The Times*, no doubt representing the views of many employers, accused it in 1846, during the great Edinburgh dispute, of being a 'conspiracy' to foment strikes and browbeat employers by 'tyrannical proceedings'.[72] It pointed out, in particular, 'the dangers of centralisation'.

> Leave the towns or districts to themselves, to manage each its own affairs. and there is a strong probability that, however little squabbles might occur occasionally, no very important or permanent dissension would interrupt the relations of employer and employed. But introduce a foreign power—one that neither has nor can have that intimate knowledge of the feelings of the parties concerned without which the soundest judgement is liable to err—appeal to such a power as this, and all prospect of a compromise is at once shut out. The great central committee after deliberating in darkness, decides in folly; and issues a fiat that can hardly ... produce any other result than the widening of a breach which, if left to itself, might have closed itself.

There is not, however, the slightest shred of evidence to support such statements. As the *Typographical Gazette* pointed out, the Executive was

> a power only appealed to when the towns *cannot* 'manage each its own affairs', that is. after remonstrance and a full local inquiry have failed to obtain an amicable understanding ... The Association in no way interferes with master and man until ... the two have been found unable to settle their differences.... The question in dispute is then submitted to the judgement of forty-five practical men working in London, Liverpool, Bristol, Edinburgh, and Dublin, nine in each city, besides officers, [and not to a] great central committee ... deliberating in darkness.

Neither did the Executive 'issue its fiat, decided in folly', but almost invariably adopted a cautious, moderate, restraining attitude, which often served to prevent serious disputes developing out of local feeling. The Association aimed, in fact, at 'the diminution of strikes', by placing strike decisions 'in the hands of a Committee, consisting of representatives of the whole Kingdom; thus rendering it impossible for any strike to take place upon an affair of trivial amount'.[73]

The Association rule was that 'in any case of dispute occurring in any town connected with this Association, the secretary of the society shall communicate the particulars to the Board for that district, who shall determine whether it is necessary to require the General Secretary to consult the whole of the Boards upon the question'. 'No society shall have power to declare any house unfair until it has been decided by the Executive.' Obviously it was the aim of the Association, by increased central control over local societies, to prevent trivial disputes developing into strikes. At the same time, of course, the Association aimed to provide the requisite funds to win strikes when they could not be prevented. Its establishment, as we shall see, aroused exaggerated hopes and was followed by an outbreak of disputes all over the country.

The second great object of the Association was the abolition of the tramp-relief system and substitution of weekly allowances to the unemployed. Each out-of-work member was to receive 6s. per week, casual earnings to be made up to 8s. No member was to be allowed any relief 'in travelling from town to town in search of employment—the object of weekly payments being to increase the comfort of unemployed members, and to supersede tramping'. But 'every member desirous of changing his locality may do so, by obtaining a certificate of membership, and a statement of his account, if any, addressed to the secretary of the town to which he is going', which would entitle him to free admission. Travelling members would, in fact, be entitled to draw their weekly unemployment allowance in whichever society town they happened to be located on a Saturday night. But the old tramp system was to be replaced by a system of labour direction along the lines laid down by 'Northern Unionist' in 1841, which would proportion the supply of hands to the demand in the various towns.

The new mode of relief would, it was hoped, keep men loyal to the Association, prevent 'ratting', render strikes more successful, and thus keep up wage rates. It would also do away with the moral and physical evils of the tramp system. To the objection that it would benefit 'the idle and ill-disposed', it was answered that 'the allowance proposed is not so great an inducement as to cause idleness'; but certain safeguards were imposed to see that unemployed and strike hands should work when possible and not defraud the Association. The usual warnings and penalties against 'ratting' were also enacted.

The meeting at Derby, which had 'unanimously agreed' upon the plan for a National Typographical Association, was primarily a Delegate Meeting of the Northern Union. Thirty-three of its members were present, as against three from London, one from Cambridge, two from Ireland, and one from Scotland. The initiative in the movement towards 'General Union' had, all along, come from the Northern Union. It remained, therefore, to secure the assent of London, Scotland, and Ireland to the proposed reorganisation.

Scotland declared in favour of amalgamation at a Delegate Meeting in August, because of the 'many growing evils affecting the profession' which made 'a radical change' necessary.[74] The S.T.A. had been completely defeated in a number of strikes. They also considered it 'the duty of each and all to sink minor differences in upholding the one great principle of Union'. Moreover, a remedy had been found for the evils of the tramp system and if they did not join the N.T.A. they would have to support their own unemployed and strike hands, who would no longer get tramp relief in England.

The London Union of Compositors also decided to participate.[75] It was pointed out that, whereas the present Union had failed, the new Association promised great advantages. It would diminish the number of strikes and at the same time ensure success, by united action, in those which could not be prevented. It would also provide just compensation to strike hands and, above all, it would abolish the tramp system and give adequate relief to the out-of-work. The L.U.C.'s underlying motive, however, in supporting the proposed scheme was that it would reduce the influx of unemployed and strike hands from the provinces and thus keep up London wage rates—admittedly 'a selfish view of the question'.

Before the Association was actually established, however, another Delegate Meeting was held in Manchester, in December 1844, to revise the proposed plan.[76] A few alterations and additions were made, chiefly to prevent abuse of out-of-work payments, but the main principles remained unchanged. The Irish Union having decided in favour of amalgamation, the N.T.A. covered the whole United Kingdom.

Its launching fortunately coincided with the end of the long period of depression and the beginning of a trade boom, which brought increased employment in the printing industry. It could never have survived, in fact it could hardly have been established, but for this favourable trade situation. For a year and a half it was able to accumulate funds, in a period of comparatively full employment and few strikes; but when depression returned in 1846 it quickly collapsed.

At first, however, expansion was rapid.[77] By June 1845 the Association had 59 branches and 4,338 members, increasing to 67 branches and 4,969 members by December. At the end of 1846 it had 74 branches and 5,418 members,[78] but had then been suffering from trade depression for about eight months. Unfortunately, there seems to be no third half-yearly report in existence. It is probable, however, that the Association reached its maximum membership in that period, perhaps 5,700.

Even so, it never included anything like all journeymen printers in the United Kingdom. In London the Pressmen and Daily Newspaper Compositors stood aloof, mainly from reasons of selfish independence. The Manchester Society also refused to join the Association, for similar reasons and because it considered the Association financially unsound.[79] In July 1846 a writer in the *Typographical Gazette* denounced the 'apathy, listlessness, and nonchalance exhibited by members of our profession in several cities and towns' in the south-western, southern, south-eastern, and eastern counties of England. 'Take, for instance, Norwich, Ipswich, Bury St. Edmunds, Exeter, and Plymouth. These are only a few; but . . . in almost all the towns where even the shadow of a printer is found, in the counties of Lincoln, Norfolk, Suffolk, Essex, Kent, Sussex (Brighton and Lewes excepted), Devon, and Cornwall, the same feeling of indifference seems to prevail.' In Wales the Association could number only three branches. These statements are confirmed by the Census Abstracts of 1841 and 1851, which show that scores of country towns containing printers were never included in the Association. Apart, moreover, from these non-union areas, there were, even in the very strongholds of the Association, a large number of 'unfair' offices and non-society men.

A few large cities formed the backbone of the Association. Nearly half its members were London compositors—2,200 out of 5,418 in December 1846. Edinburgh (580), Glasgow (353), Dublin (about 400), and Liverpool (320) accounted for another 1,653 members. The remainder were scattered among 69 branches, 54 of which had less than 30 members each.

The Association's record for the first year of its existence was one of glorious success. The first half-yearly report showed a considerable surplus of receipts over expenditure in every district and a total balance in hand of over £900. The latter had increased by the end of the second half-year to nearly £2,000 and the report was full of self-congratulatory phrases. There were, however, ominous signs from Ireland, where heavy payments had been made to unemployed hands: expenditure there had exceeded receipts by over £150 and an appeal for assistance had been made to other districts.

It was the declared policy of the Association to diminish the number of strikes and it undoubtedly adopted a conciliatory, though firm, attitude. The various District Boards and the Executive kept a close control over the branches and sought to settle all disputes amicably—by deputation, negotiation, and mutual concession. Their policy was mainly defensive. Even when it proved impossible to achieve a settlement by peaceful diplomacy, the Executive would not sanction a strike without a reasonable chance of success and required detailed information as to the state of trade, number of unemployed, non-members, and apprentices before coming to a decision.

Despite such cautious moderation, however, many disputes occurred. In the first half-year twenty-six were submitted to the Executive, in the second twenty-five, apart from those decided by individual Boards. It seems that the members, buoyed up by exaggerated belief in the strength of the new Association and assured of strike allowances, may have adopted a more independent, even aggressive, attitude towards employers. Moreover, trade was booming and the labour market favourable. In nearly all the disputes the Association secured victory or satisfactory settlements.

The disputes arose from familiar causes. The majority were due to the employment of an 'illegal' number of apprentices. There were several instances of employers attempting to reduce wage rates and one or two of their refusal to make payment for 'over-hours'. The transfer of matter from one office to another and the refusal of journeymen to compose matter for 'unfair' houses were also sources of dispute. Apart from these questions, the Boards were mainly concerned with excluding 'foreigners', insisting on the seven years' apprenticeship, fining 'unfair characters', punishing those guilty of 'misconduct', approving local rules, and extending the organisation into unassociated towns. There is no evidence of the Association trying to raise wages.

John Backhouse viewed the Association's progress at the end of its first year with

> the highest gratification . . . The practicability of the Association has now been tested by experiment; and, notwithstanding the fears expressed by some, it has been found equal to its engagements in every point of view. Its strike-members, and those who have unfortunately been out of employment, have been supported . . . The utility of the institution, in maintaining fair wages, restricting the number of apprentices, settling disputes, awakening the lethargic . . . reforming the vicious . . . is admirably and forcibly set before you in the Reports . . . and the moral influence of the Association, by producing temperance and good order will not . . . be questioned; and thus every fair and honourable employer may rely . . . on having steady and attentive workmen.

The hope was expressed that the Association would 'not only ameliorate the present evils of the trade, but . . . elevate the professors of the noblest and most valuable art upon earth to that rank and to the enjoyment of that recompense to which their employment justly entitles them'.

These extravagant hopes were doomed to rapid disappointment.

Borne along on the crest of a trade 'boom', the Association had flourished. There had been few unemployed hands to support and contributions had flowed in steadily. The brisk demand for labour had enabled the Association to enforce its principles and there had been no strikes of any consequence. When the 'slump' came in the spring of 1846, however, the Association was soon hard hit and by the close of the year was in dire straits. The 'rot', as we have seen, began in Ireland in the autumn of 1845, as a result of the terrible potato famine. A similar dearth soon prevailed in England. In July 1846 it was reported that 'from a period of great activity we have descended to a time of almost unexampled slackness; and ... the present lamentable state of trade in London, and the various other large cities in the provinces, in Scotland, and in Ireland ... approximates closely to that which existed in 1841'.[80] The country was, in fact, passing through another of those periodic commercial, industrial, and financial crises, which brought such severe suffering among wage-earners. Unemployment rapidly increased and with depression came more numerous attempts by employers to reduce wages and introduce apprentice labour. Strikes resulted, bringing an increasingly heavy burden upon the Association funds and reviving the problem of 'rat' labour.

The effects were already visible in the third half-yearly report.[81] There was still a balance in hand of just over £2,112 but expenditure had begun to exceed income. Nearly £870 had been paid to unemployed members and over £515 to strike hands. Many societies had been forced to appeal for assistance. The number of disputes had increased: forty-six had been submitted to the Executive and many houses had been 'closed'. There were several demands for increased wages, but the Boards adopted an extremely cautious policy in view of the trade depression. Apprentice-restriction was the main cause of disputes and 'closed' offices.

A Delegate Meeting was held in London at the end of March 1846. Being just prior to the slump, it resounded with self-congratulatory speeches. Very few changes were made in the rules, 'as the present position of the Association testifies that we have done well hitherto'. The chief result was a set of restrictive apprentice regulations for each district. The question of 'a limitation of the hours of labour' was also discussed, but it was deemed 'prudential' not to take any action, though regulations were made regarding payment of overtime and Sunday work. Non-society men were offered entry on easy terms in an effort 'to bring within our ranks every member of the profession'. There was a further tightening-up of the unemployment-relief regulations: branches were to require 'proof that each claimant for the relief has made proper application for work'. There are several instances in the Midland Board's minutes of unemployed hands being ordered to move or be deprived of relief if there was no prospect of work in their own towns, but the Executive eventually decided that such men could only be required to move if employment was found for them. There seems to have been little labour direction by the Boards. Tramping practically disappeared in the first year or so of the Association's existence, but as soon as depression returned we find men 'on the road' again, searching for employment.

This meeting marks the apogee of the Association's fortunes. As depression decended in the following months, its position soon became critical. A growing number of unemployed had to be supported, disputes became more frequent, and scores of houses were 'closed', thereby increasing strike expenditure. Many local societies had to be assisted and the SE. and SW. Boards had to appeal for funds. In October, therefore, the Executive were forced to double the subscription for three months. Over £1,000 had been expended by the Association on unemployment relief in the previous quarter and strike payments were almost as heavy.

Strikes had everywhere failed. As soon as members were withdrawn, employers found many men ready and willing to take their places: 6s. per week could not prevent the out-of-work from 'ratting', while non-society men abounded. Many members, therefor, began to realise the futility of strikes 'in the present state of depression and of the Association's finances', advocating 'reason and argument ... with the employer in place of force'.[82] Expedients were also suggested for 'employing the unemployed' by providing 'more work', instead of strikes. Thus we get movements for co-operative production and abolition of the 'Taxes on Knowledge'.[83]

By the end of 1846 the Association was in a parlous condition. Income for the previous half-year, deducting branch balances, came to £3,372, while expenditure had been £4,507. Societies had forwarded only £592 to the District Boards and had been forced to claim therefrom £1,622, due to their heavy unemployment and strike payments—£1,996 and £1,261 respectively. The balance in the hands of the District Boards had consequently been reduced to £402 and the Executive were forced to continue the double subscription for a further period of three months. Ninety disputes had been brought before the Executive and numerous strikes had resulted, 'in which, through the unprincipled conduct of a number of men unconnected with us, we have not always been successful'. Members were warned that they must 'avoid and prevent strikes as much as possible' and fight only against 'flagrant instances of tyranny and injustice'.

There were ominous signs that employers had got the measure of the Association and realized its weakness. A Liverpool employer had proposed to give his men an increase 'if they would sign a document to disconnect themselves from the Association. If they refused to sign ... they were to consider themselves under a fortnight's notice.' The same thing happened in London, where the hands on the *Morning Post* were required 'to sign a document, annulling their present rights and privileges'. But far more serious than either of these was the situation in Edinburgh, 'unparalleled in the history of the profession, wherein thirty-eight employers ... the professed enemies of combination ... combined to overthrow the Association'. The dispute was caused mainly by the Edinburgh branch's attempts at apprentice-restriction. Friction had also arisen over certain of their working regulations, which the employers regarded as 'insolent interference' with the rights of management.[84] The outcome was that on 28 October 1846, at a meeting of Edinburgh master printers, thirty-eight subscribed their names to the following resolutions: '1. That no Journeyman shall be taken into employment who either leaves or threatens to leave his Employer on "strike". 2. That no Journeyman shall be taken into employment without producing a certificate from his last Employer. 3. That in all cases, Masters will prefer Non-Unionists to Unionists.'

It is obvious that the Edinburgh masters had decided to combine in an attempt to crush the 'insolent interference' and 'tyrannous dictation' of the Association. Their action was, in fact, 'an attack against the very existence of the Association itself'.[85] The masters, knowing the Association's financial straits, deliberately aimed at overwhelming it by throwing over 200 men on the strike funds. Their resolutions were met in January 1847 by counter resolutions from the Edinburgh journeymen, refusing to knuckle under and threatening a strike unless the obnoxious ultimatum was withdrawn; but these were rejected and on 6 February, therefore, battle began. Over 200 men came out, involving a strike expenditure of more than £100 per week. It appears that twelve of the thirty-eight employers eventually withdrew their names from the resolutions, while a few of the strike hands secured situations elsewhere, but in April 1874 there were still 150 on the strike-roll. Their places were rapidly filled by 'rats' from London and by apprentices.

The Association was soon, therefore, in serious financial difficulties. Members fully realized that defeat in Edinburgh would mean the end of the Association and great efforts were made in nearly every town to raise funds, by voluntary subscriptions, collections, special meetings, concerts, and appeals to other trades. The various District Boards repeatedly forwarded money to Edinburgh and made urgent appeals to branches for grants from their local funds. The double subscription was again continued for another three months at the end of March and an additional contribution of sixpence per week 'during the continuance of the Edinburgh Strike' was also imposed. This, however, amounting to a 'treble levy' and coming after repeated renewals of the double subscription, aroused widespread opposition and had to be discontinued.

Unemployment was still widespread and branches were constantly appealing for financial assistance. Many were unable to pay the full amount of unemployment and strike allowances. There were frequent reports of desertion and arrears of subscriptions, while a number of smaller societies collapsed. A deficiency of over £90 in the Midland District accounts, discovered on the death of the Treasurer, caused angry feelings and division among members in Liverpool and discredited the Association generally. Principle was having to give way to expediency in disputes and the Association made repeated surrenders; but still petty strikes were numerous, mostly over apprentices. In London it proved utterly impossible to enforce the restrictions and the SE. Board was authorised to suspend them whenever expedient. This decision was very distasteful, however, to the Midland Board, which considered apprentice-limitation 'the most important feature of the national compact', abandonment of which would 'open the floodgates of abuse ... to a ruinous extent'. There were constant recriminations between the various Boards, the Midland even threatening to secede from the Association when the Executive refused to close the *Liverpool Journal* office for non-payment of arrears. Similar ill-feeling and dissension prevailed among local societies, several threatening secession or refusing to forward contributions.

This distress, these failures and divisions, formed the background to the great Edinburgh dispute. Obviously the Association could not cope with its pecuniary liabilities. Voluntary subscriptions proved insufficient and in June 1847 the treble levy was again imposed, to 'continue until the termination of the Edinburgh strike'. It merely served, however, to increase the dissension and multiply desertions. The Association was consequently 'unable to implement its engagements to the strike hands', who therefore went back on the employers' terms. The Executive were forced to acquiesce and allow the Northern Board discretionary power to open the closed offices. The strike had ended in disastrous failure, after costing the Association about £2,000.

The 'Great Amalgamation' was now bankrupt and rapidly disintegrating, but a last attempt was made to save it by a Delegate Meeting held in Liverpool in August 1847, at which radical alterations were made in organisation and finance. The Office of General Corresponding Secretary was abolished, owing to the constant friction between him and the District Boards and dislike of the 'absolute and irresponsible power' which he tended to acquire. In future the District Boards would communicate directly with each other. Increased powers were also given to the Boards, whose functions were now taken over by the local committees in London, Liverpool, &c. The general tendency, in fact, was towards decentralisation, increased independence being granted to local societies. Subscriptions, it was also decided, were only to be raised in future by approval of the members, who were to be provided with more information about Executive action. Finally, to solve the financial crisis, it was decided to raise subscriptions and make drastic reductions in out-of-work and strike payments.

These reforms merely prolonged the existence of the Association for a few more months. Members refused to pay their subscriptions and societies to forward their contributions. Soon strike and out-of-work payments had to be suspended. Branches broke up or seceded from the Association. Hundreds of members deserted. The Association was riddled with dissension and recrimination. All faith in amalgamation departed. The final collapse came early in 1848, when the SE. Committee (London) proposed that the Association be dissolved, to which the Midlands Committee 'very reluctantly' agreed.

The chief cause of failure was, of course, the trade depression, though the Association might have survived this but for its weekly out-of-work and strike payments. National, geographical, and industrial differences had also contributed to the collapse. Feelings of local independence were still strong and the Amalgamation was regarded as unwieldy. Its collapse, therefore, resulted in a re-reversion to the *status quo*. The London Society of Compositors was re-established as a local society in 1848, the Northern Union as the Provincial Typographical Association in 1849, and the Scottish Typographical Association in 1852–5. Ireland was still in misery and chaos as a result of the famine, but the Dublin Society had reorganised itself and local societies in other towns managed to maintain a precarious existence.

V. SOCIAL AND POLITICAL ASPECTS OF TRADE UNIONISM IN THE
PRINTING INDUSTRY IN THE FIRST HALF OF THE NINETEENTH
CENTURY.

There are two main but opposing social characteristics of trade unionism among printers in this period. On the one hand, typographical societies still retained much of the exclusiveness of the craft gilds, small groups of skilled and well-paid artisans, separated from the 'masses' of manual workers. As such, they concerned themselves mainly with the regulation of their own craft and remained aloof from general Labour movements. On the other hand, as the printing industry developed and capitalist competition grew, as the old gild regulations decayed and the influx of apprentices broke down the barriers of exclusiveness, printers began to feel their interests at one with those of other workers whose customary standard of life was threatened by the same economic forces. Thus there is visible among them a growing solidarity with other sections of the 'proletariat'.

Typographical societies were, as we have seen, affected by the general movement towards 'Greater Unionism' in the late twenties and early thirties, as a result of which the Northern Union was established in 1830. But, while in favour of national unions of workers in particular trades, they held strictly aloof from the movement to establish a general trades' union—of the workers, that is, in all trades—with its strands of Owenite idealism, militant aggression, and direct-action syndicalism. When, for example, the Manchester Typographical Society received a letter from the committee of the 'National Association for the Protection of Labour', the general trades' union organised in 1829–30 by John Doherty, it decided 'that the subject be considered this day six months', and there is no further mention of the matter.[86] Similarly they declined to join the 'Society for National Regeneration', organised in 1833 by Owen, Fielden, and Doherty for the achievement, among other things, of a general eight-hour day, regarding its objects as 'impracticable'.[87] Typographical societies also appear to have held aloof from Owen's 'Grand National Consolidated Trades' Union' in 1833–4, condemning its violent and revolutionary tendencies: though they sympathised with the workers fighting against capital exploitation, their attitude was one of critical superiority.[88]

When, however, they felt their interests seriously threatened in common with those of other organised workmen, they would join in combined resistance. The famous trial of the five Glasgow

cotton spinners in 1837, for example, for conspiracy, violent intimidation, and murder, followed by the Parliamentary inquiry into
workmen's combinations,[89] brought printers into line with other
trade societies and roused a sense of solidarity, especially as unionism in the Irish printing trade was particularly involved. Delegates
were appointed to joint trades' committees and subscriptions raised
for the cotton spinners' defence.

After the Parliamentary inquiry fizzled out, however, typographical societies returned to their erstwhile isolationist policy. They
took no part, as we shall see, in the Chartist agitation of the
following years. Neither did they participate in the renewed
movement towards 'Greater Unionism' in the forties—the
'National Association of United Trades for the Protection of
Labour'. The National Typographical Association sent two delegates to the first conference of the 'United Trades' in London at
Easter 1845, but the new trades' union seems to have aroused no
enthusiasm among printers, at that time busy establishing their
own Amalgamation. It was decided, therefore, not to send a
delegate to the postponed conference on 28 July,[90] and when the
question of joining the United Trades' Association was raised
again, at the N.T.A. Delegate Meeting in the spring of 1846, it
was 'not recommended' by the Executive and was eventually rejected by an overwhelming majority of the members.[91]

The *Typographical Gazette* clearly expressed the attitude of
most printers towards amalgamation with the United Trades'
Association. Such action, it was considered, might lead to the
collapse of their own Association, which had taken so many
years to build up. It had been difficult enough getting the various
typographical societies to unite. How, then, could an amalgamation
of so many diverse trades be formed? The idea was utterly impracticable. It would also lead to an outburst of strikes. Moreover,
how could the 'United Trades' decide what was a fair price for
printing? By joining that Association printers might have their
wages reduced to the general level.

It is clear that, despite the moderate aims and prudent administration of the United Trades' Association, as compared with the
'Grand National' of 1834 and the Chartism of 1838–42, printers
still regarded attempts at 'general union' as violent and revolutionary, of doubtful legality and 'savouring of a political character'.
Workmen, it was considered, should confine themselves to
organising their own trades, using moderation and justice in
dealings with employers instead of aggressive coercion. At the
same time, they should be ever ready to help others in resisting
oppression. Typographical societies did, in fact, make numerous

grants to assist other trades in strikes against reduced wages, excess of apprentices, &c.—to builders, currieris, hatters, gold-beaters, boot and shoe makers, cotton spinners, carders, fustian cutters, small-ware weavers, miners, potters, and tin-plate workers, as well as to bookbinders and typefounders.[92] But they refused to sacrifice their independence to any 'general union' or federation.

Owenite schemes of co-operation and socialism, however, did attract some disciples among journeymen printers. George Mudie, a Scottish journalist and printer, who came to London in 1820, was editor of *The Economist* (1821–2), a weekly paper devoted to the propaganda of Owenite co-operation and denunciation of the capitalist system. He also organised among London journeymen printers an 'Economical and Co-operative Society' on Owenite lines, but it seems to have received no recognition from the London typographical societies and soon ended in failure.[93]

An effort to establish a co-operative printing office in London in 1834, by 'friends of the exchange-labour system', also failed.[94] Owenite ideas were taken up by such printers as Hetherington, Cleave, and Watson, but there is no indication that these men ever took any part in typographical trade unionism. By the time they had risen to play leading roles in working-class radical agitation they were employers with their own printing or publishing offices in London. As such, they and other Owenite leaders of the working classes came in for criticism from the London Union of Compositors regarding wages on the *Poor Man's Guardian, Crisis*, and *Pioneer*.[95] Typographical societies, however, as we shall see, strongly supported them in their campaign for liberty of the press and against the 'Taxes on Knowledge', and in their efforts to secure 'improvement' and 'enlightenment' of the working classes.

John F. Bray, another of the early English Socialists, who effected in his *Labour's Wrongs and Labour's Remedy* (1838–9) a synthesis of Owenite teachings and the anti-capitalist writings of such as Thomas Hodgskin, was a journeyman printer. During the 'thirties and early 'forties he worked in several provincial towns, mostly in Leeds, and appears to have been a member of the Northern Union.[96]

Bray was a typical self-taught working man, roused by the propaganda of such as Owen and Hodgskin. There were among journeymen printers many such 'well-informed men, who, independent of their ordinary avocation as compositors, are conversant in social and political economy, in the arts and sciences, in language',[97] as evidenced by some of the articles in their trade periodicals. But only a small minority, it would appear, imbibed the Owenite gospel. Journeymen printers were eminently practical in their trade organisations and critical, therefore, of the Utopian air about Owenite Socialism. Yet though they rejected the schemes of community building and social revolution, many typographical societies were attracted by the ideas of co-operative production and working-class 'improvement'.

The efforts at co-operative production in 1820–1 and 1834 had not been supported by the typographical societies. In 1846, however, when the N.T.A. was collapsing amid widespread unemployment and strikes, many similar schemes were advocated in the *Typographical Gazette*, as a means of 'employing the unemployed' and an alternative to useless expenditure on strikes and out-of-work benefit. The outcome of these various proposals for 'co-operative printing offices', journeymen joint-stock 'typographical companies', a 'National Printing Office', or 'National Press', was the establishment in London of the *People's Newspaper*, a weekly newspaper, the first number of which appeared on 30 May 1847.[98]

About twenty strike hands and fifteen out-of-work members were employed on this paper. Unfortunately, however, 'the discontinuance of the London trade subscriptions, which were absolutely necessary for the continuance of the paper, rendered it impossible to proceed beyond the fifth number, and it was most reluctantly abandoned', after incurring a net loss of about £100. It was taken over by a typographical joint-stock company, which, however, was only able to survive by receiving 'the loan of the strike hands of the Association upon credit'. The Delegate Meeting in August therefore decided to drop it. It had never received much support from the provinces, where many members objected to the appropriation of Association funds, intended solely for trade-union purposes, to the establishment of a newspaper, 'thereby bringing the employed into competition with the employer'.

Typographical societies were strongly influenced by the various movements for 'improvement of the moral and social condition of the working classes'. They deplored 'the instability and ignorance' of the masses and disapproved of violence, preferring 'moderation' and 'reason' and advocating the education and 'enlightenment' of the people.[99] Among the objects outlined in one of the many plans for reorganisation of printers' unions in the early 'forties, it was hoped 'to improve the physical and moral condition of the members ... to discourage intemperance and immorality; to create a desire for, and a love of the practice of virtue; and thus to secure union, intelligence, and happiness'.[100] For similar ends, 'Typographical Mutual Improvement Societies' were established in the 'forties, like that at Newcastle-on-Tyne which included among its objects 'the mutual improvement of the profession generally' and 'the training of youth', and which aimed 'to promote a better knowledge of all matters appertaining to the trade, and to cultivate the moral, intellectual, and social wellbeing of all parties connected with it'. Lectures were given and a library was established.[101] A 'Reading and News Room and Library' were also established in Manchester in 1849, 'where unemployed members of the Society may find an agreeable retreat during leisure hours, and thus be drawn from the temptation of the tavern, and also the members generally may be enabled, after business hours, to assemble in a rational and desirable manner'.[102]

This 'improving' tendency—the movement towards discussion societies, reading-rooms, and libraries—was closely linked with the temperance movement of the time. There are a number of articles in the trade periodicals denouncing the evils of drink, particularly those connected with society meetings in public houses, which were both expensive and degrading.

That the evils depicted were not overdrawn is proved by the Manchester minutes and reports, with their evidence of drunken and disorderly behaviour and of the expense involved by ale at monthly meetings. In 1843, however, the society ceased to meet in a public house and rented a 'Meeting Room': beer was no longer an item of expenditure. Several other large societies also removed from the 'pot-house' in this period.

Throughout these years typographical societies maintained a definite non-political attitude, or at any rate an attitude of non-interference in party politics. There was, as yet, no distinct 'Labour Party' in the country: workmen might differ in their political views, and the introduction of politics into a trade society would therefore create division and conflict. Moreover, most working men were excluded from the franchise, while both major political parties were aristocratic in composition and outlook, so that political action seemed rather futile. Workmen placed more trust in their trade unions than in party politics, which were felt to be unconnected with trade affairs.

The Union was, in theory at any rate, a democratic organisation, in which every member had a vote. It enacted industrial laws and provided social securities. Most journeymen, therefore, looked to the Union, not Parliament, for protection and support. The State had abandoned the policy of industrial regulation for *laissez-faire*. Hence it was felt that 'to expect any interference on the part of the Legislature is futile'.[103]

Denunciations of class legislation by a property-owning, capitalist Parliament are scattered throughout trade-union periodicals and reports in this period. 'Our legislators', it was declared, 'are wrong in not doing right to all. ... They protect some, and leave us unprotected. What have we to do, then, but protect ourselves?'[104] 'All trade societies are the results of that combination of property and influence which ... governs the councils of the land—that legislative combination which, by directing its whole designs to the protection of capital, has left the working man no other resources but to combine for his own preservation.'[105]

Obviously journeymen printers felt the existing political system to be unjust and even oppressive. As individuals they were, no doubt, greatly interested in current political questions and resented exclusion from parliamentary representation. The *Compositors' Chronicle* stated that it excluded politics from its columns 'not because we consider them unworthy of regard—for we think every working man should be a politician'. The growing liberalism of government was chiefly due to the fact that 'working men think more and know more of the policy of the rulers'.[106] But from the prudential motives which we have already mentioned—the variety of political views and danger of internal conflict, the supposed non-connexion of politics and trade affairs, and also the violent and revolutionary air about working-class political movements in this period—typographical societies steered carefully clear of politics.

They appear to have played little part in the political agitation of the years 1830–2 to secure the passing of the Great Reform Bill. Neither did they participate in the Chartist Movement of 1838–42, the violent working-class protest against social oppression, which aimed to secure political power for the masses. It is probable that they regarded the movement as futile and doomed to failure, though many no doubt approved of the Chartist aims. They were also strongly opposed to its revolutionary character and advocacy of 'physical force'. Their general attitude approached closely to that of William Lovett, who, as a London cabinet-maker, also belonged to the class of skilled artisans. This is visible not only in their advocacy of 'moral force' as opposed to 'physical', but also in their desire for the education and 'enlightenment' of the working classes.

Obviously the Chartist movement—with its violent talk and violent mobs of oppressed and degraded workers, with its tendency to 'physical force' and its loud-mouthed and scheming mob orators—could have little attraction for the more educated, skilled, and aristocratic sections of the working class, including printers. There are, in fact, very few references to Chartism in the literature of typographical societies. In a brief allusion in December 1841 the *Compositors' Chronicle* expressed its opinion as to the 'futility' of Chartist attempts at alteration of the political system: 'We expect to see the mummery of 1838 renewed with the same negative result.' The editor considered it imprudent, however, to make further comment, since 'it is never desirable to damp the efforts of those who are labouring in a good cause'.

His forecast was correct, for the following summer saw strikes and 'plug plots' all end in failure and imprisonment. From these violent movements printers' unions stood aloof. It was stated in October 1842 that they could not be 'identified with the recent outbreaks which have characterised the actions of some trades' societies', that they had not been seized by 'the prevailing mania'. There had not been 'a single instance wherein a letterpress printer has either forfeited his liberty, or undergone an examination before any magistrate, for engaging in the recent tumults'. Printers were concerned solely with 'the maintenance of those generally recognised principles affecting the trade' and had 'no political aim or object in view, nor the slightest approximation to partisanship of the like nature'.[107]

It is quite certain that printers had little love for Feargus O'Connor, the Chartist demagogue. As owner of the *Northern Star,* O'Connor was, in fact, denounced as an 'unfair' employer.[108] When the paper was printed in Leeds the workmen had frequently to complain of 'irregularity in the payment of wages', and when it was tranferred to London an excess of apprentices was employed —on a paper which advocated the claims of labour!

It is probable, however, that although typographical societies steered clear of Chartism on account of its revolutionary character and demagogy, they approved of its political aims. As we have seen, they undoubtedly shared the Chartist resentment against exclusion from political representation, against landed wealth, capitalist oppression, and class legislation. The Corn Laws were regarded as an obvious example of the latter. Typographical societies strongly supported the Anti-Corn Law League against 'landlords' monopoly'. The Manchester Society, for example, resolved unanimously in February 1839 to 'petition Parliament for a total and immediate repeal of the Corn Laws'.[109] *The Compositors' Chronicle* contained all the stock arguments of the abolitionists and urged members of the trade to strive 'by every legal and constitutional means' to get rid of the Corn Laws, so as to secure cheaper bread for the working classes, increase trade, and provide more employment.[110]

Typographical societies were not, however, consistent in their application of 'free trade' ideas. Their interests were as narrow and selfish as those of the classes they denounced. Their trade policy was monopolistic and protective: their exclusion of 'foreigners', restriction of apprentices, and regulation of wages and hours were undoubtedly opposed to the principle of *laissez-faire*. They only desired 'free trade' in so far as it would benefit themselves. They demanded the removal of all duties on articles of consumption such as corn, meat, and tea, but desired the maintenance of protection for British manufacturers, particularly printing. They asked for abolition of the duty on paper, but sought to maintain that on foreign books.

The repeal of the newspaper stamp, paper, and advertisement duties and removal of restrictions on the size of newspapers would, it was hoped, cause a great expansion of the printing industry, increased employment, and higher wages. Typographical societies therefore made constant efforts to secure abolition of these obnoxious 'Taxes on Knowledge'. They repeated the arguments of those who wished to obtain cheap literature, education, and 'enlightenment' for the working classes. 'The labouring millions ought to be considered. By giving them a cheap press, you do that for their minds, which, in giving them a cheap loaf, you do for their bellies.'[111] Their real motives, however, were not 'improving' and educational, but self-interested and economic: to secure 'more work', 'employment for the unemployed', and higher wages.

In their political agitation, typographical societies adhered strictly to 'legal and constitutional means', seeking to gain their ends by steady perseverence in petitioning Parliament. There was nothing violent or subversive in their actions. Such political action as they took, moreover, was almost invariably dominated by practical, economic motives, connected with their own industrial welfare. Normally avoiding political intervention, they felt that on questions vitally affecting their particular interests and devoid of 'party' colour they had a right to make their voices heard. This is illustrated not only by their agitation against the 'Taxes on Knowledge', but also by their opposition to the various Bills introduced by Talfourd in the late 'thirties and early 'forties to extend the period of copyright, which, they protested, would check 'the diffusion of knowledge' and reduce employment in the printing trade. Typographical societies throughout the country therefore petitioned against the Bills. They were even more alarmed, in common with other trade unions, by the Masters and Servants Bill of 1844, which threatened to increase the existing legal and judicial oppression of workmen. The *Printer* strongly denounced the Bill and called on all journeymen to petition Parliament against it. Their efforts doubtless helped to defeat these measures.

Typographical societies seem to have suffered very little from legal or judicial oppression after the repeal of the Combination Laws in 1824–5. Quite frequently, in fact, they themselves appealed to the law, with success, against their employers, particularly to secure enforcement of the customary fortnight's notice or wages on dismissal from a 'regular' situation. The fact that they almost invariably restricted themselves to 'moral force' in pursuance of their aims and that the threat of a fortnight's notice was their only weapon rarely brought them under cognisance of the law. Moreover, despite many petty strikes, good relations existed on the whole between employers and employed.

NOTES

1. Howe, E., and Waite, H. E., *The London Society of Compositors* (1948), p. 26.
2. The outcome was the famous 'Interlocutor' of the Court of Session in 1805. The papers are in the Goldsmiths' Library, London University.
3. Place MSS. Add. 27,799. Extracts are given in Howe, E., *The London Compositor*, p. 251.
4. Dickson, J. J., *Manchester Typographical Society Centenary: A Souvenir* (Manchester, 1897).
5. *Compositors' Chronicle*, No. 23, June, 1842.
6. See below, pp. 90–124.
7. In 1832 the Secretary received £2 and the Treasurer 16s. annually.
8. See above, p. 83.
9. *The London Scale of Prices* (1836) provides the above information regarding Leeds and York.
10. *Compositors' Chronicle*, No. 12, Aug. 1841.
11. See below, p. 122.
12. *Compositors' Chronicle*, No. 26, Sept. 1842.
13. London, Liverpool, Manchester, and Dublin appear to have been the only societies with unemployment relief funds in 1844. (Report on the N.T.A., 10 Sept. 1844, in L.S.C. Trade Reports, 1830–47.)
14. Select Committee on Combinations, Second Report (1838). Evidence by Messrs. T. Daly, H. Courtney, and M. Ryan, pp. 96–109.
15. See *The Typographical Association*, p. 326.
16. Webb, S. and B., *op. cit.*, p. 77.
17. *Ibid.*, p. 84.
18. *An Account of the Rise and Progress of the Dispute between the Masters and Journeymen Printers exemplified in the Trial at large, with Remarks Thereon*, 1799. (Pamphlet in the Goldsmiths' Library, London University.) See also Webb, S. and B., *op. cit.*, p. 78, and Howell, G., *Conflicts of Capital and Labour* (1890), p. 91.
19. Place MSS. 27,798. *The Times*, 9 Nov. 1810. Webb, S. and B., *op. cit.*, p. 78.
20. This account of the origin of the Northern Union is drawn from the Manchester T.S. Minutes, the *Compositors' Chronicle*, no. 12, Aug. 1841, and no. 32, Mar. 1843, the *Typographical Gazette*, no. 1, April 1846, and the *Typographical Circular*, Feb. 1877.

21. Manchester T.S. Minutes. Members had to pay much higher *local* subscriptions, e.g. in Manchester, 1s. 6d. per month.
22. N.U. Half-Yearly Reports. By the early 'forties the Union included the following towns: Birmingham, Blackburn, Bolton, Bradford, Cardiff, Cheltenham, Chester, Chesterfield, Derby, Doncaster, Durham, Gloucester, Halifax, Hereford, Huddersfield, Hull, Isle of Man, Kendal, Kidderminster, Kirkby Lonsdale, Lancaster, Leamington, Leeds, Leicester, Liverpool, Macclesfield, Manchester, Merthyr Tydfil, Monmouth, Northampton, Nottingham, Potteries and Newcastle-under-Lyme, Preston, Sheffield, Shrewsbury, South Shields, Stafford, Sunderland, Wakefield, Warwick, Wigan, Wolverhampton, Worcester, and York. In addition, small towns were often included in the jurisdiction of larger ones, e.g. Rochdale and Stockport in that of Manchester.
23. *Printer*, no. 8, June 1844. The Twelfth Annual Report of the Northern Union gave the number of non-members in the branches as 275.
24. Report on the N.T.A., 10 Sept. 1844, in L.S.C. Trade Reports, 1830–47.
25. After 1838 an additional penny was required for the Tramp Relief Reimbursement Fund. See below, p. 106.
26. Some of the larger societies also had their own strike funds. See below, pp. 104–5.
27. *Printer*, no. 6, April 1844.
28. *Typographical Circular*, Feb. 1877, quoting from an 'Address' issued by the N.U. Delegate Meeting in June 1836.
29. *Compositors' Chronicle*, no. 23, June 1842.
30. N.U. Tenth Annual Report (1840).
31. *Compositors' Chronicle*, no. 12, Aug. 1841.
32. N.U. Tenth Annual Report (1840).
33. L.U.C. Annual Report, April 1842.
34. *Typographical Gazette*, no. 2, May 1846.
35. See, for example, *Typographical Gazette*, nos. 2 and 5 (May and Aug.), 1846.
36. *Compositors' Chronicle*, no. 10, June 1841.
37. To prevent this, the Northern Union established a rule that a fortnight's notice of such changes must be given.
38. Manchester T.S. Minutes, 21 Oct. 1834.
39. Reprinted in the *Compositors' Chronicle*, no. 1, Sept. 1840.
40. N.T.A. Second Half-Yearly Report, Dec. 1845.
41. *Compositors' Chronicle*, no. 23, 20 June 1842.
42. 'Address of the Delegates to their Fellow Brethren in the U.K.', reprinted in the *Compositors' Chronicle*, no. 2, Oct. 1840.
43. N.U. Eleventh Annual Report (1841).
44. N.U. Twelfth Annual Report (1842).
45. *Compositors' Chronicle*, no. 23, 20 June 1842.
46. Manchester T.S. Minutes, Aug. 1839.
47. *Ibid.*, 9 June, 1847.
48. P.M.M.T.S. Report, 4 Nov. 1898.
49. *Compositors' Chronicle*, no. 19, Mar. 1842.
50. *Printer*, no. 13, Nov. 1844.
51. N.T.A. Midland Board Minutes, 1 June 1847.
52. *Oxford Herald*, 6 July 1843.
53. 'Address' issued by N.U. Delegate Meeting in 1840, reprinted in *Compositors' Chronicle*, no. 2, Oct. 1840.
54. N.U. Rules (1840).

55. N.U. Seventh Annual Report (1837).
56. N.U. Eleventh Annual Report (1841).
57. N.U. Rules (1840).
58. *Compositors' Chronicle*, no. 14, Oct. 1841.
59. *Ibid.*, no. 3, Nov. 1840.
60. *Ibid.*, nos. 14, 15, and 16, Oct.–Dec. 1841.
61. N.U. Eleventh Annual Report, 1841.
62. *Compositors' Chronicle*, no. 22, June 1842.
63. *Ibid.*, no. 23, 20 June 1842.
64. *Compositors' Chronicle*, nos. 30, 31, and 34 (Jan., Feb., and May), 1843.
65. *Printer*, no. 8, June 1844.
66. *Ibid.*, no. 10, Aug. 1844. The rules of the Association are also to be found in the L.S.C. Trade Reports, 1830–47.
67. *Ibid.*, no. 11, Sept. 1844.
68. i.e., only half that suggested by Houghton and Backhouse. When, therefore, 'slump' came in 1846 the subscriptions had to be doubled and even trebled.
69. See L.U.C. Annual Report, 1839, and N.U. Annual Report, 1840, for the failure of an attempt by Bristol and Bath to establish a 'Western Union'.
70. Midland Board Minutes, 18 Feb. 1845.
71. L.U.C. 'Report ... on the Proposed N.T.A.', 10 Sept. 1844.
72. *The Times*, 16 Nov. 1846.
73. *Typographical Gazette*, no. 10, Dec. 1846.
74. *Printer*, no. 12, Oct. 1844.
75. *Ibid.*, no. 13, Nov. 1844. See also the L.U.C. 'Report ... on the Proposed N.T.A.', 10 Sept. 1844.
76. *Ibid.*, no. 14, Jan. 1845.
77. See the N.T.A. Half-Yearly Reports.
78. (i) *SE. District:* Aylesbury, Brighton, Cambridge, Hertford, Lewes, London, Oxford, Thames Ditton, Woking (2,417 members). (ii) *SW. District:* Bath, Birmingham, Brecon, Bristol, Cardiff, Cheltenham, Hereford, Leamington and Warwick, Newport, Stafford, Wolverhampton, Worcester (301 members). (iii) *Midland District:* Blackburn, Bolton, Bradford, Carlisle, Chester, Derby, Doncaster, Durham, Halifax, Huddersfield, Hull, Isle of Man, Kendal, Lancaster, Leeds, Leicester, Liverpool, Macclesfield, Manchester, Newcastle, Nottingham, Preston, Sheffield, South Shields, Wakefield, York (949 members). (iv) *Western District:* Armagh, Belfast, Carlow, Clonmel, Cork, Derry, Dublin, Galway, Kilkenny, Limerick, Nenagh, Newry, Omagh, Waterford, Wexford (687 members). (v) *Northern District:* Aberdeen, Dingwall, Dumfries, Dundee, Edinburgh, Glasgow, Kilmarnock, Perth, Stirling, Stranraer (1,064 members).
79. A branch of the Association was eventually established in Manchester, but failed to attract more than about a quarter or a third of the old Society's members.
80. *Typographical Gazette*, no. 5, July 1846.
81. Of which there is a financial summary in the *Typographical Gazette*, no. 9, Nov. 1846.
82. *Ibid.*, nos. 8 and 9 (Oct. and Nov.), 1846.
83. See below, pp. 128 and 132.
84. *The Times*, 16 Nov. 1846. An account of the origins and progress of this dispute is given in the *Typographical Gazette*.

85. *Typographical Gazette*, no. 15, April 1847.
86. Manchester T.S. Minutes, Jan. 1830.
87. *Ibid.*, Dec. 1833.
88. See the L.U.C. Annual Reports, 1834–6.
89. See Webb, S. and B., *op. cit.*, pp. 170–3.
90. N.T.A. First and Second Half-Yearly Reports (1845).
91. *Typographical Gazette*, no. 3, June 1846.
92. See the minutes and reports of the London and Manchester Societies and numerous references in the trade-union periodicals.
93. Beer, M., *History of British Socialism* (1919–20), vol. i, p. 205.
94. L.U.C. First Annual Report, Feb. 1835.
95. L.U.C. First Quarterly Report, July 1834. Cf. the attitude of printers' unions towards Feargus O'Connor, the Chartist leader and proprietor of the *Northern Star* (below, p. 131).
96. Jolliffe, M. F., 'John Francis Bray', *International Review for Social History*, vol. iv (1939), and 'Fresh Light on John Francis Bray', *Economic History* (*Economic Journal* Supplement), Feb. 1939. See also *Typographical Circular*, Jan. 1890.
97. *Typographical Gazette*, no. 5, Aug. 1846.
98. Printed report in L.S.C. Minutes, 19 Oct. 1847, and *Typographical Circular*, Mar. 1877.
99. See, for example, the L.U.C. Annual Reports, 1834–6.
100. *Printer*, no. 7, May 1844.
101. *Typographical Gazette*, no. 10, Dec. 1846.
102. Manchester T.S. 45th Half-Yearly Report, Dec. 1849.
103. *Compositors' Chronicle*, no. 1, Sept. 1840.
104. N.U. 'Address to the Printers of Wales', in the *Compositors' Chronicle*, no. 10, June 1841.
105. L.U.C. Fourth Annual Report, Mar. 1838.
106. *Compositors' Chronicle*, no. 13, Sept. 1841.
107. *Ibid.*, no. 27, Oct. 1842.
108. *Typographical Gazette*, nos. 3 and 4 (June and July), 1846.
109. Manchester T.S. Minutes, Feb. 1839.
110. *Compositors' Chronicle*, nos. 13 and 14 (Sept. and Oct.), 1841.
111. *Typographical Gazette*, no. 14, Mar. 1847.

Chapter 6

THE LONDON SOCIETY OF MASTER LETTER-FOUNDERS, 1793–1820*

The history of trade unionism is very fully documented and has been the subject of intensive study, and the activities and policies of present-day trade unions are under constant scrutiny. In contrast, far less attention has been paid to the development, organisation and objectives of employers' associations. Yet these have existed for as long as trade unions, and their policies have been equally as sectional and as much 'in restraint of trade', in restricting output, regulating prices, etc., as those of trade unions. They have generally escaped public scrutiny, however, and have not, like trade unions, been subject to parliamentary enquiry or judicial proceedings, until the fairly recent measures against monopolies. Their activities have usually been shrouded in secrecy and historians have not been able to discover or secure access to surviving records to anything like the same extent as for trade unions.

Nevertheless, in some industries a good deal of information has been unearthed about employers' organisations. It is an interesting coincidence that the printing and allied trades, like the printing trade unions, have proved one of the richest sources for such studies.[1] And the present writer has been able to place alongside his account of early typographical trade unionism a revealing investigation into early combination among master letter-founders, or type-founders, in the late eighteenth and early nineteenth centuries.

T H I S chapter is based mainly on a manuscript volume, previously known but little utilised, containing the minutes of a Society or Association of Master Letter-Founders which existed in London during the years 1793–1820.[2] Letter- or type-founding was still, in this period, a highly skilled handicraft, little changed since the early days of printing. It had, however, become a specialised trade, distinct from printing, so that printers, instead of making their own

---

* This chapter originally appeared as an article in *The Library* (Transactions of the Bibliographical Society), June 1955, except for the two introductory paragraphs.

types, as at first, bought them from typefounders. It included, in fact, several specialised processes: the cutting of the steel punches, the formation and justification of the matrices, the casting of the type, and the finishing processes of breaking-off, rubbing, setting-up, and dressing.

The number of persons employed in each foundry was quite small, probably not more than a dozen even in the largest. The capital value, on the other hand, was fairly high: William Caslon sold his third share in the Chiswell Street Foundry in 1792 for £3,000,[3] and when Robert Thorne was thinking of retiring in 1817–1818 he asked £8,000 for his business, though this figure was regarded as 'very high' by the Society of Letter-Founders, 'so much so indeed' that they would not make an alternative offer.[4]

Letter-founding was a jealously guarded 'art and mystery' from which outsiders were generally excluded. Punch-cutting especially had always been a highly secret craft, 'Kept so conceal'd among the Artificers of it,' says Moxon in his *Mechanick Exercises* (1683), 'that I cannot learn any one hath taught it any other; But every one that has used it, Learnt it of his own Genuine Inclination.' It was usually handed on from father to son, but workmen and apprentices employed in the foundry sometimes succeeded in discovering the secret methods of their masters. The earlier English letter-founders came mostly from metal trades requiring similar skills: Joseph Moxon (1627–c. 1690), for example, was originally a mathematical instrument maker, William Caslon I (1692–1766) had been an engraver of gun-locks and barrels, and John Baskerville (1706–75) was in the japanning trade. Until the later eighteenth century the master letter-founders usually designed and cut their own punches, but by this period, owing to increasing demand, they were employing punch-cutters as well as casters, rubbers, and dressers.

English letter-founding had risen to high standards of excellence under the Caslons, Baskerville, and others in the eighteenth century, and this country had not only ceased to be dependent for type and matrices on imports from Holland and France, but was even exporting them to the Continent. The number of typefounding firms, however, was surprisingly small. Throughout most of the seventeenth century they were restricted to four, by Star Chamber decrees and by the Licensing Act, and even after the latter's lapse in 1695 this figure was rarely exceeded: at the end of the eighteenth century there were not many more, and they were nearly all in London, where most of the printing in the country was done. The most famous letter-foundry was that established by William Caslon I in Chiswell Street. William Caslon II, who followed his father in the business, died in 1778, without a will, so his property was divided equally between his widow, Elizabeth, and his two sons, William and Henry. The chief superintendence of the foundry was in the hands of William Caslon III until 1792, when he sold his share in it to his mother and sister-in-law,[5] and set up on his own in another foundry. These two ladies carried on the business, but Mrs. Caslon senior died in 1795 and her will became the subject of some litigation, with the result that her estate was thrown into Chancery and the foundry had to be auctioned in March 1799. It was bought by Mrs. Henry Caslon, who that same year married Mr. Strong, a medical man, and soon afterwards took Mr. Nathaniel Catherwood into partnership. In 1809, however, both partners died and young Henry Caslon II assumed management of the business. He took John James Catherwood, brother of Nathaniel, as a partner in 1814, the partnership lasting until 1821.

William Caslon III, on relinquishing his share in the family business, bought another well-known London letter-foundry, that of Joseph Jackson (d. 1792), who had at one time been a workman in the Chiswell Street Foundry, but had established a business of his own in Dorset Street, Salisbury Square, Fleet Street. Caslon removed the foundry to Finsbury Square, but after becoming bankrupt in 1794 started up again in the old quarters in Dorset Street. About the year 1803 he took his son, another William, into partnership, and in 1807 he retired. William Caslon IV carried on the business until 1819, but then sold it to Blake, Garnett & Co., of Sheffield, to which town the entire stock was removed.

Another eminent London letter-foundry was that originally started in Bristol by Joseph Fry, who, among various other industrial enterprises, established the famous chocolate firm in that city. He and his partners, William Pine and Isaac Moore, sought to imitate in Bristol the example of Baskerville in Birmingham, but in 1768 they removed their foundry to London. In 1782, Pine and Moore having previously withdrawn from the business, Fry took his two sons, Edmund and Henry, into partnership, and that same year they purchased many of the punches and matrices, including most of the 'learned' and foreign ones, at the sale of James's foundry, 'the last of the old English foundries'. After the death of Joseph Fry in 1787 his eldest son, Dr. Edmund Fry, 'probably the most learned letter-founder of his day', took over and next year removed the business from Worship Street into a new foundry which gave its name to Type Street. Isaac Steele and George Knowles were taken into partnership in 1794 and 1799 respectively, but both these had apparently retired by 1816, when Dr. Fry resumed sole management. Soon afterwards he admitted his son,

Wendover Fry, into partnership. Their foundry adopted the name of the 'Polyglot Letter Foundry', on account of the wide range of type-founts, including many 'learned' and foreign ones, which they produced.

Vincent Figgins, another leading London letter-founder in this period, had originally been employed at Joseph Jackson's, where he served his apprenticeship. In the two or three years before Jackson's death in 1792 the management of the business had been almost entirely in his hands, but he lacked the necessary capital to buy it, and, as we have seen, it was purchased by William Caslon III. Helped, however, by John Nichols, the famous London printer and bibliographer, Figgins soon managed to build up a very successful foundry of his own—at first in Swan Yard, Holborn, then in West Street, Smithfield—which he carried on for many years.

Robert Thorne, already listed among the London letter-founders in 1785, in Barbican, became prominent after his purchase in 1794 of Thomas Cottrell's foundry,[6] also in Barbican. Thorne removed in 1808 to Fann Street, Aldersgate, where he carried on business until his death in 1820.

These were the most important of the London letter-foundries, but there were a number of lesser ones. Simon and Charles Stephenson had a foundry in Bream's Buildings, Chancery Lane, from 1789 to 1797. Louis Jean Pouchée, a Frenchman, started a foundry about 1810 in Great Wild Street, Lincoln's Inn Fields, at first in partnership with a man named Jennings. Richard Austin, a punch-cutter for the Stephensons and later for other foundries, established a foundry of his own in Worship Street, Finsbury, in about 1815. The rest were small, unimportant founders—Barton & Harvey, Brown, Lench (or Lynch), Heaphy, Simmons, Black, Moore, and McPhail—about most of whom little more is known than their names and addresses.

There were very few typefounders in the English provinces. After Baskerville's death (1775) there were none of any importance. Miles Swinney, printer and proprietor of the *Birmingham Chronicle* from 1771 to 1812, was also a letter-founder, but almost all provincial printers appear to have got their type from London. In the first quarter of the nineteenth century, however, three more provincial letter-foundries were established: that of Bower, Bacon, and Bower in Sheffield, started about 1810; that of Anthony Bessemer, at Charlton, near Hitchin, Hertfordshire, begun about the same time; and that of Blake, Garnett & Co., who bought William Caslon IV's foundry in 1819. These, said Hansard in 1825, 'complete the list of provincial letter-founders in England'.[7]

There were three more letter-foundries in Scotland. Until the early nineteenth century Messrs. Wilson & Co., of Glasgow, established in the 1740s by the great Alexander Wilson, 'the Father of Scotch letter-founders', as Hansard calls him, had a monopoly of the Scottish trade, but in 1807 William Miller, a foreman in their foundry, set up a rival establishment in Edinburgh, and his success, in its turn, raised up a competitor in the person of John Matthewson, who started another foundry in Edinburgh soon afterwards.[8] These Scottish letter-foundries became serious rivals to those in London, not only, as Hansard tells us (referring especially to Messrs. Wilson), because of the high quality of the type which they manufactured, but also because of 'the advantageous terms which, from the comparative cheapness of living, and the low rate of wages to journeymen in Scotland, they have been enabled to offer', so that 'most of the principal printers in London have been induced to supply themselves with a considerable portion of their chief working founts from this foundry; the letter being delivered and the old metal taken in return, without the least charge or expense on the score of carriage'.[9] Bower, Bacon, and Bower, of Sheffield, were also able to cut their prices below those in London.

This competition, as we shall see, was acutely felt by the London letter-founders, but, to judge from the various type-specimens and addresses to the printing trade issued in the later eighteenth century. there was also a good deal of competition among the London letter-founders themselves, and it was mainly to reduce this and to secure agreement on prices that the Society or Association of Letter-Founders was established. The first 'General Meeting of Letter-Founders' was held in the York Hotel, London, on 28 June 1793, soon after the outbreak of war with France, and was 'Convened for the purpose of taking into consideration the enormous increase of the Prices in the various Articles made use of in the Business of Type-Founding'. It was attended by Mrs. Caslon senior, Mrs. Henry Caslon, William Caslon, Dr. Edmund Fry, Simon Stephenson, and Vincent Figgins, that is, by all the important London letter-founders, but by none of the small ones. A letter was also read from Miles Swinney of Birmingham, 'approving of the object of this Meeting', and he was actually present at the second meeting; but that was his only attendance and, as we shall see, he soon broke away from the Society. No other provincial letter-founder joined it, so that it became a purely metropolitan body. It was usually called 'the Society of Letter-Founders', though occasionally it was referred to as 'the Association'.

The first meeting passed a number of resolutions with regard to advancing the prices of printing types, since 'for the reasons above stated without an increase is made ... it is impossible to pursue our Business without material Loss'. They therefore agreed on a list of prices ranging from 1s. 1d. per lb. for English and larger founts to 6s. 3d. per lb. for Pearl, ready money, and from 1s. 2d. to 6s. 9d. per lb. on 'running accounts' allowing one year's credit. Prices were also fixed for quotations and justifiers, two-line letters, space rules, script, music, space lines, and oriental types; flowers and blacks were to be charged the 'same as the Bodies they are cast upon', and £1. 18s. per cwt. was to be allowed 'for Old Metal in Exchange'. These prices, it was stated, 'appear to us to be as moderate as the present high Charges of Materials will admit so that a small and moderate Profit may attend our Labours and which Justice and Candour will allow when the fact is known that the addition to the prices of Printing Types does not by a considerable degree amount in an equal proportion to the advance of the Materials'. It was agreed, therefore, 'that we will not on any account charge less than the rates of Prices above set forth. But that at any time when there shall happen a sufficient reduction in the prices of the Articles of our Manufacture another Meeting shall be called to consider of an equitable and proportionate reduction in the List of Prices'. This list was to be printed, together with a circular note, and 'sent to all the Printers for their Information', with an intimation that the new prices were to come into effect on 1 July.

The London master printers, however, strongly opposed the increase in the prices of types and prolonged negotiations followed between the Society of Letter-Founders and 'the Committee of Printers'.[10] The next meeting of the Letter-Founders was held on 28 August 1793, 'in consequence of information that the late rise on Printing Types did not meet the entire approbation of the Trade'. They were 'desirous to accommodate themselves as far as in their power to the convenience of their Employers', the master printers,[11] and agreed to a revised list of prices, 'being an advance of only ten Per Cent. At the same time in order to exonerate themselves from any imputation of the late prices being exorbitant, they respectfully inform the Printers that the raw Materials of their Manufactures have risen upwards of Fifty Per Cent within the last Ten Years'. As a result of this revision, the prices of the various type founts now ranged from 1s. 1d. per lb. for English and larger to 6s. 7d. per lb. for Pearl, with similarly revised prices for quotations, two-line letters, space rules, script, music, space lines, and orientals. These were one year's credit terms; it was agreed that $7\frac{1}{2}$ per cent discount should be allowed for ready money. The allowance for 'old metal in exchange' was reduced to £1. 13s. 4d. per cwt.

This revision failed to satisfy the master printers, whose committee passed a unanimous resolution on 5 September 'that the proposed rise was not sufficiently justified by any ground of Argument stated by the Letter-Founders; and that if the rise be persisted in, it appears to them, that the Trade will be driven to the necessity of having recourse to the various other means in their Power, of supplying themselves with such Letters as they may have occasion for in future'. This resolution was forwarded on 28 September to the Letter-Founders' Society, who therefore held another meeting on 3 October to consider it. They decided to inform the master printers' committee that they were ready to 'attend' them at any time to justify the proposed increase. The master printers' committee at once expressed their willingness to receive a deputation and a special meeting was arranged on 15 October, to which the letter-founders sent Messrs. Caslon, Fry, and Stephenson as their representatives. The latter's arguments, however, failed to convince the master printers, who informed the Letter-Founders' Society in a letter dated 22 October 'that though the Letter-Founders must be the best Judges of the necessary Profits of their own Manufactures, what they have advanced does not satisfy the Committee that there is real ground for making a rise of Ten Per Cent'. This was reported to a meeting of the Society on 3 December. No resolution was passed, but it seems clear from later price-lists that the letter-founders persisted in charging the increased prices, despite the master printers' opposition.

Interest now shifted away from prices to the discount which should be allowed for ready-money purchases. It was proposed on 3 December 1793 by Dr. Fry, 'upon the suggestion of an eminent Printer', that the allowance should be raised from $7\frac{1}{2}$ to 10 per cent, but the unanimous opinion was 'that the present Discount afforded so moderate a Profit that it would be imprudent and materially injure us by any Alteration'. A similar proposal on 18 February 1794, this time by Mrs. Caslon senior, was also unanimously rejected. On 18 September 1794, however, a special meeting of the Society was summoned by Vincent Figgins, 'on Account of Mrs. Caslon having allowed £10 per Cent on the payment of a Bill contrary to the declared Agreement of this Society'. Faced with this charge, 'Mrs. Caslon said she would enquire into the fact— if true, it is contrary to the principles [upon which] she carrys on Trade and highly improper'. At the same time Dr. Fry again moved that the discount should be officially altered to 10 per cent, but, though he was seconded by William Caslon, the proposal was again rejected at an adjourned meeting on 3 October. Eventually, however, on 28 November 1794, after Vincent Figgins had been converted, the proposal was passed, despite the protests of Messrs. Stephenson, who pointed out that it had 'been seriously discussed on three previous Meetings and determined in the negative and no new Argument exhibited to occasion an alteration', a protest which was supported by Mrs. Caslon.

The next subject of discussion in the Society, at meetings on 18 and 22 December 1795 (over a year had elapsed since the last meeting), was the length of credit to be allowed to customers. The granting of more favoured terms of credit was, and still is, of course, 'an easy method by which the banished demon of competition could re-enter the house'.[12] Moreover, the extension of credit brought greater risks. It was therefore agreed 'that the Credit hitherto allowed to Printers be altered from 12 Months to 6 Months, Viz., That the Letter Founders' Bills be delivered at Midsummer and Christmas annually'.

At this same time the propriety of raising the price of Pica and English a halfpenny per pound was also considered, but 'it was held impolitic to make any advance at the present time altho' the small profit attending those Founts would fully justify the advance'. The Society also discussed less important matters, such as whether or not to give Christmas boxes in future, and whether or not to contribute to the printers' 'Weigh-Goose'.

The Society's meetings were held at first in the York Hotel, Bridge Street, and later in the New London Tavern, Cheapside. Its membership remained the same, except that the names of Charles Stephenson and Isaac Steele were added after they had become partners in the business of Simon Stephenson and Dr. Fry respectively. Miles Swinney, the Birmingham founder, had, as we have seen, been among the Society's original members. On 5 February 1796, however, Dr. Fry laid before the Society a printed list of reduced prices of printing types 'said to be the List of Mr. Swinney's prices and circulated by him', which were several pence per lb. below the Society's list. It was therefore decided that a letter should be written to Mr. Swinney reminding him of his signature to the Society's list and asking whether he was in fact going back on his bond: the Society was 'Very unwilling to suppose you would on any Account depart from it when so solemnly sanctioned', and therefore adjourned its meeting to give him an opportunity 'to do away the imputation that you are charged with'. The Society failed, however, to get a satisfactory answer from him. At a meeting on 10 June 1796, moreover, a letter was received from William Caslon informing the Society of his resignation.

These defections, especially Caslon's, together with the differences regarding discount, appear to have brought about the temporary suspension of the Association's trade activities, for there is a break in the minutes from that date until 26 December 1799. It is probable, however, that the members may have continued to meet socially from time to time and that the Society never actually broke up. When the minutes start again there is no reference to any sort of reconstitution. The meeting was attended by Mrs. Strong (formerly Mrs. H. Caslon), Nathaniel Catherwood, Vincent Figgins, and Dr. Fry. The first business was the admission to the Society of two new members, Nathaniel Catherwood, partner in the Caslon foundry in Chiswell Street, and George Knowles, in partnership with Fry & Steele. The decision of 22 December 1795 regarding six months' credit to customers was reconsidered, but, after being 'weightily discussed', was confirmed. A proposal was also made 'to raise the prices of Printing Types from Burgeois to English', but it was agreed 'that no such advance can at this time be made with propriety. Nevertheless, this Society agree to meet Mr. Wm. Caslon, at his request, on Saturday next, the 28th Inst., at the City Coffee house, to confer with him on the subject.'

At this meeting with Caslon, actually held on 2 January 1800, he agreed to rejoin the Society, in return, it appears, for their agreeing to an increase in the prices of certain founts.[13] The prices from English to Brevier would now range from 1s. 2d. to 3s. per lb. It was also decided 'to write to the house of Alex. Wilson & Sons at Glasgow, to know if they will increase their Prices to such a Rate, as will bring them so near to ours, as have [sic] hitherto been the Case'. Several other revisions of prices and trade practices were also made. It was agreed 'to allow 42/- Per Cwt. on Old Metal, weight for weight; and all above only 28/- Per Cwt'. And it was decided 'that in future, all Imperfections[14] shall be paid for on delivery; that no Discount be allowed under the Value of Two pounds; and only five Per Cent on Imperfections to any amount above that Sum'.

The letter to Messrs. Wilson & Sons,[15] dated 3 January, and their reply of 19 April 1800 are written in the minute-book. The Society, it appears, first approached Patrick Wilson, who was then in London, but was informed that 'as he had the least concern in the business, he could not say anything decisive on the subject'; but he did express the opinion 'that should a reasonable advance be made in the current Prices of Types at London ... it would soon induce an advance at the Glasgow Letter Foundry, of such a rate, as would bring their Prices fully as near to those at London, as had ever heretofore been the Case'. The London Society now asked in their letter if Messrs. Wilson would, in fact, do this. They considered that 'the enormous prices of Coals, the great advances on every sort of Iron Work, furnaces, &c, with the assessments on our Profits ... demand a rise'.

Andrew Wilson, however, though agreeing that there were good grounds for proposing an increase, considered 'that this is not the proper time to bring such a proposal before the Trade, because the printing Business is at present much cramped, by the long continuance of the War, and besides greatly injured and diminished by the late Rise on Paper.... Should you and the other Letter founders in London, however, agree to a rise, I think it highly probable that ere long, we should likewise make some addition to our present prices also.'

This letter was considered by the London Letter-Founders' Society at meetings early in May, when it was pointed out 'that the Price of Paper is falling, that Journeymen Printers are advanced in their Wages, and that the Printers are about to raise the Prices to their Employers [i.e. customers]'. In view of these and 'various other Considerations' it was decided that the proposed increase in the prices of printing types should take place.[16] This decision was communicated to Messrs. Wilson in a letter dated 14 May, but it was not until September, after two or three more letters, that Messrs. Wilson replied, stating that they would raise their prices 'at the latter end of the year'.

Meanwhile, the letter-founders' workmen—the casters, rubbers, and dressers—must have been feeling the effect of the war-time rise in the cost of living, and appear to have been agitating for increased wages, and perhaps even threatening to strike. On 1 May 1800, therefore, we find the master letter-founders taking joint action by agreeing 'that no servant be, in future, employed, unless he leave his last place, his work being finished, and clear of Debt'. On 5 May, however, they conceded a partial increase in piece-work prices for casting, deciding 'that the Price to Casters be raised to 9d. per thousand on English, Small Pica and Pica'.

This increase evidently failed to satisfy the workmen, for towards the end of the year we find the master letter-founders again discussing the question of wages. It was at first decided, on 10 December, 'that there does not seem sufficient reason to comply with the petition of the men at this time', but this decision was reversed on 22 December, when it was agreed 'to advance the Wages of casting Long Primer, Burgeois and Brevier to 8½d. per thousand; Dressers 2s. a week additional; and Rubbing to be a quarter of the Price of Casting'.

Another interesting agreement round about this time concerned the price of lead, the main raw material for letter-founding. It was decided at meetings in September and October 1800, 'that we give no more than 18s. Per Cwt. for Tea lead', presumably the lead foil used for lining tea chests. Various supplementary agreements were also made regarding the prices of type. On 8 April 1801, for example, it was decided 'in future to sell Blacks and Flowers at double the prices they have usually been sold for', a decision which was communicated to Messrs. Wilson of Glasgow, who replied that they would 'be likely to approve, and follow the example', when they would inform the London letter-founders. At the next meeting, on 6 May 1801, it was agreed 'in future to charge matrices to the Printers ten shillings each', and 'to allow 37/4 Per Cwt. for old metal in exchange; 24/- Per Cwt. for old metal not in exchange'. Agreements were also reached on 7 April 1803 in regard to the charging of 'imperfections' and 'mixed' founts.

Meanwhile the question of discount on cash purchases was again causing differences. On 10 December 1800 it was agreed, firstly, 'that no discount be allowed on Goods under the value of Two pounds'; secondly, 'that only five Per Cent be allowed on Accounts not exceeding Ten pounds'; thirdly, 'that only Seven and a half Per Cent be allowed on Accounts not exceeding Fifty Pounds'; and finally, 'that only Ten Per Cent be allowed on amounts exceeding Fifty pounds'. Then, on 6 May 1801, it was decided 'not to allow more than $7\frac{1}{2}$ Per Cent Discount for money on Goods to any amount', a return to the rate of 1793–4.

On 14 July 1802, however, William Caslon called a meeting at which he accused Dr. Fry of having 'offered to allow a Mr. Linwood, Merchant, Gt. St. Helen's, 10 Per Cent Disct. for money, instead of $7\frac{1}{2}$ according to our Agreement'. Linwood was said to have informed Caslon of this, stating that Dr. Fry, 'knowing him to be a customer of Mr. Caslon's, made this proposal to induce Mr. Linwood to deal with the Type Street [Fry's] foundery'. At a meeting on 21 July, however, Dr. Fry rejected this accusation, producing a supporting letter from Linwood, who had also made a verbal denial to other members of the Society, which therefore agreed that the charge was 'wholly unfounded'. The result was that 'Mr. Caslon desired his name might be erased from the Society which was immediately complied with'. His behaviour was considered 'highly censurable', and it was agreed that 'unless he make a suitable Apology he cannot be readmitted into our Society'.[17]

This, Caslon's second withdrawal, appears to have weakened the Society considerably again, and on 25 April 1803 it was decided 'to ask Mr. Thorne to join our association', no doubt with the idea of strengthening it, but there is no indication as to whether or not he did so at this time. The Society had, until this incident, been meeting more regularly. In its early years it met only to deal with particular questions as they arose, but on 9 July 1800 it was agreed that in future meetings should be 'held on the first Friday in every month, at 10 in the morning precisely, and any Gentleman who does not attend by 15 minutes after 10 by the house Clock, to forfeit 2/6'. This rule, however, later amended to the first Wednesday in every month, was not very closely observed, and often, when the Society did meet, there was no business to transact and the meetings were adjourned.[18] Then, at the end of 1802, came Caslon's second defection, which seems to have brought about another breakdown of the Society, for there are no minutes from 3 June 1803 to 18 December 1809.

The last business of any importance which the Society transacted was in regard to stereotype founding.[19] It was resolved on 7 April 1803 'that if any founder cast Type out of the usual way, for the purpose of Stereotype, it is materially injuring our trade: and Mr. Figgins is requested to take the matter into his Consideration, and to speak to Mr. Wilson'. The letter-founders obviously feared that the manufacture of stereotype plates would reduce the demand for movable types. Vincent Figgins complied with the Society's request and informed a meeting on 25 April 'that he would not receive any further orders from Mr. Wilson, to be cast out of the common way, without first consulting the Trade'. At the next meeting, however, on 3 June, it was agreed 'that the Resolution not to cast Types for the Manufacturers of Stereotype ... be rescinded', and that they should be at liberty to do so, 'but not to do anything towards the further improvement of that Manufactory, without a previous Communication to a meeting of this Society'.

The next meeting of the Society, according to the minutes, was not held until 18 December 1809, but again there is no indication of any reconstitution. By that date William Caslon III had retired and his son had joined the Society, while young Henry Caslon and Robert Thorne had also become members. The first business arose out of a letter 'received by each of the Founders from Mr. Didot containing proposals respecting the use of his Patent Machine'. This must have referred to the type-casting machine of Henri Didot, of the famous Paris typefounding, printing, and paper-manufacturing family, a machine which Hansard informs us was 'for casting type at the rate of 24,000 per hour'.[20] Here was another and more serious threat to the old handicraft methods of letter-founding, which, if successful, might well ruin many of the existing foundries. It was therefore 'unanimously resolved to reject his [Didot's] proposals, individually'.

A few years later, however, in 1815, the Society was again approached, this time by Léger Didot, younger brother of Henri, in regard to a similar type-casting machine. An extract from a printed paper describing this machine and its superiority over the traditional method of hand-casting is entered in the minute-book under the date 14 February 1815, together with a printed letter from T. Bensley, the well-known London printer, dated 17 November 1809, describing successful trials with type cast by the machine. The latter, it was claimed, was capable of producing 2,400 types an hour,[21] and would do the work of four hand-casters at half the cost. The machine was offered for sale to the Letter-Founders' Society, who were invited to inspect it. This they did, but they were not impressed and declined to negotiate on its purchase. The machine doubtless did suffer from practical defects, but the type-founders were strongly opposed to such inventions, which they continued to obstruct for many years.[22]

At its meeting in December 1809 the Society, in addition to considering Didot's letter, had decided to double the price of 'Superiors, Astronomical, Zodiacal, Algebraical, Geometrical, Mathematical, Physical and Genealogical Sorts'. There was no other business and the Society did not meet again until December 1810. It was then decided that meetings should be held quarterly, on the first Tuesday in March, June, September, and December, and that the office of Secretary (who was also to be Chairman) should be held for a year and served according to alphabetical order.

This meeting was occasioned by 'the great injury the Trade was sustaining from the Undersellers', William Caslon proposing, 'with a view of counteracting them', that there should be a revision of prices. A new scale was eventually agreed on: letter, spaces, and em and en quadrats would in future cost from 2s. 8d. per lb. for 6-line Pica and above, to 9s. per lb. for Pearl,[23] large quadrats to be about half this; prices were also fixed for space lines, quotations, and justifiers, space rules, Flowers, Blacks, Saxons, Greek, Arabic, Syriac, &c., and regulations were made in regard to the cost of accented letters; 9d. per lb. to be allowed 'for the overweight of old metal', and the same allowance to be made 'for old metal received in payment of accounts that are due'. It was also agreed to allow six months' credit on single orders and twelve months' on 'running accounts'.

This price revision, however, does not appear to have had much effect, for on 7 February 1812 a meeting was specially summoned 'for the purpose of taking into consideration the present state of the trade and to determine upon what steps it may be necessary to take in consequence of the Scotch and Sheffield founders sending specimens and offering types at low prices to the Printers'. The Scottish prices were from 3d. to 7d. per lb. below those recently fixed by the

London Society, while Sheffield types were from 2*d*. to 3*d*. per lb. lower still. It was therefore decided to send a letter to Messrs. Wilson & Sons of Glasgow, Messrs. Miller & Co. and Mr. Matthewson of Edinburgh, and Messrs. Bower & Co. of Sheffield. In this letter, entered in the minutes for 11–12 February, the London letter-founders complained of 'a considerable diminution in the demand for our types' in consequence of the lower prices charged by the Scottish and Sheffield foundries. They were 'well aware of the many advantages you enjoy in the manufacture of your types which our locality denies to us', but they were 'firmly resolved no longer to lose our trade by suffering ourselves to be undersold', and would, if necessary, reduce their prices to the level of their competitors'. But this they pointed out, 'must be greatly to the disadvantage of all', and they therefore suggested 'the propriety of your selling the types of your foundry at our prices, giving the same Credit and allowing the same Discount as we do'. They ended with this warning: 'Should you resolve not to sell at our prices, we ... shall sell at yours (even if you still lower them), but we leave to your consideration what loss and inconvenience must attend the ultimate settling of the Prices, at a rate which may be so highly injurious, as to render the Trade not worth carrying on.'

Answers were received from Alex. Wilson & Sons of Glasgow and Wm. Miller & Co. of Edinburgh, both dated 25 February. Miller & Co. pointed out that 'we are but new beginners and have ... to conform our prices to that [*sic*] of Messrs. Wilson of Glasgow. ... Were we to raise our prices higher than theirs ... all our customers would leave us. We have been often informed of late that they threaten to undersell us and also to give any length of Credit.' They could not, therefore, comply with the request of the London Society.

Messrs. Wilson & Co. pointed out that 'the difference between our prices and those at London are much the same as ever they were'. They considered that the dissatisfaction among the London printers was chiefly due to their 'being charged the same high prices for the types now that the regulus [antimony] has fallen from £400 to £200 per Ton. ... It surely would have been good policy in all the Letterfounders to have come forward at least a twelve Month ago, and proposed some reasonable reduction of the prices of Types,[24] this we expected would have been done, altho' we did not choose to take the lead in it.' Had the London prices been reduced, 'it would certainly have prevented some orders from being sent either to Sheffield or to us, and might have checked the *new* Foundry at London, which, if we are well informed, now sell 3*d*. per lb. below our prices. ...[25] Were we, as required by the [London] Society of Letterfounders, to sell at the same prices and to give the same Credit and Discount with them, we would ask them what inducement any Printer in London could have to apply for types to so distant a Foundry; he could have *none*; they therefore require of us to do what in justice to ourselves we can never do.... From our *situation* we must ... be under the absolute necessity of holding our prices somewhat under those of London.'

As regards the Society's threat of cut-throat competition, Messrs. Wilson pointed out that the London founders 'would lose more of their usual profits than they could ever gain, even altho' ... they abridged the sale of the few founts we used to send to London'. It was suggested that if the Society would only make their prices reasonable, 'things would go on as formerly, and ... they would have but little reason to complain of any other diminution of their business than what arose from the orders for types being divided among more Foundries than used to be at London, for surely the few we would then send would bear but a small proportion of those wanted for so extensive a market as London'.

This letter appears to have carried weight with the Society, for, after various proposals, they merely reduced the prices of the larger types, which now ranged from 2*s*. per lb. for 6-line and larger to 2*s*. 6*d*. per lb. for Great Primer, those smaller to be unaltered, 'except for founts of 1000 lbs. and upwards, which are to be charged at the Glasgow prices'; the allowance for old metal in exchange for the larger sizes to be 1*s*. per lb., for others 1*s*. 3*d*.[26]

One of the few items of interest in the Society's proceedings during the next three years, apart from Didot's type-casting machine, already mentioned, was the introduction by William Caslon junior of his patent 'Sanspareil' matrices for large letters, in place of the old sand moulds.[27] Vincent Figgins feared that 'these Types ... from their cheapness will be so generally used as almost to exclude Large Letters cast in the usual manner', but the Society decided that Caslon's invention would 'not do the trade the injury apprehended'.[28] The idea was, in fact, quickly adopted by the other type-founders. Of some interest, too, is an 'address' received in September 1813 from the journeymen 'requesting an advance in the prices paid to them', but the Society considered 'that the present state of the business will not admit of any advance being made'. Apart from these items, the minutes are mainly concerned during these years with minor matters, such as the allowance for old metal, the price of space lines, and the discount on the balance of accounts between members. Meetings were regularly held each quarter, with a few special ones as required, mostly in the 'Three Cups', Aldersgate Street.

Towards the end of 1815, the Napoleonic Wars being over and prices generally falling, the question of further reducing the prices of types became important. A proposal for a general reduction was considered at meetings in November and December, but rejected, as was a request from the Committee of London Master Printers shortly afterwards. In June 1816, however, after several further meetings, a new list of prices was agreed on, involving reductions of from 2*d*. to 6*d*. per lb. for the various founts, with similar reductions in the allowance for old metal. The regulations regarding twelve months' 'running credit' and $7\frac{1}{2}$ per cent. 'discount for ready money' remained unaltered.

Changes in the prices of types during the war and post-war years had not been uniform over all the founts. English, for example, which had been raised to 1*s*. 1*d*. per lb. in 1793, reached 3*s*. per lb. in 1810 and was now reduced to 2*s*. 8*d*. per lb. in 1816; whereas Pearl, 6*s*. 7*d*. per lb. in 1793, had only risen to 9*s*. per lb. in 1810 and was now 8*s*. 6*d*. per lb., i.e. the percentage changes had been much greater for the larger sizes.[29] This was because raw material costs were proportionately higher and labour costs lower per pound for the larger sizes, and raw material prices fluctuated much more than wages.[30]

The solidarity of the associated London typefounders is illustrated not only by their agreed policy on prices, wages, discounts, and credit, but also in other ways. Léger Didot, as we have seen, offered his type-casting machine in 1815 'to the purchase of this Society';[31] William Caslon senior in 1817 'made an offer to travel for the Society generally', to secure orders, though his offer was declined;[32] in 1818 the negotiations on the proposed sale of Robert Thorne's foundry were conducted by the Society;[33] and about the same time it was decided 'that every member of this Society do forthwith prepare a list of their customers as they consider unworthy of Credit'.[34]

The last three years in the minute-book, 1818–20, are mainly devoted to negotiations with the journeymen on wages and to the differences which they created among the Society's members. A special meeting summoned on 15 May 1818 to consider 'petitions from the men of some of the Foundries for a rise in wages', considered that it was 'not advisable to make any alteration in the present scale'. This decision was reversed at a meeting on 3 June, when a revised scale was agreed upon, but a further meeting on 8 June again decided against an increase. Another petition from the men in December was also rejected.[35]

The earlier agitation, it appears, had resulted in a strike at Dr. Fry's foundry which had been defeated by legal action, but Dr. Fry had not been generally supported by the other masters, and his proposal that the legal expenses incurred should 'be paid equally amongst the Letter Founders' received no support.[36] The result was Dr. Fry's resignation from the Society, with considerable bitterness, in December 1818, and soon afterwards he issued a list of prices several pence per pound below those of the Society.

Dr. Fry's defection was followed in 1819 by the withdrawal of William Caslon from the letter-founding business (his foundry being sold to Messrs. Blake, Garnett & Co. of Sheffield), and in 1820 Robert Thorne died, so that the Society's membership dwindled to two firms, those of Henry Caslon & Catherwood and Vincent Figgins. At the same time there was increasing competition from other London and provincial foundries. It was not long, therefore, before the Society ceased to exist, the minutes ending in June 1820 after lasting nearly thirty years.[37] That it lasted so long was due to the very favourable conditions for monopoly practices in letter-founding. A mere handful of firms were able to meet the existing demand for type, which, although essential to printing, accounted for only a small proportion of the total cost. Its price, therefore, was fairly amenable to manipulation.

NOTES

1. See M. Sessions, *The Federation of Master Printers, How It Began* (1950), and E. Howe, *The British Federation of Master Printers 1900–1950* (1950).
2. This volume was kindly loaned to me by Mr. and Mrs. A. Ehrman, of Clobb Copse, Beaulieu, Hants. It was previously in the possession of Stevens, Shanks & Son, the firm which succeeded that of Figgins, the old London letter-foundry established in 1792 by Vincent Figgins, who was a member of the Letter-Founders' Association. It is referred to in T. B. Reed, *A History of the Old English Letter Foundries* (ed. A. F. Johnson, 1952), pp. 110 and 246. Reed's work is, of course, the standard history of English typefounding, and my introductory account of the various firms of this period is based largely upon it.
3. T. C. Hansard, *Typographia* (1825), p. 352. The business appears to have depreciated considerably in the next few years, since afetr the death of Mrs. Caslon senior the whole foundry was purchased by Mrs. Henry Caslon in 1799 for £520; but this was doubtless because she and her young son already had a large share in the firm. See below, p. 139.
4. Minutes, 2 Jan. and 11 Mar. 1818.
5. Also called Elizabeth; his brother Henry had died in 1788, leaving an only son, Henry, aged two.
6. Cottrell had served his apprenticeship and been employed as a journeyman at the foundry of William Caslon I, but set up an independent foundry, at first in partnership with Joseph Jackson, in 1757. Thorne was a former apprentice of Cottrell's.
7. *Typographia*, p. 361.

8. There is some doubt as to when Matthewson began founding in Edinburgh. The above account follows Hansard, but William Chambers, *Memoir of Robert Chambers* (1872), p. 157, states that Matthewson started in the 1770s and that 'he set up the business of letter-founding in Edinburgh, which he had all to himself until the commencement of establishments with higher claims to taste in execution'.

9. *Op. cit.*, pp. 361–2.

10. The London master printers were also organised into an association at this time which not only negotiated with the Letter-Founders' Society about the price of type, but also with the journeymen compositors and pressmen with regard to wages, hours, and apprentices. See *The London Scale of Prices* (1836); E. Howe, *The London Society of Compositors* (1948), pp. 26–30 and 42–83; and M. Sessions, *The Federation of Master Printers: How it Began* (1950), pp. 205–14. Neither Mr. Howe nor Miss Sessions, however, mentions the interesting information about the early organisation of the London Master Printers which is to be found in the evidence before (1) the Select Committee on Artizans and Machinery, 1824, and (2) the Royal Commission on Trade Unions, 1868. Giving evidence before the former, Richard Taylor, a London master printer, stated that 'in my trade, the masters have always been in the habit of meeting together ... to regulate the prices [of piece-work]; and, by conferring with the men, to maintain a scale of prices which should produce an uniformity of payment ... whenever an alteration has been made, either to advance or reduce, it has been done by a combination or conference among the masters'. There had been several such conferences between 1785 and 1816. (Parliamentary Paper, Reports from Committees, 1824, vol. v, pp. 52–6.)

   Similar evidence was given before the Royal Commission on Trade Unions in 1868 by George Levey, master printer, who stated that before the establishment (1855) of the existing Master Printers' Association 'there were previous temporary associations'. There had been for many years 'a sort of committee of masters, that were appointed on each special occasion when the men required ... an increase of wages.... On all those occasions a few of the leading masters of London constituted themselves into a sort of committee in order to meet and confer with committees similarly appointed by the journeymen.' A more regular association was formed in 1836, but lapsed temporarily in 1849, to be re-established again in 1855. (Royal Commission on Trade Unions, 1868, Tenth Report and Minutes of Evidence, p. 83, QQ. 19,481–8.)

11. By 'employers' they obviously meant what we would nowadays call customers.

12. T. S. Ashton, *Iron and Steel in the Industrial Revolution* (1951), p. 182.

13. There had been no increase since that in 1793.

14. These were supplements or additional letters to a fount, which, being cast at a later date, were apt to differ from the original. See Hansard, *op. cit.*, pp. 393–4.

15. Andrew Wilson, son of Alexander, was head of the business, in which his sons Alexander and Patrick were partners.

16. The Society agreed on 9 July 1800 to increase the prices of printing types 'for exportation' by an average of about 10 per cent. above these new home prices.

17. Minutes, 3 Nov. 1802.

18. The meetings were held in various London coffee houses, especially

the Guildhall, and in the Antwerp Tavern, Threadneedle Street. The Society's membership remained unaltered: Mrs. Strong (previously Mrs. H. Caslon), Catherwood, Caslon, Figgins, Fry, Steele, and Knowles.

19. Stereotype was first introduced into this country by William Ged, a goldsmith of Edinburgh, in 1727, but was little used until after Earl Stanhope's invention of the plaster-of-Paris process about the year 1800.

20. Hansard, *op. cit.*, pp. 478–80. See also Reed, *op. cit.*, p. 355. A full account is given in the *London Journal of Arts and Sciences*, 1 May 1824. The output of a hand-caster was generally not more than 4,000 types per working day of twelve hours.

21. This was only one-tenth of the rate given by Hansard, but there is no possibility of typographical error, since the rate was also given as forty per minute.

22. See Reed, *op. cit.*, pp. 355, 306–1, and 367–9. Didot's invention was patented in England by the Frenchman Pouchée in 1823, but was eventually bought up by the founders and destroyed.

23. These prices were on average about double those fixed in 1800, so there had probably been several increases since then. There was apparently little, if any, reduction at this time, as Caslon had proposed.

24. As, in fact, William Caslon had proposed.

25. This was apparently a reference to the foundry recently established by the Frenchman Pouchée, which became known as the 'New Foundry'.

26. Minutes, 28 Apr. 1812.

27. See Reed, *op. cit.*, p. 321.

28. Minutes, 12 Jan. 1813.

29. These prices are for letter, spaces, and em and en quadrats, and do not include the variations in the prices of large quadrats, introduced in 1810.

30. The table of prices at the end of vol. ii. of Tooke's *History of Prices* includes those of lead and tin, two of the main raw materials of letter-founding. The price of lead (English, in pigs) fluctuated between £16 and £24 per fodder (19½ cwt.) in the years 1782–92. The outbreak of war does not appear to have affected the price, which remained fairly steady round about £21 per fodder down to 1800. It then rose sharply, however, reaching £41 in 1805, and remained high until the end of the war, though fluctuating between £27 10s. and £43 per fodder. After the war it fell rapidly to £18 per fodder in 1817, but then rose slightly to average about £23 in the next ten years.

The price of tin (English, in bars) was fairly steady round about £83 per cwt. in the years 1782–91, but in 1792 it rose to over £100, at which it remained until 1800, when it began to rise again, reaching £128 per cwt. in 1806 and £174 in 1810. It remained high, though fluctuating considerably, until the end of the war, after which it fell to an average of less than £80 per cwt. in 1819–20.

The close connexion between these changes in the prices of raw materials and those in the prices of type is clearly evident. Information about wages in typefounding for this period is very scanty, but it seems clear from the evidence in the Society's minutes that there were few alterations and that wages changed much less than raw material prices.

31. Minutes, 14 Feb. 1815.

32. *Ibid.*, 3 June 1817.

33. *Ibid.*, 2 Jan. and 11 Mar. 1818.

34. *Ibid.*, 11 Mar. 1818.

35. It is interesting to note the evidence given by Francis Place before the Select Committee on Artizans and Machinery in 1824, about the effect of employers' combination on wages in the typefounding trade. When asked his opinion of the effect of the Combination Laws 'as to the raising or lowering of wages', he answered: 'Generally, they have had little effect in that way.... In some *particular* trades [however], they have kept wages down too low; the typefounders, for instance. In this trade, the masters in London do not exceed ten, and a close combination at all times exists among them; and they have thus been able, by aid of the law, to keep wages very low.' (Select Committee on Artizans and Machinery, 1824: First Report and Minutes of Evidence, p. 45.)

36. Minutes, 2 Dec. 1818.

37. There is evidence, however, of its revival later on. James Figgins, for example, referred in 1873 to 'the association of type-founders which was formed in 1851, and which was dissolved in 1863' (*Journal of the Royal Society of Arts*, 21 Mar. 1873, article 'On Certain Improvements in the Manufacture of Printing Types', by J. R. Johnson, followed by report of discussion). See also *The Printers' Register*, Aug. 1868, supplement, article on 'Progress of Typography', and *The British and Colonial Printer*, 28 Apr. 1892, article on 'The "Associated Typefounders". An unsatisfactory retrospect.' These articles are mainly concerned with the letter-founders' continued opposition to the introduction of type-casting machinery.

Chapter 7

THE STRUGGLE FOR A FREE PRESS*

A F R E E press is regarded nowadays as one of the natural liberties of this country. We are apt to forget, however, how recently that freedom was achieved.[1] The early growth of printing and of the newspaper press, in the sixteenth and seventeenth centuries, was seriously restricted by fetters imposed upon it by Government and Parliament. Freedom to print was unthinkable under authoritarian royal government, with obvious dangers to the established political, religious, and social order, in a period when plots, riots and rebellions were by no means uncommon, when political and religious feelings often ran high, and when foreign dangers were ever-present. Printing, therefore, was shackled by licensing or censorship, by prosecutions for 'seditious libel', by the monopoly control of the Stationers' Company, by limiting the numbers of printers, presses, and apprentices, and by searches and seizures.[2]

The first English newspapers did not appear until the early seventeenth century, but the number of these 'news-books', 'corantos', 'diurnals', 'mercuries', and 'intelligencers' multiplied during the temporary relaxation of control in the Civil War. This freedom proved short-lived, however, for controls were soon re-established under the Commonwealth and Protectorate, and also after the Restoration, with the Licensing Act of 1662.

These restrictions were frequently evaded, however, and eventually, after the 'Glorious Revolution', the Licensing Act was allowed to lapse in 1695, the control on the number of printers and presses was ended, and the Stationers' monopoly disintegrated. In the following years printing expanded rapidly both in London and the provinces, until almost every town of any size had its printing

---

* This chapter, concerned with the eighteenth and nineteenth centuries, draws on my broader survey, ranging from the sixteenth to the twentieth century, 'Parliament and the Press', published in three parts in *Parliamentary Affairs* (Hansard Society), Vol. IX (1956), nos. 2, 3, and 4. It also utilises my article, 'Freeing the Press: the First Provincial Dailies', in the *Manchester Guardian*, 28 June 1955. I have also drawn on my researches into the printing industry and working-class history.

press and weekly newspaper, while the first dailies appeared in the metropolis.

Not surprisingly, therefore, it is commonly stated in history textbooks that freedom of the press in England dates from 1695. This, however, is very far from true: press freedom still remained very limited, mainly because of the continued operation of the law of criminal or seditious libel, with its principle that maintenance of public order and security necessitated suppression of any dangerous criticism of the established government or religion. Parliament and ministers were no more in favour of press freedom than kings had been; in fact, Parliament itself often took proceedings against offenders, especially for breach of parliamentary privilege by reporting of its debates or criticisms of its members.

Nevertheless, there was more freedom in the air, an 'itch of novelty', a desire 'to hear news and talk politicks',[3] which could not be suppressed. The metropolitan newspapers, especially the 'Grub Street' press, revelled in the political and religious controversies of Queen Anne's reign. There were constant complaints by the Government about the 'licentiousness' of the press, the 'false and scandalous libels', the 'seditious papers and factious rumours', the 'most horrid blasphemies against God and religion', which appeared in newspapers and pamphlets.[4] And there were many projected Bills for restraint of the press, since the existing law seemed incapable of preventing these 'abuses'. Parliament, however, was unwilling to restore anything like the old licensing system. Instead, it resorted to an indirect form of control, by 'the laying a great duty on all newspapers and pamphlets'. Thus was passed the Act of 1712 (10 Anne, cap. 19) imposing the first 'taxes on knowledge', as they were later called: a newspaper stamp tax of a halfpenny a half sheet and a penny a whole sheet (four folio pages), beyond which it was raised to the prohibitive rate of two shillings a sheet; a shilling duty on each newspaper advertisement; and an excise duty (in addition to customs duty) on paper varying from 4d. to 1s. 6d. per ream, according to quality.

These taxes, especially the newspaper stamp duty, struck a serious blow at the press, ruining many papers, restricting the establishment of others, and limiting the size and circulations of those which managed to survive. Their mark is branded on the front page of all newspapers, save illegal ones, for the next century and a half.

The burden of this taxation was increased in the following years. The halfpenny stamp tax and the advertisement duty were doubled in 1757, and the stamp tax was raised again, to three-halfpence, in 1776, while the paper duty was also repeatedly increased. Yet so great was the demand for news and advertising, as a result of party political controversy together with increasing trade and population, that, despite taxation, the number and circulation of newspapers continued to rise. By 1790 there were thirty-two in London, including fourteen dailies, and sixty in the English provinces (none of which, however, was a daily), while the total annual circulation, as shown by the stamp returns, nearly doubled between 1753 and 1790, from about seven and a half to fourteen millions. The average circulation of a weekly paper, however, was only a few hundred.

Taxation, by making newspaper publishing less profitable, made it more susceptible to political bribery and control. 'An eighteenth-century newspaper was not an independent organ of public opinion. Its sale was far too restricted to enable it to be entirely self-supporting.'[5] Government subsidisation became widespread and systematic in the early part of the century, leading to the creation of an 'official press', expressing the views of the Government and denouncing opposition. The Opposition, of course, also had its subsidised journals, but the party in power was able to avail itself of large official financial resources; moreover the Government could give its own papers free postal distribution throughout the country. Walpole's Government was particularly notorious for its bribery of the press, and there was a great scandal on his fall, but subsidisation continued, on a lesser scale, well into the nineteenth century.

Bribery, of course, was a great evil, but it was less evil than repressive legislation. It was a recognition, in fact, of the failure of directly repressive measures: Governments now resorted to more subtle, indirect means in order to secure popular support for their policies and to combat opposition. The law of seditious libel, however, still remained *in terrorem*, and there were repeated examples of its enforcement in the eighteenth century—warrants against suspected printers were often executed with great brutality,[6] premises being broken into and ransacked; not only were papers seized, but sometimes type as well; fines, pillory, and imprisonment continued to harass the press, although only one printer was put to death in the eighteenth century, unfortunate John Matthews, hanged for high treason in 1719; and even when prosecutions failed, arrest and imprisonment could cause great hardship.

On the other hand, there were long periods when the law was only sporadically enforced and a good deal of libellous printing went unscathed.[7] The eighteenth century witnessed the gradual development of party political controversy, in which newspapers (especially in London) figured prominently. There was nothing yet, of course, like a developed party system of government: politics was a fierce struggle between similar but rival aristocratic cliques for power, place, and perquisites. There was no such thing yet as 'His Majesty's Opposition': opposition to the King's government was still regarded as disloyal, fractious, and harmful, and was therefore to be suppressed. The party in power did not hesitate to use most dubious methods to secure its own continuance in office—bribery and corruption were one way, control of the press was another—while the party in opposition naturally sought to utilise the press against the party in power. On the other hand, both Whig and Tory parties were dominated by the landowning aristocracy and gentry, and politics was often merely a matter of the 'ins' and 'outs', or of 'court' versus 'country', between whom there were often no fundamental differences of principle; the Jacobite rebellions of '15 and '45 failed and both parties came to support the Revolutionary settlement and constitution—royal government limited by parliamentary control. More tolerance towards press criticism therefore developed.

At the same time, there was widening public interest in politics, which could not be suppressed, and which led to the breakdown of Parliament's prohibition of newspaper reporting.[8] This was got round at first by reports during the parliamentary recess, by such papers as Abel Boyers' *Political State of Great Britain* (from 1703), the *Gentleman's Magazine* and *London Magazine* (from 1732), but this was forbidden by the Commons in 1738. The growing feeling against prohibition, however, was voiced by Sir William Wyndham, leader of the opposition, who declared:

> I do not know but they [the electorate] may not have a right to know somewhat more of the proceedings of the House than what appears upon your votes; and if I were sure that sentiments of members were not misrepresented, I should be against our coming to any resolution that could deprive them of a knowledge that is so necessary for their being able to judge the merits of their representatives within doors.[9]

To do Parliament justice, it must be admitted that there was a great deal of misrepresentation, falsehood, personal abuse, and scurrilousness in the newspaper reports. But clearly the idea was developing of Parliamentary representatives being responsible to the electorate, and press reporting was an important factor in that development.

Prohibition of reporting, however, continued down to 1771, in which year the intrepid John Wilkes, in league with the parliamentary opposition, strong in the City government, and supported by many newspaper proprietors, launched a final and successful assault on parliamentary secrecy. Parliamentary reports began to appear quite openly in the London press, despite further prohibition by the Commons. The *Middlesex Journal*, at Wilkes' instigation, denounced the parliamentary rule as 'a scheme ... by the Ministry to prevent the public being informed of their iniquity'. The printers of this and other journals were arrested, but released by the City magistrates (including Wilkes), who imprisoned the Commons messenger for violation of the City franchises. The Commons replied by ordering the commitment of the Lord Mayor and another magistrate and by summoning Wilkes to the Bar of the House. Wilkes, however, steadfastly refused to appear, the imprisoned City magistrates were treated as heroes, the newspapers continued to print parliamentary reports, and the danger of popular rioting eventually forced the Government to recognise the impossibility of enforcing its prohibition. The rule was never officially rescinded, but henceforth reports were tacitly permitted, though the House continued to take action against misrepresentation or libellous attacks on its members. The Lords similarly gave way in 1775. From now on newspaper reporters were admitted into Parliament; their occupancy of the back row of the Strangers' Gallery was recognised in 1803, and a special press gallery was erected in 1831.[10] The significance of this victory was that Parliament, being now opened to public view and criticism, was forced increasingly to recognise its responsibility to the electorate.

John Wilkes had previously figured in another famous episode concerning press freedom. In the period down to 1760 Whig governments, securely entrenched in power, had shown considerable tolerance of press criticism. The opening years of George III's reign, however, witnessed a ferment in British politics, with the fall of the Whig oligarchy and the creation of Tory governments composed of the 'King's Friends', with first Lord Bute and then George Grenville as Prime Minister. Feeling was exacerbated by the conclusion of an unpopular peace with France in 1763. Opposition was strongly, even scurrilously, voiced in the press, the most outspoken being the *North Briton*, of which John Wilkes, M.P., was secretly owner and editor. The famous No. 45, of 23rd April 1763, contained such offensive criticism of the King's speech at the prorogation of Parliament that a general warrant was issued for the arrest of its unnamed 'authors, printers, and publishers', on a charge of seditious libel. Wilkes and many others were arrested, but challenged the powers of the Secretary of State in the Court of Common Pleas, which acquitted them and awarded damages, at the same time declaring general warrants, and warrants for search and seizure of papers, to be illegal. This was a triumph not only for the liberty of the subject, but also for greater freedom of political criticism in the press.

These trials, and the famous 'Junius' trials in 1770, also led to the assertion of the rights of juries to decide the criminality or otherwise of publications in libel cases, a principle which was finally conceded in Fox's Libel Act of 1792. This was important in that it now left public opinion (as represented by the jury) to decide what was criminal libel, and not the judges, who were apt to take a narrow legalistic view.[11] Chief Justice Holt had declared in 1704 that anything 'reflecting on the Government', or 'possessing the people with an ill opinion of the Government', was seditious libel.[12] Blackstone, in the 1760s, had defined 'the liberty of the press' simply as 'laying no previous restraints upon publications', by licensing, etc., but anyone publishing 'improper, mischievous, or illegal' matter—'any dangerous or offensive writings'—would be liable to prosecution under the law against criminal libel, which was 'necessary for the preservation of peace and good order, of government and religion, the only solid foundations of civil liberty'.[13] Lord Mansfield likewise stated, in 1783, that 'the liberty of the press consists in printing without any previous licence, subject to the consequences of the law'.[14]

The legal cases against Wilkes and others, however, backed by the rising tide of public opinion—though 'the mob' could so easily be manipulated—brought pressure to bear upon the courts and upon judicial interpretations of the law. Some eminent judges, such as Lords Camden and Erskine, were coming to hold more liberal opinions in regard to the freedom of the press. Lord Erskine, for example, defending Thomas Paine, prosecuted in 1792 for publication of the revolutionary *Rights of Man*, declared:[15]

> that every man, not intending to mislead, but seeking to enlighten others with what his own reason and conscience, however erroneously, have dictated to him as truth, may address himself to the universal reason of a whole nation, either upon the subject of government in general, or upon that of our own particular country:— that he may analyze the principles of its constitution,—point out its errors and defects,—examine and publish its corruptions,—warn his fellow-citizens against their ruinous consequences,—and exert his whole faculties in pointing out the most advantageous changes in establishments which he considers to be radically defective, or sliding from their object by abuse.

Paine was acquitted, but such an enlightened view was very far from being accepted by the Government, after the outbreak of the French Revolution in 1789, followed by the prolonged wars with France between 1793 and 1815. The middle and upper class Radicalism of Wilkes or the Earl of Richmond was one thing—and Pitt himself had become sympathetic to moderate parliamentary reform

—but that of Paine and other extremist Radicals, appealing to the masses, was quite another. Fears of Jacobinism and revolutionary outbreaks in this country, patriotic anti-French feeling, and the pressures of war led to the adoption of a more repressive policy by the Government, which sought to stifle all expression of radical or reforming opinion in public meetings, political associations, or newspapers. The Government not merely paid out larger subsidies to the 'official press', but sought to restrict the development of other newspapers by heavier taxation. The 'taxes on knowledge' were repeatedly increased, until in 1815 the stamp duty was 4d., the advertisement duty 3s. 6d., and the paper duty varied from 1½d. to 3d. per lb. At the same time Acts were passed in 1798–9 requiring, among other things, the registration of all printing presses, while increased penalties were imposed for printing, publishing, or even possessing unstamped papers. The Government's aim was to stamp out 'treasonable and seditious practices'. Thus there was a great increase in the number of prosecutions for criminal libel: in the two years following the outbreak of war with France in 1793 there were more such prosecutions than in the preceding twenty years. There was, in fact, a systematic attempt to destroy Radicalism, since it might cause subversive action among 'the lower orders'. The Government was able, moreover, to secure popular patriotic support in this policy: 'Church and King' mobs attacked the offices of reforming newspapers, such as Matthew Faulkner's *Manchester Herald*, which was destroyed by an 'anti-Jacobin' mob in 1793.

There is no doubt, however, that Radicalism was spreading among the working classes. Repression of the Radical press was accompanied by the Combination Laws of 1799–1800, suppressing trade unions. E. P. Thompson considers, in fact, that there was now developing a revolutionary combination of political radicalism and trade unionism, under the combined effects of the French Revolution, war, and the Industrial Revolution.[16] The evidence for such a direct link, and for the involvement of trade societies in political activity, is extremely thin: the great majority of trade societies, both now and later, appear to have confined themselves fairly strictly to trade affairs concerning wages, hours, apprentices, etc., and not to have meddled in politics. But there is no doubt that many working men, including trade unionists, if not trade societies as such, were becoming increasingly interested and active in politics.

This movement was largely suppressed or driven underground during the war, but revived in the later stages of the war and in the post-war years, after 1815. Wartime trade dislocations and post-war slump, combined with bad harvests, high food prices and the effects of industrialisation, produced a dangerously explosive situation. The country was convulsed in the distressed years 1815–20 by Radical agitation demanding political and social reform. The working classes became increasingly vocal and their discontent found expression in mass meetings and cheap, unstamped, Radical newspapers.

As a result of the increased stamp duty, raised to 4*d.* in 1815, the price of newspapers was pushed up to 6*d.* or 7*d.*, which, as was intended, put them quite beyond the means of the lower and lower-middle classes, except in coffee-houses, 'pubs', and reading rooms, and squashed popular papers out of existence. Only the upper-class press could survive, with very restricted circulations: at the beginning of the nineteenth century the leading London daily, the *Morning Post*, averaged only 4,500 copies a day, while the circulations of most provincial papers were numbered in hundreds rather than thousands. One or two provincial dailies did struggle into existence, but only briefly survived. The number of weeklies, however, continued to increase: by 1836 there were over seventy newspapers in London and nearly two hundred in the English provinces, while the total annual circulation in the United Kingdom had risen to nearly thirty-six millions.

Nevertheless, there is no doubt that taxation was having a restrictive effect. Forces were at work in the late eighteenth and early nineteenth centuries, which, but for repressive taxation, would probably have led to a much greater development of the newspaper press. Population was rapidly growing; education and literacy were spreading; the rapid expansion of trade and industry was increasing the demand for newspaper advertising; liberalism and radicalism were swelling the demand for political reform and arousing increasingly widespread interest among the middle and lower classes; while, at the same time, the invention of the steam-driven cylinder-printing machine and the improvements in transport were making for a rapid expansion of newspaper production and sales.[17] It was only to be expected, therefore, that the newspaper stamp, advertisement, and paper duties should be denounced as harmful fetters on the free expression of public opinion, as damaging to trade, and as 'taxes on knowledge'.

This outcry became part of the wider Radical agitation for political reform in the years after 1815, an agitation waged not only by means of political meetings and petitions, but also by unstamped pamphlets and newspapers, against a government which continued to maintain a reactionary, repressive policy. Cobbett gave the lead by legally evading the stamp duty, publishing his *Weekly Political*

Register (first started in 1802 and costing 1*s*. 0½*d*.) as an open sheet or pamphlet in 1816 at twopence a copy, at which price it was bought in tens of thousands by working-class readers. His famous 'twopenny trash' was quickly followed by other cheap pamphlets, such as Wooler's *Black Dwarf*, Hone's *Reformists' Register*, Wade's *Gorgon*, and Carlile's *Republican*, all attacking the existing social structure, clamouring for political reform, and even advocating violent revolution. Other more moderate, middle-class, Whig or Radical stamped papers also took up the cause of reform, like Cowdroy's *Manchester Gazette* and the *Manchester Observer*, and similar publications in other towns.

The answer by Government and local magistracy was a further spate of prosecutions for criminal libel against printers, publishers and sellers, and the passage of 'gagging' Acts in 1817 and 1819. Two of the infamous Six Acts in the latter year were intended to put down 'blasphemous and seditious libels' and 'to restrain the small publications which issue from the press in great numbers and at a low price', by bringing them within the definition of a newspaper and thus obliging them to pay stamp duty.

This legislation, together with numerous imprisonments, seems to have stunned the Radicals for a few years. Their newspapers, now having to be stamped, had to raise their price to sixpence, which either brought about their collapse or considerably reduced their circulations. Economic recovery in the 1820s also caused the reform movement to slacken off. Attempts on the part of Joseph Hume and a handful of other Radical M.P.s in 1825 and 1827 to secure repeal or reduction of the newspaper stamp and advertisement duties gained little support in the unreformed Parliament, though some slight concessions were obtained.

The tide of reform was rising, however, among the middle as well as the working classes. In Manchester, for example, according to Archibald Prentice, 'a small band' of middle-class reformers had begun to form from about 1812 onwards, and they found expression in the 'twenties in newly-founded reforming newspapers such as the *Manchester Guardian*, started in 1821, followed in 1828 by Prentice's *Manchester Times*. It was under growing public pressures that the ruling Tory party abandoned its policy of 'Eldonite reaction' in favour of 'Enlightenment' and introduced reforms of the tariff system and corn laws, the penal code, prisons, and metropolitan police, and finally emancipated Dissenters and Catholics from most of the disabilities under which they had so long suffered. Towards the end of 1830 petitions from Manchester calling for the repeal or reduction of the newspaper stamp duty were presented to Parliament by Lord Morpeth,

Edward Strutt, and others, who obtained a promise of amending legislation from the Duke of Wellington's Government. But the Tories fell from office soon afterwards.

On the question of parliamentary reform, the Tories had refused to move, and so, under the new Whig government, there began the great struggle over the Reform Bill. The fight for a free press was intimately related to this political Reform Movement: the press, despite its limited circulation, was the main instrument of mass propaganda in the hands of the reformers, who realised that a free press was indispensable to the free expression of public opinion and a more democratic form of government; and political reform, it was hoped, would lead to the removal of legal restraints on the freedom of the press, which had been imposed primarily to prevent 'seditious' political criticism of the old regime. Brougham declared that the press was 'the only organ of public opinion' capable of dictating to the Government, since 'none else can speak the sense of the people'.[18] The swelling tide of opinion in favour of a free press found expression in the writings of middle-class Radical philosophers like Jeremy Bentham, James Mill and John Stuart Mill, while Radical M.P.s such as Joseph Hume, Edward Lytton Bulwer, and J. A. Roebuck gave vigorous support to the movement in Parliament. This was a 'respectable' move-ment, emphasising the need for popular education, diffusion of knowledge, etc., and also using free-trade arguments for removal of fiscal restrictions. Among the working classes, at the same time, there was a growing realisation that a cheap press was the main channel for dissemination of radical, socialist, and trade-union ideas: from the late 1820s onwards, there was a huge increase in working-class periodicals, under the influence of the reform agitation, the Owenite co-operative movement, and the outburst in trade-union activity during these years.

The new Whig Government, however, though it quickly brought in a Reform Bill, disappointed the Radicals by failing to do any-thing about the 'taxes on knowledge'. The Whigs, in fact, as the agricultural labourers and trade unions soon discovered, were as harsh in their attitude towards 'the lower orders' as their Tory predecessors had been.

There was only one course of action, therefore, left open to the Radicals: to defy the law. And so began the great 'battle of the unstamped'.[19] Carlile and Cobbett were still active, bringing out the unstamped *Prompter* and *Twopenny Trash* towards the end of 1830, but the most outstanding figure in this campaign was Henry Hetherington, with his *Penny Papers for the People* and the *Poor Man's Guardian*, 'established, contrary to Law, to try the power of "Might" against "Right". Price 1*d*.'. 'Defiance is our only remedy', said Hetherington: only thus could they uphold 'this grand bulwark of all our rights, this key to all our liberties, the freedom of the press—the press, too, of the ignorant and the poor'. Other working-class Radicals who were prominent in the struggle —printing, publishing, or selling unstamped papers—included William Carpenter, James Watson, John Cleave, and William Lovett, future leaders of London Chartism. The 'battle of the unstamped' was, in fact, mainly a working-class struggle, with emphasis on political and social rights, deliberately defying the law and often revolutionary in tone, quite different from the middle-class parliamentary agitation. It was supported, however, by middle-class Radical booksellers such as Abel Heywood, of Manchester, who was imprisoned for selling unstamped publications.

The Whig Government, in fact, pursued just as repressive a policy as the Tories had done, trying to stop the flood of publications by prosecutions, fines and imprisonments. During the years 1819–30 there had been over 200 summary convictions for selling unstamped publications; in the next five years there were some 700.[20] But in vain: the law simply could not be enforced. The 'infamous unstamped' abounded everywhere, filled with reports of working-class political and trade-union activity and clamouring for reform. The passing of the Reform Bill did little to reduce their demands, especially those of the more extreme Radicals, who regarded it as a betrayal, since it merely enfranchised the 'mongrel aristocracy' of middle-class manufacturers, shopkeepers, etc., the 'millocracy' and others who were exploiting the workers. The upper- and middle-class newspapers did not, generally speaking, lend much support to the agitation against the 'taxes on knowledge', in fact most were opposed to abolition as being likely to flood the country with cheap, popular newspapers, which would not only compete with themselves but disseminate dangerous revolutionary ideas.

In Parliament, however, at the same time as the 'battle of the unstamped' was being waged, Radical M.P.s such as Edward Lytton Bulwer, J. A. Roebuck, Joseph Hume, and Daniel O'Connell were conducting a repeal campaign, aided from outside by Francis Place and George Birkbeck. Motions were brought before Parliament, backed by hundreds of petitions, demonstrating the harmful effects of the 'taxes on knowledge' in restricting trade, hampering popular education, and causing the propagation of illicit and revolutionary unstamped papers.

This agitation soon achieved substantial successes. First of all, in 1833, the Government reduced the advertisement duty from

3s. 6d. to 1s. 6d., and then, in 1836, in addition to reducing the paper duty to a uniform three-halfpence a pound, cut the newspaper stamp duty to a penny, with a halfpenny on advertising supplements. These successes, of course, were only partial, and the Radicals were not satisfied—resentment being strong against what Lord Brougham called 'the last, the worst, penny' of stamp duty which still remained—but there was little immediate prospect of achieving more, especially in view of the Government's budgetary difficulties in the subsequent trade depression. Moreover, reforming energies in the following years were absorbed in other, wider, and more exciting movements either for the People's Charter or for Corn Law Repeal. Agitation against the remaining 'taxes on knowledge', therefore, died down until the late 'forties.

Meanwhile, the Government gradually came to realise that prosecutions for criminal libel or for selling unstamped papers were neither effective nor politic, since they merely gave publicity and martyrdom to the victims and exacerbated prevailing discontent. The forces of freedom and public opinion could not be suppressed. So the 'prosecuting system' was allowed tacitly to lapse, though the law remained unchanged, except that Lord Campbell's Libel Act in 1843 entitled anyone criminally prosecuted for defamatory libel to plead the truth of the matter charged, if it was for the public benefit that it should be published. Judges eventually came to give a much more liberal interpretation to the law. In 1868, for example, liberty of the press was defined as 'complete freedom to write and publish, without censorship and without restriction, save such as is absolutely necessary for the preservation of society'.[21] Tolerance and freedom of expression also triumphed in the religious as well as in the political sphere, prosecutions for blasphemous libel becoming a thing of the past, while the remaining legislative disabilities imposed on non-conformists (Protestant, Catholic, and Jewish) were gradually removed and people were allowed to worship, or to be atheists, as they pleased. Political and religious persecution fell—as they had risen—together.

Meanwhile, the reductions in taxation of 1833 and 1836 had given a great stimulus to the growth of the newspaper press. According to *Mitchell's Newspaper Press Directory*, the number of newspapers published in the United Kingdom increased from 397 in 1836 to 563 in 1851, while the stamp tax returns show that the total circulation more than trebled. This was chiefly on account of the lowering of newspaper prices, which were now generally fourpence or fivepence, while some popular periodicals were selling for threepence and twopence, or even less, often by evading the stamp duty. Several leading provincial newspapers, including the *Manchester Guardian*, became bi-weeklies, but no daily newspaper was yet published in England outside London (though one or two were established in Dublin and Glasgow).

The 'forties saw the triumph, though not the completion, of Free Trade in Britain, culminating in the repeal of the Corn Laws —a triumph for those who believed in the removal of restrictive taxation. This victory naturally revived the demand for the abolition of the 'taxes on knowledge'. The demand was, in fact, strongly supported by the leading members of the 'Manchester School', Richard Cobden and John Bright. As Cobden declared in 1850,[22]

> So long as the penny [stamp duty] lasts, there can be no daily press for the middle or working class. Who below the rank of a merchant or a wholesale dealer can afford to take in a daily paper at fivepence? Clearly it is beyond the reach of the mechanic and the shopkeeper. The result is that the daily press is written for its customers—the aristocracy, the millionaires, and the clubs and news-rooms. The great public cannot have its organs of the daily press, because it cannot afford to pay for them. The dissenters have no organ for the same reason. The governing classes will resist the removal of the penny stamp, not on account of the loss of revenue—*that* is no obstacle with a surplus of two or three millions—but because they know that the stamp makes the daily papers the instrument and servant of oligarchy.

It is not surprising that, with sentiments such as these, Cobden and other middle-class Radical M.P.s should have joined in agitation on this issue with working-class Radicals and Chartists. Such an alliance had never been fully achieved against the Corn Laws, but it was against the 'taxes on knowledge'.[23] In 1849 a Newspaper Stamp Abolition Committee had been founded, including such veteran campaigners as Henry Hetherington and James Watson, in addition to John Dobson Collet (secretary), Richard Moore (chairman), G. J. Holyoake, and other Chartists, while Francis Place was treasurer. This mainly Chartist body was merged in 1851 into a wider Association for Promoting the Repeal of the Taxes on Knowledge, with T. Milner-Gibson, M.P., as president, Moore chairman, Collet secretary, and Place treasurer, and including on its committee such Radical M.P.s as Cobden, Bright, Hume, Scholefield, and Ewart. Most newspaper proprietors supported the Association against the advertisement and paper duties, abolition of which would obviously benefit existing journals, but not against the stamp duty, which protected them against cheap Radical competition.[24] The paper trade also joined in the campaign, and so did journeymen printers' trade societies.

The campaign against the 'taxes on knowledge' followed—not surprisingly in view of its leadership—the successful example of the Anti-Corn-Law League, organising mass propaganda by means of pamphlets, public meetings, petitions, and parliamentary motions. Its victory was inevitable, now that Free Trade had triumphed: successive Governments admitted the evil of the taxes, but could not abolish them wholesale because of the consequent loss of revenue. It was ten years, in fact, before the last of them was removed: first, in 1853, the advertisement and supplement duties; then, in 1855, the penny stamp; and finally, in 1861, the paper duty. At last the press was free!

The effect was immediate and striking: newspapers sprang up like mushrooms, dailies were established, and weeklies, bi-weeklies, and tri-weeklies multiplied. The total number in the United Kingdom grew rapidly from 563 (17 dailies) in 1851 to 1,294 (84 dailies) in 1867. The expansion was much less striking in London, however, than in the provinces. London already had a dozen or more well-established dailies; the only important new-comer was the Liberal *Daily Telegraph* in 1855, the first 'respect-able' newspaper to be produced for a penny. It was followed by several other penny dailies, but most proved short-lived; the only successful rival, in fact, was the Tory *Standard*, until the *Daily News* reduced its price.

In the provinces, on the other hand, new daily papers proli-ferated. In 1853 there was still not a single daily newspaper in England outside London, but in that and the following year, following repeal of the advertisement duty, and also with the excitement of the Crimean War and the first telegraphic news reporting, several were established, though not very successfully. In 1855 and the following years, after repeal of the stamp duty, daily newspapers sprang up in most provincial towns of any size. The most successful were old-established weeklies or bi-weeklies, like the *Manchester Guardian, Liverpool Daily Post, Leeds Mercury*, etc., but many entirely new ones were set up. By 1867 there were thirty-three in the English provinces, almost all morning papers; but from about that time onwards evening papers became increasingly numerous, so that by 1913 there were eighty-one, as against forty-two morning papers, in the provinces. A similar expansion occurred in Wales, Scotland, and Ireland.

Within a few years of stamp repeal, most daily newspapers reduced their prices to a penny. At the same time, they were able considerably to expand their reading and advertising space, the abolition of the advertisement duty resulting in a rapid growth of newspaper advertising. The consequent increase in their circulations and advertising revenue rendered them independent of political subsidies. In London, within twenty or thirty years, the *Daily News* and *Daily Telegraph*, with circulations up to 150–200,000, had surpassed *The Times*, while in the provinces the leading dailies had raised their circulations to 30–40,000.

They were not, however, papers for the masses, but catered mainly for the better-educated and more serious-minded of the middle and working classes. Liberal or Conservative in politics, they included nothing like the Radical working-class papers of the first half of the nineteenth century, which had fought the 'battle of the unstamped' and advocated revolutionary political and social reforms. The upper and middle classes, in fact, still controlled the press, as they did Parliament. And when dailies for the millions did come, from the end of the nineteenth century onwards—after the workers had been enfranchised and a national system of elementary education had been established—their owners became 'press lords' and these publications, with their catchy headlines, sensationalism, and trivialities, had little in common with those of Cobbett, Carlile, and Hetherington. But this, apparently, is what the masses wanted, and still want, as the fate of the *Daily Herald* and the success of the *Daily Mirror* have demonstrated.[25]

NOTES

1. In addition to the classic nineteenth-century histories of journalism by Andrews, Fox-Bourne, Grant, and Knight Hunt, the following books are suggested: A. Aspinall, *Politics and the Press, 1780–1850* (1949); C. D. Collet, *History of the Taxes on Knowledge* (1899); L. Hanson, *Government and the Press, 1695–1763* (1936); H. Herd, *The March of Journalism* (1951); S. Morison, *The English Newspaper, 1622–1932* (1932); F. S. Siebert, *Freedom of the Press in England, 1476–1776* (1952); W. H. Wickwar, *The Struggle for the Freedom of the Press, 1819–1832* (1928); for recent works by Hollis and Weiner, see below, p. 166, n. 19.

2. In addition to Siebert, *op. cit.*, see W. M. Clyde, *The Struggle for the Freedom of the Press from Caxton to Cromwell* (1934), and J. B. Williams, *History of English Journalism to the Foundation of the Gazette* (1908).

3. *British Mercury*, No. 369, 1712.

4. See, for example, the *Commons Journal*, Vol. XVII (1711–14), pp. 28, 31, and 251.

5. Aspinall, A., *Politics and the Press, 1780–1850* (1949), p. 66.

6. The Secretaries of State could issue special or general warrants for search and seizures, executed by the 'messengers of the press'; general warrants, as distinct from special, were made out against unnamed 'authors, printers, and publishers' of alleged libels, so that a large number of suspects could be arrested and examined in order to discover the real culprits, a practice particularly dangerous to 'the liberty of the subject'.

7. See G. A. Cranfield, *The Development of the Provincial Newspaper, 1700–1760* (1962).

8. The House of Commons first sanctioned official publication of its 'votes and proceedings' during the Exclusion Bill crisis of 1680–1, and this practice was continued after the 1688 Revolution, but reprints in newspapers were forbidden and no reporting of debates was allowed. The House of Lords would not even permit official publication of its votes. Transgressions of these bans entailed liability to punishment for breach of parliamentary privilege.

9. *Parliamentary History*, X, 802–3.

10. It was still possible, however, for either House to exclude 'strangers' and go into secret session, but this became very rare, especially after popular riots in 1810 caused by Parliamentary exclusion of the press during a committee on the unsuccessful naval expedition to Walcheren.

11. Previously it was for the judge to determine whether or not a publication was libellous; the province of the jury had been limited to determination of the facts as to authorship, publication, and meaning.

12. *14 State Trials*, 1128.

13. Blackstone, *Commentaries* (1769), IV, 151–2.

14. *21 State Trials*, 1040.

15. *22 State Trials*, 414.

16. E. P. Thompson, *The Making of the English Working Class* (rev. edn., 1968).

17. A. E. Musson, 'Newspaper Printing in the Industrial Revolution', *Econ. Hist. Rev.*, 2nd ser., Vol. X, no. 3, April 1958.

18. *Parliamentary Debates*, 3rd series, VIII, 268 (7 Oct. 1831).

19. Wickwar, W. H., *The Struggle for the Freedom of the Press, 1819–32* (1928). Recently two more intensive studies have appeared: P. Hollis, *The Pauper Press: A Study in Working-class Radicalism of the 1830s* (1970), and J. H. Weiner, *The War of the Unstamped: A History of the Movement to Repeal the British Newspaper Tax, 1830–1836* (1970). These have added a great amount of detailed information, but have not necessitated any modification of my general account.

20. Wickwar, *op. cit.*, p. 30.

21. Fitzgerald, J., in *R.* v *Sullivan* (11 Cox C.C. 49).

22. Morley, J., *The Life of Richard Cobden* (1881), Vol. II, p. 421.

23. There had, of course, been earlier collaboration during the 'battle of the unstamped'.

24. The *Manchester Guardian*, for example, as it became increasingly Whiggish, ceased to denounce the stamp duty. It considered the penny stamp reasonable, in view of the free postage that went with it, and regarded the outcry against the 'taxes on knowledge' as 'cant'. It was afraid that abolition might lower the character of the press and lead to the publication of 'mischievous opinions'.

25. On the modern press, see Musson, *Parliamentary Affairs*, Vol. IX (1956), No. 4. It may be pointed out, however, that sensationalism, crime, sex, and trivialities were also commonplace in eighteenth-century newspapers. See Cranfield, *op. cit.*, especially Chap. 4.

Chapter 8

THE IDEOLOGY OF EARLY CO-OPERATION IN LANCASHIRE AND CHESHIRE*

THIS year, 1958, marks the centenary of the death of Robert Owen, the father of Co-operation and Socialism in Britain.[1] It is fitting, therefore, that we, here in Manchester, should now look into the motives and ideas of the early co-operative movement in Lancashire, as it developed under his inspiration.[2] Lancashire has good claims to be regarded as the cradle of British Co-operation. It was in Manchester that Robert Owen began his career in cotton-spinning and so became acquainted with the evils of the early factory system and began to develop his ideas of social reform. It was in Manchester that the first Co-operative Congress met in 1831, and it was in Liverpool that the first Co-operative Wholesale Company was started that same year, a year which also witnessed, at Birkacre, near Chorley, the most ambitious attempt at co-operative production during the early Owenite period. Co-operative societies probably existed in greater profusion at that time in Lancashire than in any other part of the country, except perhaps in London and the neighbouring West Riding. Later on, in 1844, the Rochdale Pioneers revived Co-operation and in the 1860s the Co-operative Wholesale Society was founded in Manchester.

These later developments have been intensively studied and written about, but the earlier history of Co-operation in Lancashire, in the late 1820s and 1830s, has been largely neglected, though it contains some of the most interesting co-operative achievements of the period. No doubt London and Brighton did much to spread the co-operative gospel during these years, but it was in the industrial North that Co-operation found most vigorous and practical expression. It is significant that of the first seven Co-operative Congresses (1831–5) listed by Holyoake five were held in Lancashire and the West Riding.[3] There is a widespread tendency, however, to regard Lancashire co-operation as beginning in 1844 with the Rochdale Pioneers, whereas in fact there was little that was new

* From the *Lancashire and Cheshire Antiquarian Society's Transactions*, Vol. LXVIII (1958).

or pioneering about them: their society was merely a revival of the Owenite Co-operation of the earlier period. It is here that we must look for the roots of the movement.

Co-operation did not, of course, begin with Owen.[4] There had been co-operative corn-mills and trading companies in the late eighteenth century. Of these, there was at least one in Lancashire, a co-operative trading company established in Oldham in 1795, the main purpose of which was the bulk purchase of cheap foodstuffs.[5] There may have been other such societies, but there seems to be no surviving evidence of their existence. Co-operation in Lancashire, apart from isolated early experiments of this kind, was of later development, beginning in the 1820s under the inspiration of Robert Owen and other Socialist writers, such as William Thompson, John Gray, and J. M. Morgan.[6] Co-operative ideas were not, in fact, of native Lancashire growth, but were introduced from outside. There is abundant evidence in the literature of the period of how strongly influenced Lancashire co-operators were by Owenite ideas. They had clearly read many of the books and pamphlets produced by Owen and his followers: they had read such periodicals as the *Co-operative Magazine*, the *British Co-operator*, the *Free Press*, the *Associate*, and the other co-operative publications sent out from London in the late 1820s, especially by the London Society for the Promotion of Co-operative Knowledge, and they were also influenced by early provincial co-operative periodicals like the *Brighton Co-operator* and the *Birmingham Co-operative Herald*. They were visited in 1830 by the indefatigable William Pare, secretary of the First Birmingham Co-operative Society, and the first co-operative missionary, who lectured in most of the chief Lancashire towns.[7] About this time William Carson, another missionary, also originally from Birmingham, came to settle in Lancashire, where he soon became one of the leading figures in the co-operative movement.[8] Later on, Thomas Hirst, of Huddersfield, toured and lectured extensively in Lancashire and Cheshire,[9] and J. Whittaker came from London to lecture on labour exchanges.[10] Soon co-operative societies began to spring up all over the north-west, and active measures were taken by Lancashire and Cheshire co-operators themselves to spread the gospel even into the smallest towns and villages and to attract wider support from the working classes generally. They developed their own propagandist organs, such as the *Chester Co-operator* (1830), the *Lancashire Co-operator*, later the *Lancashire and Yorkshire Co-operator* (1831–2), and the Liverpool *Bee* (1832–3), while support was given to the co-operative cause in local trade-union periodicals such as the *United Trades' Co-operative Journal* (1830), the *Voice of the People* (1831), the *Poor Man's Advocate*, and the *Union Pilot and Co-operative Intelligencer* (1832). Manchester particularly was a centre from which co-operation was spread into the surrounding area by missionary lectures and printed literature, organised by the 'Manchester and Salford Association for the Promotion of Co-operative Knowledge', or, more shortly, the 'Manchester and Salford Co-operative Council', which originated in a central committee set up in April 1830,[11] and which established the *Lancashire Co-operator*.

Co-operation in Lancashire, as in other growing industrial areas, was a product of the prevailing economic and social circumstances. Steam-driven machinery was creating the factory system, destroying the old domestic industries and throwing thousands of hand-workers out of employment, while the bulk of the population was coming to live in rapidly-growing industrial towns. There has been considerable difference of opinion upon the social effects of this transition, as to whether it resulted in improvement or deterioration of working-class living standards; but whatever the facts may have been, there is little doubt as to what the mass of the people— or at any rate their articulate representatives—*thought* was happening. There was a strong feeling that the working classes—the 'useful', the 'industrious', the 'productive classes'—'the source of all wealth'—were being harshly exploited by their wealthy, profiteering, capitalist employers, under the system of commercial competition, which resulted in excessive hours of work, child labour, depressed wages, unemployment, slum housing, and all the concomitant evils of ignorance, drunkenness, and crime.

The co-operative and trade-union literature of Lancashire in this period is full of such ideas. Hundreds of quotations could be given, but a few must suffice to provide their flavour. 'Enormous wealth on the one side', the *United Trades' Co-operative Journal* pointed out, 'characterises the higher orders of society, deplorable poverty, and in thousands of instances positive and absolute want, on the other side, characterise the working orders of society.' The basic cause of the existing social evils was the 'erroneous arrangement of our domestic, social, and commercial affairs, by means of which machinery is made to compete with and against human labour, and of course to the detriment of the human labourer, instead of co-operating with him, and for him, to his advantage and comfort'.[12] 'There can be no wealth without labour,' the *Lancashire Co-operator* stated: 'the workman is the source of all wealth ... Who has raised all the food? The half-fed and impoverished labourer ... Who built all the houses, warehouses, and palaces, which are possessed by the rich, who never labour or produce any thing? The workman ... Who spins all the yarn and makes all the cloth? The spinner and the weaver ...' Yet the workers were hungry, ill-housed, and ill-clad: 'the labourer remains poor and destitute, while those who do not work are rich, and possess abundance to surfeiting'.[13] 'We can fairly trace that all the miseries which society suffers are mostly owing to the unfair distribution of wealth ...'[14] The rich were being made richer, the poor poorer. Machinery had forced down wages and caused labour redundancy: it had producd an abundance of cheap goods, but the poor could not buy them and so there was apparent over-production and unemployment. Here we have the germs of an under-consumption theory: 'we opine there is a large and overwhelming [potential] demand, but unfortunately those who want articles of clothing etc. with which our warehouses are crowded, possess not that necessary article called money wherewith to purchase them'.[15] The existing monetary system, in fact, was a fundamental part of capitalist exploitation: 'money is our enemy', it was stated, for it was the means whereby the present social inequalities had been created and were perpetuated, depriving the workers of the produce of their labour and giving great wealth to the idle capitalists.[16] 'The introduction of money into society was ... a deep-laid scheme of the drones to enable them to live in idleness.'[17] Production was regulated not by the needs of the people, but by money prices and profits.

These were not the only evils from which the workers suffered and of which co-operators bitterly complained. Merchants and shopkeepers joined with industrial employers in exploiting the wage-earners. All these made profits which were extracted from the produce of labour. The workers were swindled by the system of credit in 'badger' shops, by short weight and adulterated goods, and by the payment of wages in 'truck', i.e. in kind (food, clothing, etc., at inflated prices or of inferior quality), instead of in coin of the realm. The whole of society, in fact, in the view of co-operators, was corrupted by being based on the false principle of individualism, with its desire for private profit, selfish accumulation of property, and cut-throat competition.

Co-operation offered a remedy for all these evils. Men, so Owen pointed out, are creatures of circumstances: their characters are made for them and not by them. Since, therefore, individualist competition created all the ills of existing society, a social revolution, a 'New System of Society', was necessary. Co-operation, or Socialism, as the Owenite creed was later to be called, would substitute unity and brotherhood for selfishness and competition, it would ensure a fair distribution of work and of wealth, it would banish unemployment and poverty, provide for sickness and old age, educate children, and make all men virtuous and happy. The evils of life in existing industrial towns would be remedied by the establishment of village communities, based on the principles of 'mutual co-operation, united possessions, and equality of exertions, and of the means of enjoyments'.[18] Such communities would be rationally planned, with a proper balance between agriculture and industry. Trade would be based upon a new monetary system: labour being the source of value, payment for work would be in 'labour notes', which could be exchanged for goods in 'labour exchanges', thus giving to the workers the whole produce of their labour. These Owenite ideas permeated co-operative literature and efforts in Lancashire.

At first Owen sought to secure the support of the upper and middle classes for his schemes, but without much success. Funds were raised for the establishment of a few co-operative communities, such as those of Abram Combe and Alexander Hamilton, at Orbiston, near Motherwell, in 1825–7, but they proved unsuccessful. There is said to have been an earlier scheme in 1822 for a community on Merseyside, with financial support from Mrs. William Rathbone and other Liverpool philanthropists, but it was never brought to practical fruition.[19] Owen himself despaired of success in England and left for America, to carry out his plans at 'New Harmony'; but here, too, he met with complete failure.

Owenism was faced with a dilemma. How was it possible to create entirely new circumstances under existing circumstances? How could a new and perfect system of society be built in the existing imperfect state of society? How could men be made virtuous and co-operative when they were steeped in the existing vices of private gain and competition? How could land and capital be obtained when both were monopolised by the aristocracy and middle classes? One of the most insuperable difficulties in Owen's community schemes was the great quantity of capital which he maintained would be necessary: at the third co-operative congress, in London, April 1832, he said that '6,000 *l.*, 20,000 *l.*, or even 60,000 *l.* would be of little avail' for the establishment of a community, and that they would have to borrow capital from monied men. William Thompson said that Owen refused to make a beginning with less than £240,000.[20]

Many working men did not agree with Owen on this issue. They did not wish to be under the control—however paternal—of capitalists, even such as Owen, and they did not think that such vast sums were necessary. They wanted to make a small start, with a little capital and land, and to run their own affairs on democratic lines. From these beginnings they thought that they would eventually revolutionise the whole social system. But in their discussions of community schemes they seldom faced squarely the practical difficulties involved. John Finch, of Liverpool, for example, speaking at the London congress in April 1832, declared that to bring the co-operative system into operation, 'We want labour, knowledge, virtue, capital, and land. Of labour there is ... a superabundance. Knowledge is the next thing we want', and this could be achieved through education. But he stopped there and did not explain how virtue, capital, and land were to be obtained.[21]

Nevertheless, the community idea gained a great deal of support in Lancashire, certainly among the leading co-operators, though perhaps not among the rank-and-file membership. The ultimate ideal of most of these early societies, as of the later Rochdale Pioneers, was the establishment of a new system of society based on co-operative communities. Lancashire co-operators were prominent in the discussions on this subject at the various co-operative congresses.[22] Elijah Dixon, one of the Manchester leaders, seconded the proposal for the establishment of a co-operative community at the first congress, held in Manchester in May 1831, and several Lancashire leaders—the Rev. Joseph Marriott, of Warrington, Joseph Smith and George Mandley, of Manchester and Salford, and also John Doherty, the Manchester trade-union leader[23]— were among those elected by the second congress, at Birmingham in the following October, to draw up a prospectus for such a community. John Finch, of Liverpool, declared that co-operative principles 'can be fully developed only in a state of community conducted and formed on the principles of united capital, labour, and expenditure, of an equality of rights, and of the means of enjoyment'. At the third congress, in London, April 1832, the Lancashire delegates again spoke strongly in favour of an 'incipient community'. William Carson, of Pemberton, near Wigan, said that 'after reading the works of Messrs. Owen and Thompson, the people were anxious to commence a community', and that 'many persons in Lancashire had serious intentions of forming a community', e.g. at Worsley and Liverpool. The Rev. Joseph Marriott declared that 'if it were necessary he would give up his profession, and with his family enter such a society'. Joseph Smith also urged immediate steps towards the formation of a community, to 'prove to the world that we are no visionaries; but determined, practical, and honest men'.

This enthusiastic talk in congresses, however, did not produce much practical result. Even some of the enthusiasts appear to have had doubts about the practicability of such schemes. The Rev. F. Baker, of Bolton, regarded the community scheme as 'somewhat visionary, because human nature is not yet honest, generous, and wise enough to be satisfied with the little which her wants require'.[24] George Mandley, of Manchester, though a supporter of Owen, thought that his ideas were 'not attainable in large and densely populated cities', such as those which the Industrial Revolution was creating.[25] And Edmund Taylor, from Birkacre, 'thought a great many who took the subject [of a community] up, did so very rashly. They talked of getting on the land, but said little of the principles upon which they were to associate. Their minds were not sufficiently matured', and there were considerable differences of opinion amongst them.[26]

This back-to-the-land aspect of co-operation, however, had a strong appeal for many urban workers—for the most part fairly recent migrants from the countryside—living in the new industrial towns. There was a tendency to idealise the rural past and to make comparisons between the depressed urban wage-earners of the present day and the 'bold and virtuous peasantry' of old, 'their country's pride', returning after a hard day's toil to 'a peaceful cottage, a plentiful table, and an affectionate family of children', whereas their descendants now lived in the filth and vice of crowded cities, in poverty, depravity, and misery.[27] The evils of the factory system were also strongly denounced by co-operators.[28] It was often pointed out that there were millions of acres of waste land in England which could be cultivated by the poor. Co-operative community schemes were frequently described as 'home colonisation' projects, in opposition to Malthusian proposals for emigration designed to get rid of 'surplus' population. This idea of utilising waste land gained some support in the upper ranks of society, as witnessed, for example, by the establishment of the 'Agricultural Employment Institution' in 1832, 'for affording employment to the unemployed poor in the cultivation of [waste] land', a scheme for 'Home Colonisation' along the lines of the 'Poor Colonies' at Frederiksoord in Holland. Lancashire co-operators supported this scheme, though they preferred, of course, their own plan for co-operative communities.[29]

One of the staunchest advocates of the back-to-the-land idea was Elijah Dixon, of Manchester. We are told that he 'held strong views upon the subject of waste lands of the country, which he thought ought to be utilised' for co-operative agriculture.[30] 'Co-operators,' he declared, 'would affect [sic] but little towards their amelioration were they not allowed to cultivate the LAND for themselves.'[31] He therefore urged them to rent or purchase land; at the same time he strongly attacked the existing land monopoly, which he traced back to the Norman Conquest. He appears to have been one of the main supporters of a proposed 'Social Community Company' in Manchester in the autumn of 1832, whose purpose was to raise capital by weekly subscriptions 'for the laudable purpose of purchasing land and eventually employing themselves' in a co-operative community.[32] One of the members was said to have made 'a beautiful model of a Co-operative Community'.[33]

What became of this scheme is not known, but we are told that at one time Dixon (doubtless with other co-operators) 'built a farm-house at Chat Moss [west of Manchester] and cultivated a tract of land there, in order that he might show what could be done even with such apparently unpromising material. How far he succeeded I never knew.'[34] This may perhaps be the same project as that referred to by Holyoake, who states that in 1830 'a few co-operators in Manchester took 600 acres of waste land upon Chat Moss, and they contrived to cultivate it. England had not a drearier spot in which to begin a new world.'[35]

Another and more successful Lancashire agricultural co-operator was E. T. Craig, who became secretary and organiser of the famous community founded by the Irish landowner, J. S. Vandeleur, at Ralahine, county Clare. Vandeleur, inspired by Owenite ideas, came to England in 1831 to get assistance in the establishment of this co-operative 'colony' on his estate, and recruited Craig in Manchester,[36] where he was then president of the 'Owenian' co-operative society.[37] Ralahine was frequently held up to Lancashire co-operators in the early 'thirties as a successful example of co-operative agriculture, but it ended in catastrophe in 1833 with the ruin of Vandeleur, due to gambling, and his flight to America.

The weakness of all these ambitious community schemes was that they depended on the philanthropy of landowners and other wealthy capitalists, who possessed almost all the land and capital of the country. The Marxist solution, of course, was to be the expropriation of these exploiting classes by a violent revolution of the masses. But few if any of the early Owenite co-operators and socialists appear to have harboured such thoughts, though there was certainly a widespread feeling at the time that a 'crisis' was approaching. There was undoubtedly a lot of bitter class feeling among co-operators in Lancashire and elsewhere, as we have seen, but most of the leaders urged pacific, conciliatory, constitutional measures to achieve their ends, for which purpose they sought to bring about a union of all classes. Their chief weapon was education,[38] the 'diffusion of knowledge', and moral persuasion. The *United Trades' Co-operative Journal*, for example, urged that the working classes should seek to become more intelligent, more charitable, more temperate, and more economical, and warned them against methods of violence: improvement could be secured only by 'peace and harmony among all classes of men'.[39] Elijah Dixon, though he denounced the wealthy landowners, 'wished not that they should be dispossessed of it', but merely 'entreated them' to allow the poor to use some of their waste land.[40] The editor of the *Lancashire and Yorkshire Co-operator* deplored expressions of class enmity and urged 'a more conciliatory spirit', since employers themselves were often helpless in the face of competition. Co-operators should be 'charitable', 'brotherly', and eschew 'party feelings'.[41] John Finch, of Liverpool, stated that one of the first principles of the co-operative system was that the existing social injustices were to be blamed, not on individual landowners and capitalists, but on 'the system under which we live; and, therefore, that no individual ought to be deprived of the least fraction of property'.[42] At the same time the Rev. J. Marriott, of Warrington, declared that 'We, as Co-operators, as friends of our fellow men, do not come here as levellers; we do not come here to deprive any human being of any of his or her property'. They advocated, not 'the greatest happiness of the greatest number', but 'the greatest happiness of all'. Men are made what they are by circumstances beyond their control, so co-operators ought to regard all their fellow-creatures 'not with enmity, not with bitterness, but with love'. It was 'one of the fundamental principles of co-operation to embrace all ranks and conditions of men'.[43]

For these reasons, Lancashire co-operators deplored such violent methods as machine-breaking and strikes. In regard to machinery, their attitude was not one of merely negative opposition: they did not object to machinery as such, but to maldistribution of its benefits. Machine-production, it was repeatedly pointed out, had made possible plenty for all; but to achieve this the workers must co-operate and 'work for themselves', with their own machinery, instead of for capitalist employers. 'The working classes must unite to make machines their servants, or machines will annihilate them.'[44]

Lancashire co-operators did get some upper- and middle-class support for their various schemes. John Finch, an iron merchant, was the leader of the co-operative movement in Liverpool, with some support from the Rathbones, one of the chief merchant houses in the port, and from other middle-class sympathisers.[45] In Manchester and Salford, Benjamin Heywood, Esq., M.P., lent benevolent aid, particularly to the school of the First Salford Co-operative Society, towards which many other leading citizens also contributed;[46] he was also the patron of a co-operative society established at Irlam o' th' Heights.[47] Several ministers of religion

in Lancashire were also strong supporters.[48] Lady Noel Byron, wife
of the poet, and a warm supporter of co-operation, gave generous
financial assistance to various Lancashire societies.[49] We also
find Manchester co-operators in correspondence with middle-class
sympathisers in London, such as Harriet Martineau, Elizabeth
Wright Macaulay, and Thomas Wayland (of Lincoln's Inn).[50]

This upper-class support, however, was not very extensive and
working-class co-operators had to rely mainly upon their own
resources. 'Union is strength' was one of their mottoes. Only by
co-operative effort could they acquire the capital necessary for their
schemes. 'Union and saving will accumulate it.'[51] The working
classes, especially in Lancashire, had already shown this to be
possible in friendly societies and savings banks, and there was also
experience of corporate organisation in trade societies and chapels.
But they could not quickly amass the huge sums which Owen
required for his community schemes. They would have to start in a
very small, practical way.

During Owen's absence in America (1824–9), so William Lovett
tells us, the leaders of the working-men who were in favour of
Owenism and also of political Radicalism began to establish
co-operative stores, the movement being widely diffused by the
establishment in London in 1829 of the British Association for the
Promotion of Co-operative Knowledge. When Owen returned from
America, 'he looked somewhat coolly on those "Trading Associations", and very candidly declared that their mere buying and
selling formed no part of his grand "co-operative scheme"; but
when he found that great numbers among them were disposed to
entertain many of his views, he took them more in favour, and
ultimately took an active part among them'.[52]

The first such co-operative societies in Lancashire and Cheshire
were established in 1829, mostly inspired by London and Brighton.
The movement spread rapidly and in the early 'thirties trading
societies of this kind were to be found in every town in the area,
sometimes several in the same town. At the beginning of May 1830,
for example, eleven were listed in Manchester and Salford,[53] and
altogether sixteen are said to have been established there.[54] In
the Bolton neighbourhood, nine societies were reported in the
middle of 1832.[55] Societies were even established in outlying
villages.

The co-operative shop or store, however, was merely a beginning, a means to a much larger and loftier end, which was to be
achieved by gradual stages. The co-operative programme was
frequently described in co-operative periodicals. The *Lancashire*

and Yorkshire Co-operator, for example, pointed out that co-operative societies were

> formed by individuals uniting together and paying a certain sum weekly, to raise a fund for the ultimate purpose of purchasing or renting land ... and erecting thereon comfortable houses, schools, etc. and workshops, furnished with the most improved machinery; but as all this cannot be come to at once without a sufficient fund, or running into debt, the following seems to be the surest way of succeeding:— 1. To raise a fund by the weekly subscriptions of members, and likewise by donations, benefits, collections, etc. 2. To open a store for the purpose of retailing to members and others, the common necessaries and conveniences of life ... Every one might bring their various articles (which they had manufactured) into the store, and would receive notes representing their value, and payable on demand, in such goods as might be in the store ... 3. To purchase raw materials, and employ the members of the society, who choose or who cannot get work otherwise ... 4. To procure land ... and send out some of the members to cultivate the same, and to erect comfortable habitations, workshops, schools, etc.; and to send out from time to time, such fit persons as choose, and are approved of by the society, to work at the different trades [until a complete co-operative community was formed].[56]

These were the stages in co-operation: formation of a society and capital fund—co-operative store—co-operative production—labour exchange—co-operative agriculture, and finally a complete community. Scores of co-operative societies and stores were established in Lancashire and Cheshire during these years. Most of them never progressed, however, beyond the selling of groceries. Indeed it is doubtful whether the bulk of their members ever really aimed at going much farther: to them the co-operative society was principally a means of getting reasonably good quality goods at fair prices. Their more idealistic leaders often complained of the lack of knowledge of true co-operative principles among the rank-and-file. At the second co-operative congress, for example, several Lancashire speakers urged missionary effort to overcome the prevalent ignorance. The Rev. Joseph Marriott deplored the fact that 'nearly 99 out of every 100 Societies were still ignorant of the principles of Co-operation', and that there were many who were 'not favourable to community'. George Mandley complained that 'there were many Societies which were clearly not Co-operative'.[57] Early in 1832 it was stated that 'a true or comprehensive knowledge of the real principles of co-operation remains extremely limited'.[58] The *Lancashire and Yorkshire Co-operator* similarly regretted that 'even in our own societies, the great principles of our system are by many little known—by less, understood'.[59]

The great majority of co-operative societies in Lancashire and Cheshire, then, never approached the Owenite ideal. Several trade unions, however, did engage in co-operative production—the Manchester dyers, for example[60]—chiefly as a means of employing out-of-work or strike members. There was also some exchange or barter of co-operative manufactures, the most outstanding project in this field being the 'North West of England United Co-operative Company' established in Liverpool, as a result of the first co-operative congress, held in Manchester in May 1831.[61] This was to be a wholesale trading company, making bulk purchases for retail societies, and also providing a centre for the exchange of co-operative manufactures. The idea of a labour currency, however, with 'labour exchanges' or 'labour exchange banks', does not seem to have caught on in the north-west, either because the principles of labour-value theory and labour notes were not properly understood, or because they were regarded as impractical, especially as most Lancashire workers were producing textile goods and so could not operate an exchange system.[62] The *Lancashire and Yorkshire Co-operator* supported the idea, the Manchester District Council being in favour of it,[63] but nothing practical appears to have been accomplished in this direction. Of attempts at community —the ultimate Owenite ideal—there were very few. The Manchester scheme at Chat Moss[64] appears to have been a complete failure. More successful, for a few years, was a combined attempt at co-operative production and community by the calico printers' trade society, or Block Printers' Union, under the leadership of their secretary, Ellis Piggott, in a printworks on an estate at Birkacre, near Chorley, which had once belonged to the great cotton-spinner, Sir Richard Arkwright.[65] This project—which has attracted almost no attention in histories of co-operation—employed about 300 of the society's members and was the biggest project of its kind in the whole country during this period. It collapsed, however, after about two years.

There was a close connection during these years between trade unionism and co-operation. This is evidenced by the names of some of the trade-union periodicals, such as the *United Trades' Co-operative Journal* and the *Union Pilot and Co-operative Intelligencer*, in which articles explaining and supporting co-operation often appeared. And as we have seen, several trade unions launched their own schemes of co-operative production. John Doherty, the great Lancashire trade-union leader, declared himself a warm supporter of Owenism—'that beautiful system', as he called it[66]— and of co-operative societies, in the various journals which he edited in the early 'thirties. But there were occasions when differences of opinion arose between co-operators and trade unionists, principally upon the relative merits of their respective organisations as a means of working-class salvation.[67] Co-operators tended to regard strikes, for example, as a futile waste of money, which they considered would be better employed in co-operative schemes. On the whole, however, good feeling prevailed and much mutual assistance was given. As Thomas Foster, one of the leading Manchester trade unionists, put it: 'the two systems were not incompatible with each other. Both union and co-operation might go together. The one would assist the other.'[68] Thus at the second co-operative congress we find Thomas Oates, representative of the *Voice of the People*—organ of the National Association for the Protection of Labour, the general trades' union launched by Doherty in Manchester in 1829—strongly supporting co-operation, while the congress reciprocated by urging all co-operators to support the *Voice of the People* and by electing Doherty, the editor, on to the committee for establishing a co-operative community.[69]

The most strongly reiterated theme or slogan of co-operators in this period was 'Knowledge is Power'. Being deprived of knowledge, most of the working classes were kept ignorant of the causes of the social evils from which they were suffering, of the oppression and exploitation of the capitalist system, and of the means whereby their conditions might be improved. Remove this ignorance by means of education—by schools, periodicals, pamphlets, and lectures—and the working classes would soon realise their wrongs and unite in action to obtain their rights. Above all, they should be given co-operative knowledge, knowledge of the 'new system of society', and of the means by which it might be achieved.

There was also another, though related, motive behind the co-operative emphasis on education. Owen taught that men are made what they are by circumstances: hence the mass of the people, brought up uneducated and ignorant, were morally imperfect and so easy dupes of drunkenness, immorality, and crime. The whole of society, in fact, was rotten through lack of proper education and moral training. Matters could be improved only by giving the people these things. Moreover, the education should be of an appropriate kind, with emphasis on practical training. Owen himself had placed great emphasis on education as an instrument of social reform and had pioneered educational methods nowadays usually associated with the names of Continental reformers such as Pestalozzi, de Fellenberg, and Froebel; his schools at New Lanark had become internationally famous.

These ideas exercised a profound influence upon leading Lanca-

shire co-operators, who repeatedly emphasised the prime importance of removing popular ignorance and spreading knowledge—
not merely teaching people to read and write, though that was
important, but also providing social knowledge, based on the
writings of Owen, Thompson, and others. The motto of the *Lancashire and Yorkshire Co-operator* was:—

> Numbers without Union are Powerless—
> And Union without Knowledge is Useless.[70]

Following the example of London, the Manchester and Salford
co-operators set up an 'Association for the Promotion of Co-operative Knowledge',[71] organising lectures, distributing periodicals, and
assisting in the formation of co-operative societies. Great stress was
laid on 'missionary' work for spreading the co-operative gospel,
and Manchester was made the centre for such activity in the
north-west by the second and third co-operative congresses. Most
societies held discussion meetings, to which non-members were
invited, and several established libraries, reading-rooms, and
schools in which members' children and also members themselves
were given education, usually in the evenings. The schoolrooms
were also used for society meettings and lectures.

Articles on education frequently appeared in the co-operative
periodicals. It was urged that the working classes should establish
schools of their own, instead of sending their children to church
schools, under upper-class control, and that the teaching should
be more practical and recreative, including industrial crafts and
agriculture, instead of mere book-learning by rote.[72] Such an
education would best fit children for life in a co-operative community. J. Read, of Rochdale, suggested that co-operative societies
throughout the country should 'form themselves into District
Associations, including all societies within 20 miles square, and
that each member subscribe 5s. for the purpose of commencing an
Industrial School in the most central and eligible situation in each
district'.[73] Some Lancashire co-operators had ideas of establishing
a national state system of education. John Finch, of Liverpool, for
example, proposed to the third co-operative congress that they
should 'apply to the legislature' for the establishment of 'a national
system of education'. The schools should be boarding schools, providing training in agriculture and industry. 'They should provide
their own food, and make their own clothes'—in fact they should
'fully support themselves, and by their means the whole population
would be trained up in, or be prepared for, a perfect state of
community'.[74]

At this same congress, William Carson, of Wigan, was the proposer of a resolution that they should press upon Parliament 'the great necessity of removing all impediments to the cheap diffusion of knowledge, and promoting ... the establishment of schools, libraries, and reading-rooms, in every town and village in the United Kingdom'.[75] Co-operative societies and other working-class associations were restricted in their educative efforts by the infamous 'taxes on knowledge', particularly by the 4d. newspaper stamp duty. They therefore participated in the agitation then being waged against these imposts.[76]

Among the most serious obstacles to the spread of Co-operation were the rationalist, anti-religious opinions of Owen, its founder. Or it might be said that Co-operation seemed like a new religion, with Owen as its high priest, threatening established Christian beliefs. In Lancashire and Cheshire, however, it appears that many —perhaps most—co-operators, while accepting Owen's social philosophy, did not share his anti-religious opinions. Indeed, they considered that Co-operation, with its emphasis on brotherhood and justice, was based on Christian principles. Many regretted Owen's anti-religious views. John Finch, of Liverpool, for example, a sincere Unitarian, urged Owen to desist from attacks on Christianity, 'because I am anxious that so good a cause [as Co-operation] should not be hindered in its progress by dissertations upon subjects which to me appear to have no necessary connection with any one principle' of Co-operation.[77] On the other hand, Finch stated about a year later that he was dissatisfied with all religious sects, because of their illiberal dogmatism, and that he regarded 'the whole host of parsons, as interested advocates of error'. He publicly deplored the fact that the existing social system, with all its evils was 'not merely permitted to exist, but is lauded ... as the very height of human wisdom', by Christian philosophers, statesmen, and political economists. He considered these evils contrary to both reason and true religion, which concur in teaching that universal happiness can never be achieved unless each man will 'love his neighbour as himself'.[78] Finch was, in fact, a profoundly religious man, but anti-clerical, an opponent of narrow theological sectarianism and of what he regarded as aberrations from true Christianity, upon which the co-operative system was founded.[79]

Other Lancashire leaders were also 'Christian co-operators'. Thus William Carson, of Wigan, declared that 'though many had been prevented [from] joining the cause of co-operation from supposing that it included none but Deists among its members, in the part of the country from which he came, people co-operated from Christian principles. He himself was a Christian co-operator, and certain he was, that there was no inconsistency between Christianity and co-operation. They had, however, excluded all sectarianism both in politics and religion, as they determined to preserve a charitable feeling to all.' Carson was glad to see 'that they had now among them churchmen and dissenters, and ministers of every Christian denomination'. He wished, 'on behalf of thousands, to state, that they were neither Atheists nor Deists, but Christians, and acted on Christian principles'.[80]

Elijah Dixon, of Manchester, lived up to his name, as a prophet and missionary of Christian co-operation. In a speech at Eccles, for example, we are told that he delivered 'a most powerful and eloquent address, in which he quoted a variety of beautiful passages from Scripture, proving Co-operation to be practical Religion'.[81] He is said to have been a great advocate of 'Universalism': 'He could prove, or he believed he could prove, by ample references to the New and Old Testaments, that ultimately all, sinners with saints, would be saved.'[82]

Clearly the opinions held by some of the leading Lancashire co-operators might well incur the hostility of orthodox religion. Thus Carson was dismissed from a situation with an architect employed by the Church Commissioners, 'because I had rendered myself obnoxious ... by the active exertions I made in aid of co-operation'.[83] The Salford Co-operative School was 'very much objected to by the clergy of the town, particularly by a Mr. Frost, who ... stated from the pulpit, that the parents would go to hell if they sent their children there'.[84] Several ministers of religion, however, gave warm support to co-operation in Lancashire and Cheshire. The Rev. Joseph Marriott, of Warrington, was one of the leaders and joint chairman of the first co-operative congress, in Manchester. At the London congress in April 1832 he urged that they should 'remember the great principle of religion, that man should love his fellow as himself. Community and co-operation would tend most effectually to the development of this principle. This he conceived to be the cause of true religion; and he sincerely regretted that so few of the ministers of religion were to be found in the ranks of its advocates.' 'Can there be a more holy cause than this?' he asked, and he wished that 'the ministers of all sects and denominations ... would unite to preach our doctrines'.[85]

The Rev. F. Baker, a Unitarian minister, was one of the pioneers of co-operation in Bolton,[86] and there are several references to co-operative lectures in Methodist chapels, sometimes leading to the formation of co-operative societies. Co-operative 'missionary' work owed a good deal to the examples of various religious bodies, especially the Methodists, with their itinerant preachers and distribution of tracts. Christians of all denominations appear to have co-operated freely in many societies. A particularly remarkable case of such co-operation was the joint editorship of *The Bee* in Liverpool by 'three editors—one a Churchman [unknown], the second a Catholic [M. J. Falvey], and the third a Unitarian [J. Finch], who seem if not in all things to agree, yet most cordially to agree to differ'.[87] On the other hand, several societies appear to have been troubled and even broken up by religious differences. At Chester, for example, it was stated that 'sectarian opinions on Religious subjects have been allowed to creep in and have retarded the operations of the Society not a little'; and at Nantwich also the members were 'split about religion and divided themselves into two Societies'.[88]

The editor of the *Lancashire and Yorkshire Co-operator* stated that 'we can under no pretence whatever, admit into our pages attacks on Christianity, nor can we suffer them to be the vehicle of theological disputation'.[89] Yet in this same number there was printed an extract from the *Moral Reformer* strongly attacking priests, particularly those of the Established Church, for having helped to shackle the minds of the people and for having participated in their oppression and exploitation. In a later number there was an apology for such articles, which had caused offence to some co-operators, and it was stated that the Manchester and Salford Association for the Spread of Co-operative Knowledge, responsible for publication of the *Co-operator*, had a rule by which 'all attacks upon the prevailing religion of this country are ... prohibited'. The few articles in question had 'either been inadvertently admitted or inserted in order to oblige some warm and useful friend to the cause, but from whom on some points they might differ in opinion'.[90] Similarly, the First Salford Society declared that at its regular weekly lectures 'on no account will any attack on the existing religion of the country be permitted ... nor will anything be allowed that is likely to promote religious controversy'.[91] On the whole, despite a few upheavals, religion appears to have caused little division among Lancashire and Cheshire co-operators, who seem for the most part to have combined Owenite Co-operation very easily with Christian principles.

Religion and education were the main forces behind the temperance movement of this period, and it is not surprising, therefore, that co-operators were usually among its supporters. Drunkenness was then a serious social evil, the cause of much poverty, misery, and crime, while it deprived workers both of the will and the means to take associated action to revolutionise the existing social system, of which it was a product. Realisation of these facts was very strong among Lancashire co-operators, one of whose main objects was to remove such moral and social evils. They constantly urged the working classes to be temperate and thrifty. Co-operative social gatherings frequently took the form of 'tea parties', where intoxicating liquors were banned, and the workers were urged to give up the practice of holding trade-union and friendly society meetings in public houses; instead they should take rooms of their own. A society schoolroom, it was pointed out, could be used as 'a lecture-room, or reading-room, or for meetings of societies, which will transact their business in it much better than at *public houses*'; members would thus have 'a place of resort for rational amusement during their hours of idleness', instead of drinking, smoking, and degrading themselves in 'besotted ignorance'.[92] Schools and the diffusion of knowledge would greatly improve moral standards.

Co-operation would thus help to remove intemperance. 'Where a co-operative society was formed,' said William Carson, 'the public house was generally the sufferer.'[93] Indeed, according to John Finch, 'every Co-operative Society was ... a Temperance Society also', and he persuaded the fourth congress to pass a resolution deeply lamenting 'the immorality and crime occasioned by the vice of drunkenness', extolling 'the good effects which have been produced by ... temperance societies', and strongly recommending all co-operators 'to give them every encouragement in their power'.[94] Finch was, in fact, not only one of the leading Lancashire co-operators, but also one of the outstanding figures in the temperance and total abstinence movements, acquiring the title of 'King of the Teetotallers'.[95] Most co-operators seem to have shared his views.

Lancashire co-operative societies do not appear to have taken any active part in the Radical political movement, which reached such a pitch in the struggle over the Reform Bill in the early 'thirties. Politics, like religion, were often excluded from their discussions, partly because of the differences in opinion which might disrupt a society, and partly because some shared Owen's view that political reform was a chimera and that the essential thing was first of all to create a new social system. On the other hand, there is little doubt that the great majority of co-operators were sympathetic towards Radicalism and that some were active politically. The *United Trades' Co-operative Journal* thought that 'a crisis is evidently approaching, and come it must soon', which was bound 'to produce some great changes in the political and social arrangements of Great Britain'.[96] The first co-operative congress, in Manchester, referring briefly to the Reform Bill, expressed 'a sympathy commensurate with its importance', but pointed out that it would not get at the deep-seated social evils, which could be removed only by the co-operative system.[97] Joseph Smith, one of the leading Salford co-operators, on the other hand, thought that 'If we could but get a fair representation in Parliament, our interests advocated, and the evils we endure fairly placed before the legislature, our cause ... would be successful'.[98] Elijah Dixon was for years one of the most prominent Manchester Radicals: he was arrested in 1817 on a charge of high treason, but released after an imprisonment of two or three months; he was present at Peterloo; and he was one of the most active local Radicals in the 1830s during the Reform Bill agitation and later on in the anti-Poor-Law and Chartist movements. He was, in fact, 'a typical Lancashire Radical of the old school'.[99] No doubt many other individual co-operators were active Radicals; but there is no evidence of any political action by the co-operative societies as such.

All this co-operative activity in Lancashire and Cheshire suffered a severe setback in 1834, with the general collapse of working-class movements, but a few societies survived and in the later 1830s there was a revival of Owenite Socialism, marked by the building of Halls of Science in various towns and by further attempts at founding a co-operative community. The ideas and personalities in this revival were much the same as in the preceding period. The Rochdale Pioneers and the co-operative movement which they successfully established were based on the principles and practices of these earlier co-operators.

NOTES

1. In addition to Owen's own *Life* and the biographies by Lloyd-Jones, Podmore, and the Coles, see J. F. C. Harrison, *Robert Owen and the Owenites in Britain and America*, (1969); S. Pollard and J. Salt (eds.), *Robert Owen, Prophet of the Poor*, (1971); J. Batt (ed.), *Robert Owen, Prince of Cotton Spinners*, (1971).
2. This paper is devoted mainly to a general survey of early Co-operative *ideology* in Lancashire and Cheshire, in the period 1829–34, and refers only briefly to Co-operative *practice* in stores, workshops, exchanges, schools, and communities. The author proposes to publish a book on the whole subject of early Co-operation in Lancashire and Cheshire before the Rochdale Pioneers (1844).
3. C. J. Holyoake, *The History of Co-operation in England* (2 vols., 1875), I, 182–91.
4. For the general history of Co-operation, see Holyoake, *op. cit.*; B. Potter, *The Co-operative Movements in Great Britain* (1891); B. Jones,

Co-operative Production (1894); Catharine Webb (ed.), *Industrial Co-operation* (3rd ed., 1907); F. Hall and W. P. Watkins, *Co-operation* (1937); G. D. H. Cole, *A Century of Co-operation* (1944).

5. William Rowbottom's Diaries, *Annals of Oldham, 1787–1830*, edited by S. Andrew, printed in the *Oldham Standard*, 1887–9. E. Butterworth, *Historical Sketches of Oldham* (1856), 151.

6. For discussions of their writings and influence, see M. Beer, *History of British Socialism*, I (1919), chaps. v–vii, and G. D. H. Cole, *History of Socialist Thought*, I, *The Forerunners, 1789–1850* (1953), chaps. ix and x.

7. Holyoake, *op. cit.*, I, 144–6, 358–9; *Bolton Chronicle*, 27 March and 3 April 1830; *United Trades' Co-operative Journal*, 10 and 17 April 1830.

8. He appears to have moved from Birmingham first of all to Leeds, where he established several co-operative societies, before settling in the Wigan district in 1830. *Weekly Free Press*, 27 Dec. 1830; *The Co-operator*, 1 Feb. 1829; *United Trades' Co-operative Journal*, 2 Oct. 1830; W. H. Brown, *Wigan Welfare and the Jubilee History of the Wigan and District Equitable Co-operative Society Ltd.* (Wigan, 1939).

9. See, for example, *Lancashire and Yorkshire Co-operator*, March 1832.

10. *Crisis*, 22 Sept. 1832.

11. *United Trades' Co-operative Journal*, 1 and 8 May 1830; *Lancashire and Yorkshire Co-operator*, April 1832.

12. *United Trades' Co-operative Journal*, 6 March 1830.

13. *Lancashire Co-operator*, 25 June 1831.

14. *Lanacashire and Yorkshire Co-operator*, 26 Nov. 1831.

15. *Ibid.*, October 1832. Cf. *United Trades' Co-operative Journal*, 10 April 1830 (Wm. Pare's lectures).

16. *Ibid.*, 26 Nov. 1831.

17. *Ibid.*, Oct. 1832.

18. *Resolutions, etc., passed at the first meeting of the Co-operative Congress, held in Manchester*, May 1831.

19. W. H. Brown, *A Century of Liverpool Co-operation* (1929), 32–3.

20. *Proceedings of the Third Co-operative Congress*, London, April 1832.

21. *Ibid.*

22. See the congress reports.

23. Doherty was not present at the Congress, but Thomas Oates attended as the representative of the *Voice of the People*, of which Doherty was editor.

24. *Lecture on Co-operation*, Bolton, 19 April 1830 (reprinted from the *Bolton Chronicle*).

25. *Proceedings of the Third Co-operative Congress*, London, April 1832.

26. *Proceedings of the Fourth Co-operative Congress*, Liverpool, Oct. 1832.

27. *Lancashire and Yorkshire Co-operator*, May 1832.

28. See, for example, *ibid.*, April 1832.

29. *Ibid.*, Sept. and Oct. 1832.

30. J. Johnson, *People I Have Met* (n.d., reprinted from the *Isle of Man Weekly Times* in the latter half of the nineteenth century), 139.

31. *Lancs. & Yorks. Co-operator*, May 1832 (supplement).

32. *Ibid.*, Sept. and Oct. 1832.

33. *Proceedings of the Fourth Co-operative Congress*, Liverpool, Oct. 1832.

34. Johnson, *op. cit.*, 139.

35. Holyoake, *op. cit.*, I, 155.

36. W. Pare, *Co-operative Agriculture ... the History of the Ralahine Co-*

operative Agricultural Association, County Clare, Ireland (1870), 14. See also Craig's own *History of Ralahine* (1882).

37. *Lancs. and Yorks. Co-operator*, April 1832.
38. See below, pp. 185–7.
39. *Op. cit.*, 6 March 1830.
40. *Lancs. & Yorks. Co-operator*, May 1832 (supplement).
41. *Ibid.*, June 1832.
42. *Proceedings of the Third Co-operative Congress*, London, April 1832.
43. *Ibid.*
44. *Union Pilot and Co-operative Intelligencer*, 10 March 1832.
45. W. H. Brown, *A Century of Liverpool Co-operation* (1929), *passim*; R. B. Rose, 'John Finch 1784–1857: A Liverpool Disciple of Robert Owen', *Trans. L. & C. Hist. Soc.*, CIX (1957), 159–84.
46. *Lancs. & Yorks. Co-operator*, July 1832.
47. *Proceedings of the Fourth Co-operative Congress*, Liverpool, Oct. 1832. On Benjamin Heywood's social-reforming activities, see *A Schoolmaster's Notebook* (ed. E. & T. Kelly, Manchester, 1957), especially pages 76–9, concerning the purchasing of food and clothing for his tenants at wholesale prices—perhaps under co-operative inspiration.
48. See below, pp. 187–9.
49. E. C. Mayne, *Life and Letters of Anne Isabella, Lady Noel Byron* (1929), chap. xxii, and W. H. Brown, *Brighton's Co-operative Advance 1828–1938* (Manchester, 1938), chap. vi, 'Lady Byron, the Godmother of Co-operation'.
50. *Lancs. & Yorks. Co-operator*, April and May 1832.
51. *Lancs. & Yorks. Co-operator*, 3 Sept. 1831.
52. W. Lovett, *The Life and Struggles of William Lovett* (edn. of 1920), 41–4.
53. *United Trades' Co-operative Journal*, 1 May 1830.
54. *Proceedings of the Third Co-operative Congress*, London, April 1832; *Lancs. & Yorks. Co-operator*, Sept. 1832.
55. *Lancs. & Yorks. Co-operator*, July 1832.
56. *Op. cit.*, 10 Dec. 1831.
57. *Proceedings of the Second Co-operative Congress*, Birmingham, Oct. 1831.
58. *Poor Man's Advocate*, 4 Feb. 1832.
59. *Lancs. & Yorks. Co-operator*, June 1832.
60. *United Trades' Co-operative Journal*, 27 March 1830; *Union Pilot and Co-operative Intelligencer*, 28 April 1832; *Lancs. & Yorks. Co-operator*, March, Aug. & Sept. 1832; *Crisis*, 22 Sept. 1832.
61. *Resolutions, etc. passed at the first meeting of the Co-operative Congress*, Manchester, May 1831.
62. See, for example, the report of the Manchester 'Owenian' Society to the third congress (*Proceedings*, London, April 1832); J. Whittaker's report (*Crisis*, Sept. 1832); and a discussion in Salford (*Lancs. & Yorks. Co-operator*, Oct. 1832).
63. *Lancs. & Yorks. Co-operator*, May (supplement), July, and Sept. 1832.
64. See above, p. 180.
65. *Proceedings of the Third Co-operative Congress*, London, April 1832; *Crisis*, 27 Oct. 1832; *Lancs. & Yorks. Co-operator*, Aug. 1832; J. Graham, *History of Printworks in the Manchester District from 1760 to 1846* (MS. in Manchester Cen. Ref. Lib., n.d., 1846?), 352; T. C. Porteous, *A History of the Parish of Standish* (Wigan, 1927), 42.
66. *United Trades' Co-operative Journal*, 17 April 1830.

67. See, for example, *ibid.*, 17 April, 8 May, 19 June, August and September 1830.
68. *Ibid.*, 7 Aug. 1830.
69. *Proceedings of the Second Co-operative Congress*, Birmingham, Oct. 1831.
70. Cf. that of the *Brighton Co-operator*: —
   Knowledge and Union are Power:
   Power directed by Knowledge is Happiness:
   Happiness is the end of Creation.
71. See above, p. 175.
72. See, for example, the *Lancs. & Yorks. Co-operator*, 7 Jan. 1832.
73. *Ibid.*, April 1832.
74. *Proceedings of the Third Co-operative Congress*, London, April 1832.
75. *Ibid.*
76. See, for example, the *Lancs. & Yorks. Co-operator*, 3 Sept. 1831.
77. Letter to Owen, 29 June 1831 (written on the back of a report of the first Co-operative Congress, now preserved in the Co-operative Union Library, Manchester). Cf. his views expressed to the third Co-operative Congress (*Proceedings*, London, April 1832).
78. *Crisis*, 10 Nov. 1832.
79. For Finch's conflict with orthodox religious opinions, see Rose, *op. cit.*
80. *Proceedings of the Third Co-operative Congress*, London, April 1832; *Crisis*, 28 April 1832.
81. *Lancs. & Yorks. Co-operator*, May 1832 (supplement).
82. Johnson, *op. cit.*, p. 138.
83. *Crisis*, 28 April 1832.
84. *Ibid.*, 22 Sept. 1832.
85. *Proceedings of the Third Co-operative Congress*, London, April 1832.
86. He entertained the co-operative missionary William Pare when he visited Bolton in March 1830, and soon afterwards delivered two lectures on co-operation (*Bolton Chronicle*, 24 April and 8 May 1830). These lectures were reprinted in a series of penny pamphlets under the general title of *The Universal Pamphleteer* (nos. 46 and 47).
87. *Crisis*, 5 Jan. 1833.
88. *A Political Reflector*, 19 March 1831 (one of Wm. Carpenter's *Political Letters*).
89. *Op. cit.*, 10 Dec. 1831.
90. *Ibid.*, April 1832.
91. *Ibid.*, Sept. 1832.
92. *Lancs. & Yorks. Co-operator*, 7 Jan. 1832. Cf. John Finch's letter to the *United Trades' Co-operative Journal*, 6 March 1830.
93. *Proceedings of the Third Co-operative Congress*, London, April 1832.
94. *Proceedings of the Fourth Co-operative Congress*, Liverpool, Oct. 1832.
95. See P. T. Winskill and J. Thomas, *History of the Temperance Movement in Liverpool and District* (1887), P. T. Winskill, *The Temperance Movement and its Workers* (1891–2), and Rose, *op cit.* Finch gave some very interesting evidence before the House of Commons Select Committee on Drunkenness, 1834, H.C. (559), viii.
96. *Op. cit.*, 6 March 1830.
97. 'Address' of the delegates, in *Resolutions etc. passed at the first meeting of the Co-operative Congress*, Manchester, May 1831.
98. *Proceedings of the Third Co-operative Congress*, London, April 1832.
99. Johnson, *op. cit.*, 138–9.

Chapter 9

ROBERT BLINCOE AND THE EARLY FACTORY SYSTEM*

THE *Memoir of Robert Blincoe* is a classic document of the Industrial Revolution, revealing the worst horrors of child labour under the early factory system. Soon after its first appearance, indeed, its publisher claimed that it was 'now a standard work, to which future ages may refer, as to a specimen of the Christian character of some of the people of England, at the commencement of the nineteenth century'.[1] Litton Mill in Derbyshire was thereby made notorious as one of the blackest examples of factory slavery. The *Memoir* declared, in fact, that the condition of the 'white infant-slaves' in the cotton spinning mills of England was far worse than that of the negro slaves on the American cotton plantations.[2]

Earlier historians of the Industrial Revolution such as the Hammonds and Mantoux severely condemned the exploitation and ill-treatment of helpless child labour in the first cotton mills. More recently, however, various scholars have made reassessments of the social effects of the Industrial Revolution, and have presented the early factory owners in a more favourable light.[3] It is worthwhile, therefore, to read again such documents as Blincoe's *Memoir* and other related evidence, including the numerous volumes produced by Parliamentary Committees and Royal Commissions of enquiry into the factory system, to try to arrive at a balanced judgement upon this question.

Blincoe's *Memoir* first appeared in a Radical weekly paper, *The Lion*, Vol. 1, Nos. 4–8, Jan. 25–Feb. 22, 1828, printed and published by Richard Carlile at 62, Fleet Street, London. In the thirteenth number, of March 28, it was announced that the *Memoir* was 'now on sale, in a separate pamphlet', though apparently not published by Carlile.[4] The author was John Brown, a native of

---

* This a revised and extended version of an article by the author, with the same title, in *Derbyshire Miscellany*, February 1958. Since then, some important new evidence has been produced by Dr. S. D. Chapman, who, however, appears to have been unaware of my earlier reassessment, to which he makes no referenc: S. D. Chapman, *The Early Factory Masters* (1967), pp. 199–209. This evidence is discussed below.

Bolton and writer of numerous other works, now little known.[5] He states in the *Memoir* that it was 'in the spring of 1822, after having devoted a considerable time to the investigating of the effect of the manufacturing system, and factory establishments, on the health and morals of the manufacturing populace, that I first heard of the extraordinary sufferings of R. Blincoe. At the same time, I was told of his earnest wish that those sufferings should, for the protection of the rising generation of factory children, be laid before the world.'

By that date the state of factory children had attracted considerable public attention and sympathy. Sir Robert Peel had secured the passing of an Act in 1802 to protect the 'health and morals' of parish apprentices in the textile mills, and in 1815, stimulated by Robert Owen, he had introduced another Bill to amend and extend this Act, to include 'free' as well as pauper children. After a great deal of enquiry and debate another Act was passed in 1819. But this applied only to cotton mills, it still permitted excessive labour, and it was never effectively enforced. Agitation continued sporadically during the 'twenties and then boiled up into a ferment during the early 'thirties, resulting in the Acts of 1831 and 1833.

John Brown, however, was dead by this time, having committed suicide a few years after writing Blincoe's *Memoir*. Richard Carlile apparently acquired possession of his papers and decided to publish the *Memoir* in his periodical *The Lion*. He did so without consulting Blincoe himself, who, as we shall see, was still living, in Manchester. Blincoe, not unnaturally, was 'at first, inclined to be angry about it'. After explanation, however, 'he became good humoured, and acquiesced in the propriety of its being published'.[6]

When the factory agitation was at its height in the early 'thirties, Blincoe's *Memoir* was republished by John Doherty, the trade-union leader who was very prominent in the factory reform movement in Manchester. Doherty, originally a cotton-spinner himself, was by this time a small printer and publisher at 37 Withy Grove, Manchester, and made repeated attacks upon the factory system in his weekly paper, *The Poor Man's Advocate*, at the same time reprinting Blincoe's *Memoir*, in 1832.[7]

Robert Blincoe was born in about 1792 and placed in St. Pancras workhouse, London, in 1796, an illegitimate child, whose mother died shortly afterwards. In 1799 he was sent with a batch of about eighty pauper apprentices, in two large waggons, to Lowdham Mill, near Nottingham, belonging to Messrs. Lambert, cotton spinners, hosiers and lace-workers. He states that the children were misled by the parish officers with glowing accounts of their future prospects, so as to produce a ready acquiescence. They were quickly disillusioned, however, by conditions at Lowdham Mill —bad and insufficient food, hard work (first picking up loose cotton from the floor, then winding rovings), for fourteen hours a day on average (excepting Sundays), with continual beatings from the overlookers, and frequent accidents from the machinery, Blincoe himself losing part of the forefinger of his left hand. When he tried to run away he was caught, brought back, and flogged. After the 1802 Act, however, there were considerable improvements, and looking back, after his later experiences, Blincoe considered that on the whole he had been comparatively well-off in Lowdham Mill.

Soon after these reforms, unfortunately, the mill stopped working and Blincoe was transferred, with most of the other apprentices, to Litton Mill, near Tideswell, belonging to Ellice Needham, of Highgate Wall, near Buxton, Derbyshire. Here he was subjected to the most frightful conditions and barbarities, despite the recent Act 'and in the face of the visiting Magistrate whose visits were ... too frequently directed to the luxurious table of the master, to admit even a chance of justice to the apprentices'. Blincoe and his fellow sufferers were totally unaware of the Act and had no idea that the magistrates came to redress grievances. 'So great was the terror of the poor ignorant apprentices, no one dared to complain', and Blincoe could not recollect that the magistrates 'ever gave themselves any other trouble, than merely going over the mill. Everything was previously prepared ... The worst of the cripples were put out of the way ... The magistrate could never *find out* any thing wrong, nor hear of a single individual who had any complaint to make.' The 1802 Act was, in fact, 'a dead letter'.

The food at Litton Mill was grossly insufficient, so much so, indeed, that the apprentices tried to steal meal from the master's pigs, scavenged refuse dumps, and gathered hips and nuts from the woods. They also lacked clothing, were rarely washed, and slept in overcrowded conditions. The hours of work averaged sixteen a day, often without breaks for meals. The work was unskilled —picking up cotton, piecing, and winding—for the obligations in the indentures as to teaching the apprentices the whole trade were ignored. Many of the apprentices died of fever and other diseases, but there was always a plentiful supply of more cheap apprentice labour to replace them; the survivors were usually undergrown, deformed, and unhealthy. Atrocious cruelties were inflicted upon them, not merely to drive them at their work, but out of sheer sadism. Blincoe's life was 'one continued round of cruel and abitrary punishments'. He was continually beaten, so that 'his body was never free from contusions, and from wounds'. It was also a common thing to be kicked, picked up by the hair or ears and thrown to the ground, or to have his ears pinched till the blood ran. Moreover, the ruffianly overseers vied with each other in devising new 'sports', such as tying him up above a machine, so that he had continually to raise his legs to prevent them being caught in the machinery; fastening weights to his ears and nose, and many other bestialities. These doings were not, as was often apparently the case, unknown to the mill-owner, for Needham and his sons encouraged and joined in such barbarities. It was not until towards the end of Blincoe's apprenticeship, when he grew rebellious and fled to lodge complaints with the local magistrates, that these cruelties were relaxed.

Blincoe's story seems almost unbelievable in its horrors, but Brown stated that Blincoe was 'in his language, temperate; in his statements, cautious and considerate': indeed, he repeatedly admonished him 'to beware, lest a too keen remembrance of the injustice he had suffered should lead him to transgress the limits of truth'. Blincoe's statements were also confirmed by others who had suffered with him in Litton Mill.[8] When the *Memoir* was published, Blincoe, having read it, stated that it was 'true, so far as it went; but that the enormities practised in Litton Mill were much greater than those related in the memoir'. He still bore scars on his head, face, and ears as witness to the cruelties inflicted upon him, yet said that he himself 'was not so ill-treated as many others were at the same mill'.

A few years later Blincoe confirmed the truth of the *Memoir* in sworn evidence before Dr. Hawkins, of Manchester, printed in the second report of the Royal Commission on the Employment of Children in Factories.[9] He showed Dr. Hawkins his deformed knees and the scars of ill-treatment in Litton Mill, but said that there were 'many far worse than me at Manchester'.

Plentiful evidence was, indeed, provided before this Royal Commission, and also in other enquiries, both official and unofficial, to show that Blincoe's story was not an isolated example. For this reason it has frequently been referred to by modern authors, since Mantoux and the Hammonds, as an illustration of the worst horrors of the early factory system. Even in his own day, in fact, Blincoe acquired notoriety in the factory reform movement: his deformities and scars were exhibited in public demonstrations in Manchester and a woodcut of him appeared in the *Poor Man's Advocate*. Mrs. Frances Trollope, mother of T. A. Trollope, appears to have based a good deal of her novel, *The Life and Adventures of Michael Armstrong, the Factory Boy* (1840) on Blincoe's *Memoir*; she and her son visited the northern factory districts in 1839, where they met Doherty, Oastler and other leaders of the factory reform movement.[10] Mrs. Trollope's novel may well be regarded as nineteenth-century 'melodrama', as Dr. Chapman says, but the *Memoir* itself is authentic and its general condemnation of the early factory system is supported by a vast amount of reliable contemporary evidence. There is no doubt whatever that many children *were* exploited and ill-treated in the early textile mills, that they were used as cheap factory labour, that their hours of work were far too long, that accidents, ill-health, and deformities were common, and that cruel punishments were often inflicted. There is no doubt that, as the *Memoir* asserts, the owner of Litton Mill, 'although perhaps one of the worst of his tribe, did not stand alone'.

Modern defenders of the factory system, however, have argued, as did contemporary factory owners, that the evils were exaggerated and there is no doubt that some of the evidence (especially that before Sadler's Committee in 1832) was biased and inaccurate. Bad conditions were by no means universal. All factory owners were not cruel exploiters, for some reduced the hours of work in their mills, established reasonable working conditions, and prevented infliction of cruelties. Some also provided good accommodation, food, and clothing for their apprentices. Conditions were worst in the older, smaller mills, especially water-mills in isolated hilly areas—like Litton Mill, 'at the bottom of a sequestered glen, and surrounded by rugged rocks, remote from any human habitation'. In such mills, owing to the difficulty of getting adult labour, large numbers of parish apprentices were employed. In such places, moreover, there was little protection from the magistrates. Blincoe pointed out in his evidence of 1833 that ill-treatment of children was worse 'in country places' than in towns like Manchester, 'where justice is always at hand'. Some of the worst employers belonged to the first generation of factory-owners, who achieved wealth by ruthless methods. On the other hand, it is evident from Blincoe's and other evidence that adult operatives, not the employers, were frequently responsible for the cruelties to children.

The evils of child labour were not confined to the textile mills. In many other trades, such as coal-mining, the metal trades, and potteries, conditions were equally bad if not worse, as revealed by the Children's Employment Commissions of the early 'forties and the 'sixties. Textile mills were the first to be subjected to legislative control because child labour was employed in them on such a large scale, and because the evils were more apparent, more inspectable, and more easily regulated in large factories than in small workshops. Exploitation of child labour was not a new thing.

Children had long been employed in domestic industry for excessive hours and under bad conditions. Parish apprenticeship dated back to the first half of the sixteenth century and had long been subject to grave abuses, having degenerated into a means of relieving the poor rates by the parish officers, on the one hand, and a means of getting premiums and cheap labour by employers, on the other. The system of 'settlement' had encouraged churchwardens and overseers to dump their pauper children in this way on other parishes.

The growth of the factory system, however, did increase the evils of parish apprenticeship. Children were now employed in far greater numbers and in greater proportion to adults than previously, owing firstly, as already mentioned, to the difficulty of recruiting labour for the early factories, and secondly because many of the factory processes were well-suited to child labour.[11] As Blincoe's *Memoir* points out, however, most working parents were at first very loath to place their children in the textile mills, so that recourse was had to parish apprentices in increasing numbers. They were now, as never before, sent off in waggon loads from the great cities—like Blincoe and his fellows from St. Pancras in London—to mills far distant from their parents or friends, and were thus remote from protection, save by the local magistrates. It was to remedy this evil, that an Act was eventually passed in 1816, limiting the distance to which London children could be sent to 40 miles.

By this time the evils of parish apprenticeship had greatly diminished in the textile trades. The 1802 Act caused many factory owners to give up taking apprentices, and with the development of steam mills in urban areas there was less necessity for such labour, since adults and 'free' children were now readily available. The 1807 returns of factory visitations in Derbyshire show that the use of 'free' child labour had superseded parish apprenticeship in almost all the local mills. Such mills as still employed parish apprentices were the smaller and less satisfactory concerns.[12] Conditions in the newer, bigger mills were a good deal better than in the older, rural water-mills. Blincoe himself testified in 1833 that such atrocities as he had experienced were now of rare occurrence, though the evils were still such that he would rather have his own children transported than put them into factories. Parish apprenticeship had almost disappeared from the textile trades by the early 1830s, though it still survived strongly and with many evils in some other industries, such as coal-mining and the metal trades.

Reassessment of the early factory system thus enables us to view Blincoe's *Memoir* in a more balanced way. Moreover, Dr. Chapman has recently produced new evidence about Litton Mill, which, he argues, proves the *Memoir* to have been exaggerated and unreliable. Unfortunately, however, it appears that in defending the early factory masters he himself is not entirely free from bias. He points out, rightly, that we must judge the *Memoir* against the standards of that day, and that 'cruel punishments to children were not unusual in the eighteenth century'; some of the punishments described in the *Memoir* were even advocated by 'progressive educationists', such as Lancaster, early in the nineteenth century. Indeed, Dr. Chapman suggests that Ellice Needham, owner of the Litton mill, was himself an enlightened educationist in copying such 'progressive' ideas as hanging weights round Blincoe's neck or suspending him above the machinery, though he concedes, almost in the same breath, that 'this bestial behaviour cannot be condoned'! He points out, moreover, that Needham was not, as the *Memoir* alleged, 'like most of the fraternity' of early factory owners, of 'obscure' origins, 'said to have arisen from an abject state of poverty' to a position of wealth by ruthless exploitation, but that he came of a well-known local landowning family. He admits, however, that Needham was a not-very-successful first-generation millowner,[13] in an area which, by the early nineteenth century, was unfavourably situated geographically to compete with the more rapidly developing industry in Lancashire and elsewhere; in fact, almost from the start, Litton mill appears to have been a struggling and not very profitable concern, of the type which commonly tended to exploit child labour most ruthlessly, especially where, as at Litton, adult or 'free' child labour was not readily available. Was it, as Dr. Chapman asserts, merely 'popular prejudice' which caused Litton and other such mills in that area to be so detested that for many years they could not recruit local labour? He actually admits that a great deal of this unpopularity arose from the fact that, at a time when the system of parish apprenticeship was tending to be abandoned elsewhere, Litton and one or two other mills nearby continued, 'for more than thirty years', to exploit this system of cheap labour by importing apprentices and then discharging them after completing their time, often to become a burden on the local poor rates.

   Dr. Chapman also admits that 'some of the allegations made in the pamphlet are supported' by two reports of county magistrates appointed to inspect mills under the provisions of the 1802 Act. This interesting new evidence, of 1807 and 1811, leads him to the following conclusion: 'There can be little doubt that apprentices at Litton suffered from long hours, monotonous diet and crowded living conditions. However ... brutal treatment, inadequate cloth-

ing and filthy accommodation are not mentioned. Nor is sickness
and death referred to.' These reports cast some doubt on the
assertions in the *Memoir* that 'the magistrate could never *find out*
anything wrong, nor hear of a single individual who had any complaint to make', that the apprentices were totally unaware of the
Act and had no idea that the magistrates came to redress grievances, that they were too terrified anyway to dare to make complaints, that the inspecting magistrates were entirely in the pocket
of the millowner, and that the Act was completely 'a dead letter'.
But Blincoe was here referring to the situation in his early years at
Litton and does state that conditions later improved, after he
himself had complained to the magistrates; moreover, inspections
were very infrequent and may well have been perfunctory, failing
to reveal the worst abuses, as Blincoe asserted.

Dr. Chapman also produces evidence from the Tideswell burial
registers to show that apprentices did not die in such numbers
as suggested by the *Memoir*, though it appears that epidemic fever
did strike down some of them. He also points out, from contemporary evidence regarding other mills in Derbyshire and elsewhere,
that Litton does not seem to have been notably worse than some of
its contemporaries; he admits that some of these other mills were
'notorious ... for their ill-treatment of apprentices', but considers
that the attacks on these, too, were by politically-minded trade-
unionists, etc. who had an aversion to the factory system. On the
other hand, Dr. Chapman has no hesitation whatever in supporting
the respectable evidence of John Farey, who, in his survey of Derbyshire in 1807–9, declared that, from his own observations and
enquiries, he could confidently assert that factory apprentices were
generally well cared for, and that he had not come across 'even sus-
picious hints to the contrary in any instance'; Farey was 'not disposed to think ... that their employ is as unhealthy as some have
represented'. These statements Dr. Chapman accepts unreservedly
as those of an unbiased, objective, outside observer, though one
would like to know the social composition of Farey's local reader-
ship and who his sponsors were. Even on Farey's own evidence, it is
apparent that there were widely-held popular opinions to the
contrary, and it is difficult to believe that these opinions were
entirely prejudiced and without foundation. It is notable that Dr.
Chapman, whilst regarding Farey's views as 'scrupulously fair',
pours doubt, by contrast, on evidence by Blincoe and other critics
of the factory system as being biased, 'calumnious', politically-
motivated and unreliable. 'There can be little doubt', Dr. Chapman
concludes, 'that the *Memoir of Robert Blincoe* was written by a

gullible sensationalist, whose statements must be treated with the utmost caution'.

To the present writer, however, it seems doubtful that this conclusion is based entirely on academic objectivity. Moreover, some of Dr. Chapman's other statements are equivocal. 'There is, of course, no denying that at Litton Mill hours were long, work tedious, diet monotonous, punishment harsh and accommodation crowded, but such conditions were not originated by the factory masters.'[14] This is, indeed, an argument often employed by defenders of the factory system, but the fact that exploitation previously existed in handicraft trades under the domestic system does not therefore sanctify it under the factory system: two blacks do not make a white. It is true that contemporary social and moral standards were low, and that ill-treatment of parish apprentices was no new thing, but mass exploitation of the kind and on the scale in which it developed in the early cotton mills had *not* previously occurred. The worst examples, Dr. Chapman admits, were in such places as Litton and other small, remote, less competitive country mills, especially in those whose owners were lacking in capital and managerial skills. 'Ellice Needham, and his workers with him, were the unhappy casualties of rapid technical and economic change in a highly competitive industry.' In other words, it is implied, Needham and his kind resorted to exploitation of cheap apprentice labour in efforts to remain competitive. Is it, therefore, justifiable to dismiss the *Memoir* of one of these 'unhappy casualties' as merely 'sensationalist' and politically motivated, and to regard Carlile and Doherty, who printed it, as the one 'a violent partisan' and the other a 'well-known agitator'?

The *Memoir* was, as Dr. Chapman admits, supported to some extent by the reports of visiting magistrates, who were not—at least this much must be conceded to Blincoe—very likely to be prejudiced in the wretched apprentices' favour. Needham, so Dr. Chapman informs us, participated in the well-to-do social life of the district, mixed with the local landowners and manufacturers, enjoyed entertaining, was a friend of the Vicar of Tideswell, and a leading member of the town's Anglican congregation. It is not therefore entirely unreasonable to suppose that he was perhaps able to influence the local magistrates to some extent. Even so, their reports indicate that all was far from well at Litton mill, and it is by no means improbable that the worst abuses were hidden from them.

Blincoe's *Memoir* may, indeed, be regarded as biased *ex parte* evidence. But so, too, was that of contemporary factory owners and their hireling doctors who alleged that it was positively beneficial to children to be employed for twelve, fourteen or more hours per day! It is worth reiterating that the exploitation of child labour in factories was strongly condemned not only by Sadler's Committee but also by the Royal Commission of 1833 (critical though it was of some of the previous evidence), and by every later committee and commission of enquiry, as well as by many independent observers. There is, in fact, an overwhelming mass of circumstantial evidence to support Blincoe's condemnation of certain factory owners, though it must be re-emphasised that his case should not be regarded as typical, but as an example only of the worst exploitation.

It is pleasant, however, to discover that Blincoe, despite his early sufferings, lived to enjoy comparative comfort in later life. After completing his servitude at Litton Mill, apparently in 1813, he remained there for about a year as an adult operative, but then left to drift from mill to mill in Derbyshire, Cheshire, and finally Manchester. By 1817, however, he had grown sick of exploitation as a wage-earner, yet, being very thrifty and living sparsely, had managed to save enough money to set up on his own as a small cotton-waste dealer in Manchester. After marriage in 1819, he occupied a shop at 108 Bank Top, but gave this up in 1824, to live at 2 Edge Place, Salford, and invested some of his capital in cotton-spinning machinery in Ormrod's mill, near St. Paul's Church, Tib Street. A fire, however, entirely destroyed the machinery and almost ruined him. Indeed, in the autumn of 1827, just prior to the publication of his *Memoir*, Carlile discovered that, 'having engaged in some kind of shop, he [Blincoe] had become insolvent, and was, or had been, confined in Lancaster Castle for debt'. The Manchester Directory for 1830, however, shows him as a weft and cotton-waste dealer at 32 High Street and shopkeeper at 407 Oldham Road. When his *Memoir* was republished in 1832, he was said to be residing at 19 Turner Street, where he kept a small grocer's shop, and was also engaged in manufacturing sheet wadding and as a cotton-waste dealer. In his evidence of 1833 he stated, 'I rent power from a mill in Stockport, and have a room to myself; my business is a sheet wadding manufacturer'.[15] He then had three children, the eldest aged thirteen, but was careful to send them to school and keep them out of the cotton mills.

The directories of the later 'thirties show him still as a wadding manufacturer and cotton-waste dealer, at 5 and 19 Turner Street, his private residence then being 23 Garden Street, Ardwick. By 1843 his business was at 4 Turner Street, his private house at 4 Bellevue Street, Hyde Road. Thereafter he disappears, apparently having either died or failed in business, but he has left in his *Memoir* an enduring epitaph.

NOTES

1. *The Lion*, Vol. I, No. 13, 28 March 1828.
2. It is worth noting that this comparison was made some years before Richard Oastler's famous 'White Slavery' letter in 1830.
3. See, for example, F. A. Hayek (ed.), *Capitalism and the Historians* (1954), especially the chapter by W. H. Hutt on 'The Factory System of the Early Nineteenth Century', which originally appeared in *Economica*, March 1926. See also Chapman, *op. cit.*
4. Abel Heywood, the Manchester printer and publisher, stated in 1888 that the memoir was 'published by W. M. Clarke, of Paternoster Row, London', not by Carlile, *Manchester Notes and Queries*, 30 June 1888. No copy of this pamphlet appears to have survived.
5. *Manchester Notes and Queries*, 14 July 1888.
6. *The Lion*, 28 March 1828.
7. Dr. Chapman is confused regarding the facts of publication. He states that the impact of the *Memoir*, first published in *The Lion*, was 'so considerable that it was reprinted in *The Poor Man's Advocate* the same year', and that later, in 1832, John Doherty republished it as a separate *Memoir*. The facts, however, are as stated above: the *Memoir*, first printed in *The Lion*, early in 1828, was immediately published also as a separate pamphlet; it was this pamphlet which Doherty reprinted in 1832; it was never reprinted in the *P.M.A.*, which did not, in fact, exist in 1828.
8. One of these confirmations, by John Joseph Betts, who became secretary of the cotton spinners' trade society in Ashton-under-Lyne, is printed at the end of the *Memoir*.
9. *Parliamentary Papers*, 1833, XXI, D.3, 17–18.
10. See T. A. Trollope, *What I Remember* (2nd ed., 1887), pp. 7–13, and M. A. Sadleir, *Trollope, A Commentary* (1933), pp. 93–4. These facts and references were provided in a 'Note' to my article of 1958. They have since been further investigated by W. H. Chaloner, 'Mrs. Trollope and the Early Factory System', *Victorian Studies*, Vol. IV (1960–1).
11. Derbyshire, where Blincoe suffered, had been the scene of the earliest exploitation of child labour in textile factories. William Hutton has left an account of his sufferings, as an apprentice in the first English silk-throwing mill, built by the Lombe brothers near Derby in the years 1717–21. (*History of Derby*, p. 160.) Arkwright also employed child labour in his first factory, also built on the Derwent, in the early 1770s.
12. *Reports of the Society for Bettering the Condition of the Poor*, V, App. 24, pp. 171–8.
13. Needham, Frith & Co. started spinning in about 1782, after nullification of Arkwright's patent in the previous year. Litton mill was, in fact, modelled on that built by Arkwright in 1779 at Cressbrook, nearby on the River Wye.
14. Cf. above, pp. 201–2.
15. Dr. Chapman cynically observes that Blincoe's early experience under factory masters does not appear to have deterred him from becoming one

of them'. He neglects, however, to mention Blincoe's own statement that it was his experiences of exploitation, not only as an apprentice but also as an adult wage-earner, in various factories, that determined him to become independent. Dr. Chapman might also have noted that there is no evidence whatever that Blincoe ever practised, as an employer, the evils that had previously been perpetrated on him, and that he still continued, in fact, to denounce the exploitation in cotton mills, and supported the factory reform movement.

Index